THE ARCHAEOLOGY OF

Native-Lived Colonialism

THE ARCHAEOLOGY OF COLONIALISM IN NATIVE NORTH AMERICA

Series editors
Lisa Frink and Aubrey Cannon

THE ARCHAEOLOGY OF
Native-Lived Colonialism

Challenging History in the Great Lakes

Neal Ferris

THE UNIVERSITY OF ARIZONA PRESS

Tucson

The University of Arizona Press
© 2009 The Arizona Board of Regents

www.uapress.arizona.edu

Library of Congress Cataloging-in-Publication Data

Ferris, Neal, 1960–
    The archaeology of native-lived colonialism :
challenging history in the Great Lakes / Neal Ferris.
        p. cm. — (The archaeology of colonialism in
native North America)
    Includes bibliographical references and index.
    ISBN 978-0-8165-2705-2 (hardcover : alk. paper)
      1. Ojibwa Indians—Ontario, Southwestern—Antiquities.
    2. Delaware Indians–Ontario, Southwestern—Antiquities.
    3. Iroquois Indians—Ontario, Southwestern—Antiquities.
    4. Great Britain—Colonies—America—History.
    5. Excavations (Archaeology)—Ontario, Southwestern.
    6. Ontario, Southwestern—Antiquities. I. Title.
    E99.C6F48   2009
    971,3'2—dc22   2008032146

♻
Manufactured in the United States of America on acid-free, archival-quality paper
containing a minimum of 30% post-consumer waste and processed chlorine free.

14   13   12   11   10   09   6   5   4   3   2   1

This work is dedicated to
Little G, Little B, and Little I: Manina, Fionntan and Maeve.
You guys make me so much more, leaving me incapable of
ever truly expressing what it all means.

Contents

Figures

Tables

Foreword

COLONIALISM STUDIES IN ARCHAEOLOGY ARE BEGINNING to flourish and mature. The series The Archaeology of Colonialism in Native North America is a timely project that reflects the developing focus in archaeology on the complex character of colonialism in Indigenous North America. There is an increasing theoretical and methodological focus on the complexities of the colonial experience—the myriad strategies and experiences of both the descendant and colonial communities and how archaeology can illuminate the specifics and generalities of their interactions and transformations. We are at the beginning of an understanding of colonialism that goes beyond a simple model of encounter and event and have begun to grapple with the entire scope of colonialism.

This series is dedicated to documenting in detail the contingent nature of colonialism—the complex interactions of people and their material, social, and intellectual worlds. Our primary goal is to highlight research that illuminates the colonial histories of particular cultural contexts and is also connected to broader insights concerning the processes, patterns, and impacts of colonialism. One of the most fascinating and fruitful aspects of this work is a fresh interest in the role of Native North Americans in the processes of colonialism. Archaeologists have come to be willing to engage in dialogue that positions Native people at the center of cultural change and persistence.

The series particularly represents research that stresses the connectedness of the precolonial and colonial—studies that recognize that colonial change did not happen in a cultural vacuum and that change is based on local conditions and historical trajectories seated in precolonial cultural forms. This way of looking at cultural transformation gives archaeology a model for evaluating how the prehistoric may differ from the historical and ethnological. Much of archaeological reasoning about and model building of the past is directly related to ethnographic structures of historical and present-day cultures. Given that colonialism has restructured what we observe, a full appreciation and accounting of the complex mechanisms and outcomes of the colonial process are essential to our interpretation of the material record.

We believe Neal Ferris's book is an ideal inaugural book to launch and represent our series. Drawing on a developing body of scholarship in colonial studies, the author integrates multiple lines of evidence and examines issues of change, continuity, accommodation, and resistance among Indigenous groups in the region of Lakes Ontario and Erie. Ferris demonstrates how "Native-lived histories," though affected by colonial processes, reveal that groups managed to maintain a consistent sense of cultural self through (and despite) centuries of Euro-North American interaction, interference, and influence.

—*Lisa Frink and Aubrey Cannon*

Preface

IN MANY WAYS THIS STUDY HAS BEEN FOR ME a coming together of various seemingly disparate interpretive research strands that I have managed to pursue over the last two decades while serving as the southwestern Ontario regional archaeologist for the province. Indeed, the ability to weave together a long-term narrative from this diverse array of research has largely arisen from the unique purview I had as a government archaeologist: seeing and reviewing the culture history findings of southwestern Ontario uncovered through the day-to-day workings of researcher, avocational and consultant. This afforded me an opportunity not only to see the comprehensive picture of the archaeological record as it was coming out of the ground but also to imagine a deeper narrative to that long-term history.

The path I've followed to this study began twenty-five years ago as an undergraduate, when I first developed an interest in the archaeology of "contact." That perhaps was inevitable, given I was then at McMaster University, where in the late 1970s and early 1980s some students and faculty were working on the archaeology of the 17th century southern Ontario Iroquoians, exploring how European contact shaped and influenced that record.

I recall at the time—though perhaps this is more an after-the-fact revising of subjective memories—wondering about the tropes that dominated those explorations of the record: of contact as dependency, assimilation and loss of identity, of Native peoples abandoning traditional lifeways and material culture and developing, instantaneously, an obsessive desire for copper kettles and glass beads. Nonetheless, I did accept as a given that major culture change had occurred by the mid 17th century, and that it could be readily found in the material traces being dug up and analyzed. I also accepted as unassailable the idea that all this change came exclusively from the immediate European impact on Indigenous people—which was, after all, a central truth that dominated most research at the time.

Following my undergraduate days, my own research interests took me elsewhere, as I was fortunate to work closely with a colleague and friend, fellow government archaeologist Ian Kenyon. His own interests were my entrée into a poorly explored area of Ontario archaeology: Native-occupied sites from the 19th century (e.g., Kenyon and Ferris 1984; Ferris 1989).

A secondary consequence of this work was again to wonder about archaeologies of contact. I wondered why, if Native archaeology as reflecting cultural coherency supposedly ended in 1650, were groups like the Anishnabeg Ojibwa living in wigwams in the 19th century and following traditional settlement-subsistence regimes? That led me to wonder what archaeology could say of the Indigenous peoples from the Great Lakes who by 1650 had collectively experienced thousands of years of ancient past, AND then continued to experience centuries of history beyond "contact" to become the communities that exist in the region today? So when I returned to McMaster in 1999 to undertake a PhD, it was to explore such questions.

I initially thought that a major challenge was going to be addressing the contradictions I assumed would exist in the Aboriginal archaeology for the centuries leading up to European contact, and the archaeology left well after, since I imagined great disruption and substantive change in the 17th century. If I wanted to explore a long-term archaeological narrative for southwestern Ontario that could connect ancient to recent pasts, I assumed I would have to talk about latent memory markers, oral traditions or other nontangible links that appeared to bridge a material divide.

And yet as I began looking for these tenuous links, I found that I didn't have to. I was surprised to find what wasn't evident: no major changes, and by this I mean no discontinuities, in archaeological manifestations between 1500 and 1750. Rather, the long-term synthesis I pulled together of the archaeological record revealed strong continuities in settlement-subsistence and material culture use consistent with earlier centuries. Any change occurred logically from within that continuity: the constant revision we see at any time through the archaeological record along with the usual inter-site variability. Moreover, when I looked specifically at data previously cited as evidence of response to European influences, I found that the appearance of those changes generally predated a possible beginning to a European influence in the region, and were much more logically interpreted as consistent with continuing expansion of Aboriginal-centric, sociopolitical community complexity.

What past research assumptions appeared to reflect more than anything else was that conventional archaeological interpretations had fixated on the 2 to 8 percent of non-Indigenous artifacts found on dwelling sites pre-1650, as well as the abundance of these items, along with Indigenous exotics, in burial contexts. Disruptive change was simply assumed to exist. The key assumption at play was that archaeological data had to echo the dramatic tales and tragedies prominent in the written records from the period.

In other words, by applying a strictly archaeological perspective that reached back well before the arrival of any Europeans in the Northeast, and also reached forward into the 19th century, the story of the Native-lived experiences through this whole period became something much different than what I had assumed it to be. It "made sense" of those 19th century Ojibwa patterns that seemed contrary to what Native people were supposed to be about by then. And, significantly, it made understanding the Indigenous experiences through the rise of the colonialist state in the 19th century something very different: people who were still active agents acting on their historically informed understandings of who they were and the way the world worked, and acting on that perspective to try to shape hoped-for futures.

Critically, what I found was that this long-term perspective that archaeology imposes on understanding the past, one that offers a complex, contextually contradictory, continuous historical narrative, also links past *and* present. The families and communities whose archaeological histories I was telling from the 15th, 17th and 19th centuries are not ancient relics, but ancestors of people who live and participate within the same community my family and I also participate in today. To me this realization highlighted a broader relevancy, linking the past to the present and beyond to provide insight and revise understandings of contemporary experiences (our current habitus and understanding of how the world works). So, recognizing the Native-centric lived experiences of Indigenous peoples as viable and active agents both in the past and in the present, for example, means that a contemporary understanding of the past as a colonialist conquest is problematic and exclusionary in our contemporary, multicultural setting of a quasi postcolonial North America. After all, I am fairly certain that those I know from Six Nations, Oneida, Delaware and Anishnabeg communities in southwestern Ontario today would argue, and argue strongly, that they remain a viable people who simultaneously share our very materialistic world, while maintaining a distinct, self-defined identity in that world.

This contemporary relevance was brought home viscerally for me as I defended my dissertation in 2006, at about the same time that my day job as a bureaucratic archaeologist began to entangle me in issues related to the ongoing reclamation/occupation of land by peoples from the Six Nations Iroquois in the southern Ontario town of Caledonia. People from Six Nations believed that the land had been improperly surrendered in the 19th century. Their action, they stated over and over again, was a necessary reclamation—taking back what had been taken away from them as a result of the failure of the Canadian Crown to respect Iroquois sovereignty. So here was a contemporary manifestation of an Indigenous people asserting sovereignty and negotiating the legacy of a particular instance of catastrophic bureaucracy, entirely consistent with the same assertions of sovereignty Joseph Brant and other Six Nations individuals made before and after arriving on the Grand in 1784 (see chap. 5).

As well, the land had been in the early stages of a housing development that had been surveyed by consultant archaeologists, who had documented many sites, including a Late Woodland Inter-Lakes settlement. Questions of how well those sites were conserved, whether burials had been missed, and why the Six Nations had not had a say over what happened to this ancient heritage, became a major issue the Crown had to address. Now, I knew through my encounters as a result of my job that the regular addressing of archaeological conservation within land use development up to that point rarely included consultation with nearby Aboriginal communities, and in some hands could be more rote and expedient than thorough and focused on documenting the past. Moreover, I also knew that the imposition of archaeological conservation sometimes leads to encounters with non-Native individuals who strenuously object to having to pay to document Native archaeology, using sometimes hurtful language to complain that the archaeological record is little more than road gravel and trash, and not relevant to the people developing and altering the land. Why, such people typically ask, do they have to bear the financial burden of documenting something of no interest to them and of no relevance to their heritage?

So for me, the experiences that played out around the Caledonia reclamation/occupation demonstrated the continuing relevancy of the past to define the present, and the continuing constraint historical biases and contemporary conventional research assumptions about Indigenous experiences create to exclude Native people from national and regional histories today. It also demonstrated the very contemporary need for revision to that understanding of the past to give it back the relevancy needed to revise attitudes in 21st-century Canadian society. Archaeological histories, I strongly feel, can provide that revision to get beyond the paradigm of colonizer and histories of exclusion, to recognize the artifice and harm this construct continues to perpetuate. After all, it seems unimaginable that contemporary Aboriginal issues such as those reflected at Caledonia can ever be resolved when the root causes arising from contested histories remains unaddressed.

Acknowledgments

I HAVE BEEN AIDED AND GUIDED BY MANY PEOPLE along the way over the last 20 years. I would like to acknowledge and thank them here. They include: Fred Dreyer, David Faux, Victor Gulewitsch, Tom Hill, Dean Jacobs, Darlene Johnston, Sue, Kathleen and Melissa Kenyon, Laurie Leclair, Jim Rementer, Linda Sabathy-Judd, Charlie Shawkence, Darryl Stonefish, David White, Paul Williams, and Dave Zellen. Also Scott Beld, Charles Cleland, Christine Dodd, Dena Doroszenko, Bill Fitzgerald, Bill Fox, Conrad Heidenreich, Heather Henderson, Susan Jamieson, Kurt Jordan, Eva MacDonald, Rob Mann, Carl Murphy, Trudy Nicks, Bob Pearce, Rosemary Prevec, Brian Ross, Patricia Rubertone, Howard Savage, Mike Spence, Gary Warrick, Ron Williamson, Stan Wortner, and Alison Wylie. Dave Robertson kindly worked my graphics into something the press could use. Thanks also to the Burton Historical Room at Wayne State University, Fairfield Museum, Museum of Ontario Archaeology, University of Toronto faunal lab, Ontario and Canada Public Archives, City of Brantford Public Library, Six Nations Woodland Centre, Royal Ontario Museum, and the Walpole Island Cultural Centre.

I also want to thank series editors Aubrey Cannon and Lisa Frink, Allyson Carter and other staff at the University of Arizona Press, two anonymous reviewers, and Meredith Fraser, who all helped bring this manuscript along. Aubrey was also my dissertation supervisor and needs to be thanked for helping open my eyes to an archaeological perspective that took me far beyond the narrow confines of Ontario archaeology, while also showing me how Ontario archaeology should go far beyond those confines.

Special thanks to Lyn Hamilton and Michael Johnson, former employers, who gave me the opportunity to pursue archaeological research on the job, saw it as my catalyst beyond, and didn't object to that being my preference over a career in management. Special thanks in memory to Greg Curnoe and especially Ian Kenyon, both of whom so shaped who I am. Ian's friendship and support, along with Bill Fox's, is what ultimately gave me a focus and direction in archaeology. In many ways, I hope this work pays homage to Ian's contributions and continues his legacy. Greg's enthusiasm for archaeology and history, and unqualified encouragement, came at a time when I really needed to be reminded that archaeology has given me a privileged way of looking at the world. I would like to think this work would have become welcome fodder for many more hours of chatting in his studio.

THE ARCHAEOLOGY OF
Native-Lived
Colonialism

I

Introduction

THIS BOOK IS ABOUT READING THE PAST through an archaeologically informed perspective—archaeological history—to construct an understanding of how Native communities in southwestern Ontario negotiated the rise of colonialism in the 18th and 19th centuries through a process of changed continuities: that is, they maintained identity and historically understood notions of self and community, while also incorporating substantial material changes and revision to those identities. As such, archaeological histories can play a critical role in revising our approach to the past by reading history through archaeology: situating the past as the prosaic and daily decisions and choices that individuals, families and communities make, informed by the way the world works at that moment based on past knowledge and future expectations.

A unique and important dimension to the archaeological perspective offered here is the ability it gives the researcher to contextualize the specifics of Native-lived experiences during the rise of a colonialist state, and tie them to much deeper archaeological histories. In effect, it situates a relatively brief sliver of Indigenous history within wider archaeological trends connected to an ancient past. This is why it is as important to understand the archaeological histories of the initial centuries of Indigenous-European interaction in the lower Great Lakes and the centuries prior to the beginning of that interaction, as it is to explore the patterns arising from the late 18th and 19th centuries.

This wider context aids significantly in revising understandings of Native-lived histories by revealing them to be complex strategies for accommodating contingencies, and informed by individual and community-specific historical realities. Any particular responses to historical specifics thus become actions either informed by historical knowledge of the way the world works, or active revision to that knowledge, rather than a-historical reactions shaped by the external motives and values of the colonialist state. Understanding changes through the era of contact and colonialism as the agency of Native communities provides a richer archaeological history of the lives lived for people of southwestern Ontario through this time, one that ultimately connects the results of this study to the aim of revisionist perspectives on Native history emerging in both archaeological and anthropological histories (Lightfoot 2005b:13).

Trapped in essentialist assumptions of Native decline and ruin, past conventional approaches to the study of European-Indigenous "contacts" have failed to demonstrate the value archaeology of Indigenous colonialisms can contribute to the broader discourse within archaeological theory and practice. This broader discourse has advanced to recognize in the archaeological record the material manifestations and dynamic interplay of social structures and processes operating within and between households, communities and nations, and the maintenance and continuous revision of identity at the individual, family and community level over the long-term (e.g., S. Jones 1997; Pauketat 2001). These are critical foci to archaeological research, regardless of temporal or geographic setting. As such, the revised approach provided here can test the validity of these broader archaeological emphases, and offer meaningful comparisons for patterns found in broadly different colonial settings (e.g., Deitler 2005; Lightfoot 2005a; Stein 2005).

The Archaeological Setting

The focus of this work is on the changing continuities of Indigenous groups within the lower Great Lakes generally and southwestern Ontario specifically. Southwestern Ontario is defined here as the north Erie peninsula: that portion of present-day southern Ontario west of Lake Ontario and bordered to the south by the north shore of Lake Erie, to the west by the Detroit and St. Clair Rivers and Lake St. Clair, to the west and north by Lake Huron and Georgian Bay, and to the east by the Niagara Escarpment (see figs. 1.1 and 1.2). This region is characterized by a broadly similar landscape of drainage systems flowing into the Great Lakes, and temperate woodland environment.

Throughout much of the ancient archaeological record, there appears to have been at least two broad archaeological traditions present in the region, falling on either side of a line drawn somewhere between the present-day cities of Chatham and London, Ontario (e.g., Ellis and Ferris 1990). This divide is embodied during the post-1000 AD Late Woodland by archaeological manifestations known as the Western Basin Tradition (Murphy and Ferris 1990) and the Ontario Iroquoian (Wright 1966) or Inter-Lakes Tradition (Ferris 1999). Though the boundary between these two traditions fluctuated,

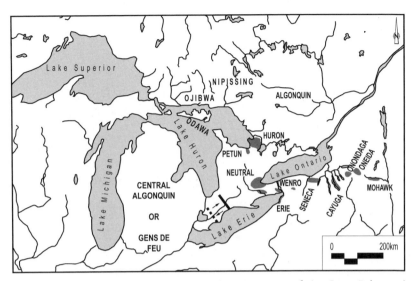

FIGURE 1.1. Southwestern Ontario situated within parts of the Great Lakes and Northeast, depicting general locations of Aboriginal nations around AD 1600. Note: As discussed in chapter 3, the solid line in the north Erie peninsula depicts the farthest extent east for precontact Western Basin Tradition Late Woodland archaeological manifestations (ca. AD 1000), while the dashed line depicts the farthest extent west for archaeological manifestations of the Inter-Lakes Late Woodland Tradition (ca. AD 1500).

and indeed they appear at some times to overlap or contract, there are distinct differences that were maintained throughout the Late and Terminal Woodland within settlement-subsistence, mortuary patterns and material culture (Ferris 2006; Murphy and Ferris 1990; Watts 2006). Archaeological data from both the Terminal Woodland and early historic records suggest that at least the immediate precontact manifestations of these archaeological traditions are connected historically to people of broadly Anishnabeg or Algonquian-like (to the west) and Iroquoian-like (to the east) cultural lifeways.

This archaeological-geographic divide blurred after settlements contracted in the latter 16th century and the 17th-century Neutral Iroquoians dispersed just after 1650. Iroquois settlement returned to the region within a decade or two, while Algonquian-speaking Anishnabeg, such as the Potawatomi and more distant Ojibwa, settled in the region by the end of the 17th century. Huron-Wendat (or Wyandot) settled along the Detroit River at about the same time, and the Six Nations Iroquois returned in the 1780s, while Oneida Iroquois settled west of London in the 1840s.

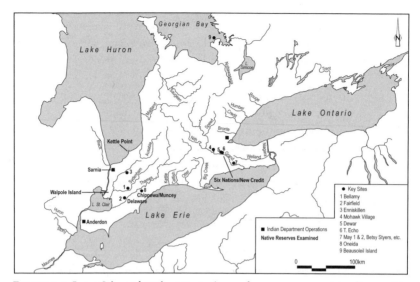

FIGURE 1.2. Late 18th- and 19th-century sites and reserve communities discussed in subsequent chapters.

Finally, with the exception of the Detroit River corridor, the region was free of permanent European settlement until later in the 18th century. Subsequent expansion of a colonialist settlement was entirely within the aegis of the British Empire, creating a broadly similar Euro-Canadian history for the region through most of the 19th century.

Coming to Terms with Terminology

An inherent challenge in a study bridging archaeological record and historical narrative is to find ways to consistently and meaningfully refer to the people whose long-term archaeological history is being constructed. I am referring here to the people who were not of the colonizer—a diverse array of groups sharing broad and distinct cultural identities as Indigenous people, demonstrated through historical, oral, archaeological, spiritual, racial or self-asserted fact. These people, collectively, resided in the Americas continuously from time immemorial to the present day, and exclusively prior to the arrival of people from Europe or elsewhere.

I will consciously use terms in this study to consistently convey distinct concepts. Generally, I use the phrase "Aboriginal nations" as a political collective and "Native people, families or communities" as descriptors. The former is intended to convey a broad sense of sovereignty encompassing Native families and communities, though I agree with Shoemaker (2004:7) about the lack of clarity "nation" imparts. But what I am trying to convey with "Aboriginal nation" is the notion of a collective sociopolitical entity, such as the Huron or Iroquois confederacy; a distinctiveness that is also reflected in the historic record as meaning more than a single community.

Of course "nation" and "confederacy" meant different things at different times to different people. For example, the Iroquois Confederacy at various times was made up of the Seneca, Mohawk, Oneida, Cayuga and Onondaga, and then Tuscarora. But were the Huron or Neutral a confederacy or more singular "nations?" And what of the multiple villages and smaller settlements within discretely defined Iroquoian territories? Was each a "nation" or a community? Certainly distinct village communities of "Huron" rejected the actions of fellow Huron communities at specific historic moments, as was also the case for the Iroquois (e.g., Heidenreich 1971; Richter 1992).

In part, understanding distinctions between community, nation and confederacy arises from the historic record. But what are the implications of using these terms backwards into the archaeological past? Certainly, I cannot refer to "the Huron" or "the Six Nations" when examining the archaeological record centuries earlier. So, to negotiate around terminological traps, I've chosen to emphasize "community" to refer to any collective at the village level, and "nation" only when referring to a broader-than-village collective. Terms like "Huron," "Neutral" and "Iroquois" will be reserved for the historical context when these terms were used. While not a completely satisfactory solution, it at least offers a consistent distinction throughout this work.

A greater complexity emerges when talking of Native people who are not of Iroquoian association. In the Great Lakes, there was a diversity of people historically who were referred to by specific tribal designations (e.g., Sauk, Potawatomi, Ojibwa, Odawa, etc.), or as the "Western nations" or "Gens de Feu" (e.g., Aquila 1983; Heidenreich 1988), in research as Central Algonquian-speaking peoples, and self-referentially as Anishnabeg (e.g., Cleland 1992b:39). Generally, autonomy operated at a village or territorial community level, though there was also a broader collective of multicommunity entities (e.g., Ojibwa), and even a greater collective (e.g., Gens de Feu). Attempting to apply standardized terms in either the ancient or historically recorded eras can only be arbitrary. So again, I use the term "community," reserving "Aboriginal nation" for contexts of broader geosocial collectives consistent with historical designations for time and place.

Similar terminological risks arise when referring to the Late and Terminal Woodland archaeological record for southern Ontario. Conventionally, most of this period in southern Ontario is thought of as ancestral Iroquoian, and time periods have been assigned historically derived political-ethnic labels by archaeologists (e.g., Ellis and Ferris 1990; Wright 1966). While I have no argument with the notion that historically known Iroquoian groups such as the Huron and Neutral were descendants of those who shaped the region's archaeological patterns in the preceding centuries, there is a huge conceptual difference between archaeologically defining cultural traditions and linking these with temporally specific sociopolitical designations. As such, I prefer to rely on archaeologically "neutral" designations—Western Basin Tradition for southwestern-most Ontario and Inter-Lakes Tradition for the east (see Ferris 1999)—when talking of the Late and Terminal Woodland archaeological manifestations belonging to the region's Indigenous ancestors.

Lastly, in the context of community, terms like "territory" are also vague and caught up with notions of ownership, sovereignty and conflicting European and Native values, all of which varied through time. Clearly, there was a strong communal sense tied to territory for all Native communities/Aboriginal nations in this region (e.g., Cronon 1983; Shoemaker 2004:15). Conceptually, though, notions of territory as a singular, bounded, exclusive sociopolitical space likely did not exist per se for communities. Rather, there would have operated several conceptions of space, including a closer, communal "possessive" territory of and for the community that subsumed, firstly, hearth and home and the immediate vicinity of residential settlements, and secondly, cemetery locations, planted fields and resource extraction locales. Beyond that, there likely were various conceptions of territory that may or may not have been communal at a broader collective of nation (e.g., Iroquois or Ojibwa territory). These encompassed hunting territories, travel networks within, between and beyond these areas, and land infrequently or irregularly visited. Also, such space likely would have been traversed by others, and so embodied a sense of "shared" or "contested" space. Given the movements of people over the last millennium, notions of "sovereign territory" most certainly would have changed through time, becoming points of dispute between communities or nations. Nonetheless, given differing categories of "possessive" territory, actions such as vacating an area of permanent settlement should not be assumed to mean "abandonment," though an area could conceptually have shifted from close to distant space, and could be more open to contested use, with territorial sovereignty extending to several distinct Aboriginal nations (e.g., Brandão and Starna 1996). Finally, there also were likely quite variable conceptions of land and territory between more seasonally mobile groups and more sedentary agriculturalists. Unless specifically referring to territory at a wider sovereignty, however, I will use the term to convey a sense of land and landscape as understood at the community level.

Organization of the Book

Chapter 2 provides an outline of the specific theoretical and methodological issues that have faced researchers examining cultures in contact and Indigenous peoples within and without colonial settings. I will also review how advances in the conceptual framework for this research have given rise to a reflexive critique of past conventional understandings of Native behaviors in response to European contact. This will also allow me to underscore the particular theoretical and methodological emphasis I will apply to the rest of the thesis.

The following three chapters explore the specific experiences that portions of three Aboriginal nations had during the rise of the colonialist state in southwestern Ontario. To demonstrate how those experiences were historically informed actions, I will provide a deeper, long-term context that extends back to the initial generations of people who interacted with Europeans, and even further back into the more ancient archaeological histories that shaped and influenced the lives of these Native peoples through the 19th century.

Chapter 3 reviews the Ojibwa of southwestern Ontario through the 19th century. I examine patterns of traditional lifeway continuity seen in the early 19th century, which were connected to the deeper Anishnabeg archaeological histories in southwestern Ontario. These patterns are compared with the Ojibwa ability to resist change and maintain traditional seasonal mobility up through the mid–19th century, as well as their adaptive responses to the loss of that ability in the late 19th century. This chapter also outlines the broad historical trends that shaped the emergence of colonialism in the region: the dramatic population increases, landscape alteration, and administrative framework of a colonial state for the colonial populace—trends that all Native communities and families had to negotiate as the region changed from a frontier to the colonialist state that would eventually become Canada.

Chapter 4 explores a potential counterpoint to the Ojibwa pattern: the archaeology and history of the refugee Delaware, who settled among the southwestern Ontario Ojibwa as a Moravian missionary–sponsored community in the 1790s. By examining the same features of archaeological history as reviewed for the Ojibwa, this chapter explores if the Delaware had a significantly different (i.e., more acculturated or dependent) way of life at the start of the 19th century than the Ojibwa, and if their response to the changes that occurred in the region throughout the 19th century were more extreme.

Chapter 5 examines the Iroquoian archaeological histories from southwestern Ontario, and how those are reflected in how the Iroquois negotiated emergent colonialism when they returned to southwestern Ontario in the 1780s. The then Six Nations Iroquois were a series of complex societies that variably interacted with each other and the colonialist "other" as their communities became enclaves in this region during the 19th century. By examining the same features of archaeological history as explored for the Ojibwa and the Delaware, this chapter reveals how Iroquois families integrated tradition and the contemporary colonial world to develop innovative ways of revising and maintaining identity.

Chapter 6 concludes by tying together the generalities arising from these more detailed archaeological histories, and considers the implications of these findings.

2

Imagining Different Pasts

ARCHAEOLOGICAL HISTORIES OF NATIVE-LIVED COLONIALISMS

Constructing the Past

To UNDERSTAND HOW AN ALTERNATIVE HISTORY is constructed from the archaeological record to speak to Native-lived experiences before and after the emergence of a colonialist landscape in southern Ontario, I first need to review the constructionist nature of telling the past.

The reflexive critique that has emerged within the historically oriented social sciences in recent decades encompasses an ongoing struggle to understand what we are intentionally and unintentionally doing in the acts of creating, constructing and telling the past. This critique questions how we can understand a time, a place or a people all removed from our own experience and contact. For Collingwood (1946:282), this is the contemporary and always revisionist challenge of "doing" history—creating the past in the act of imagining it through our selective valuation and use of particular documents and relics. It is a constantly revising process of (re)collecting multiple, contradictory, momentary, and subjective perceptions and traces that negotiates past and present to create narratives of longer duration (Ricoeur 1984; J. Thomas 1996; Wylie 2002).

Nonetheless, situating interpretive order onto this foreign place is achieved every day as historians, archaeologists and others attempt to negotiate these temporal fractures and present, explain or understand past cultural processes and human behaviors that occurred beyond living memory. Of course, the extent to which this is done self-consciously or intuitively, critically or blithely, is where much of the angst and the undermining of interpretation emerges, especially since there is not necessarily a common sense across these disciplines of what history is, or what is meant by "doing history." For present purposes, central to an active definition is adequately capturing the notion that historical methods are the act/art of selectively organizing and prioritizing fragmentary information representing many transitory and often contradictory voices within particular spatial and temporal contexts (Borofsky 2000; Collingwood 1946; Rubertone 2001). What the reflexive critique demands is an awareness that when we weave our self-selected historic factoids into a narrative belt to supposedly reveal a kind of "truth" to the story being told, we impose assumptions and subjectivities that are shaped by our intent and contemporary biases (Tilley 1993).

In addition to recognizing the subjectivity inherent in imagining the past, the reflexive critique has also emphasized historicizing that past, by recognizing the contexts of time and tradition as central to understanding patterns at any moment within that past (e.g., Ohnuki-Tierney 1990; Sahlins 1983, 1985). The result is a reframing of history as anthropology, with a focus on local and detailed context to provide "thick" or "deep" meaning to cultural patterns over time (Silverman and Gulliver 1992:36). Historicizing the past also means reading complementary patterns of both revision and reinforcement into longer term trends—in other words seeing change *and* continuity as an interconnected whole (Sahlins 1985:144). And for the recent past of contested narratives between colonizer and colonized, an anthropological history also seeks to tell histories of the "other," the excluded voices from a written record dominated by class, wealth, power and the colonizer (e.g., Axtell 1992; Faubion 1993; Krech 1991; Trigger 1986a).

Despite this trend, revision has only variably permeated the literature examining the Indigenous populations who experienced the colonial expansion of European powers into other continents over the last half millennium. Much of this work can, at times, be an unreflexive telling of Indigenous change based on the historical record generated by the colonizers. There may be attempts at telling the history of European settlement from the perspective of Indigenous peoples, but nonetheless, the principal plot is a colonizer's history that portrays the period as a unidirectional march toward Indigenous assimilation and obscurity.

Constructing Contacts & Colonialisms

Many past, unreflexive constructions of European contact and colonialism in North America have been aided by a-historical perspectives of Indigenous groups and have assumed rapid and dramatic change occurred immediately upon first contact. These notions are deeply imbedded in "negative master narratives," as Kurt Jordan (2002) has characterized for much of the conventional, postcontact historical writing from the Northeast; i.e., notions of culture change buttressed by concepts of acculturation and dependency. These concepts, and the way they have shaped Native history, are reviewed below.

Acculturation Master Narratives. Originally framed as a way to study processes of change between and among different peoples in contact (e.g., Herskovits 1938; Redfield et al. 1936), acculturation has come to mean the directed change of, in particular, nonwestern cultures in contact with western cultures (e.g., Foster 1960; Linton 1940). Models of acculturation have emphasized a clear progression from "timeless" precontact societies through rapid change triggered by exposure to more "advanced" donor cultures (i.e., European), leading to both a loss of cultural distinctiveness and a dependence on the dominant society for livelihood and even identity.

Acculturation as cultural subordination is entirely consistent with conventional historical interpretations of the impact of European colonial expansion across the globe. And while this understanding of history has been fully criticized (e.g., Axtell 1984; Deitler 2005; Trigger 1986b; Washburn and Trigger 1996), the assumed consequence of it—Indigenous cultures helplessly being enveloped in acculturation processes imposed by culturally and materially superior European societies—has proven to be an entrenched and central theme in constructing these Indigenous pasts. The resulting histories from these master narratives adopt the "negative" tone of decline and ruin, in effect the inevitable outcome of an omnipresent European influence on all Native thoughts and motivations.

Of significance in these kinds of acculturation histories has been the normative view of cultures (Cusick 1998:131). Here, change is systemic and responsive only to external stimuli, denying internal agency or history in processes of change (Albers 2002; Rubertone 2000). As well, it has meant that the transfer of cultural elements from donor (read dominant) to recipient (read subordinate) is demonstrable through the presence or absence of anything to do with the donor. This, as Cusick (1998:130) points out, implies that the degree of acculturation could be measured by an inventory of "acculturative" traits present, and so has a strongly material (read archaeological) dimension, previously embraced as the means to document acculturation archaeologically (e.g., Quimby 1966; Quimby and Spoehr 1951).

Implicit in notions of acculturative change is change *to* something and away *from* something else. Thus, change occurs because of contact, and in the absence of contact, there is no change. This reinforces the notion of an ethnographic present—Indigenous cultures being without history prior to European contact—which denies the archaeological fact that change and contact between groups was and is a continuous process (Borofsky 2000; Faubion

1993; Trigger 1981). This effectively marginalizes Indigenous histories and makes them little more than reactive background noise to the main story of European advancement during the contact era (Paynter 2000b; L. Smith 1999).

Clearly, there is a lot of baggage to disengage. Over time, acculturation has come to be narrowly equated with the subordination and assimilation of groups by European powers, contributing to the entrenchment of a negativist historical narrative and assumptions becoming facts for many researchers. If explored, these assumptions appear to originate from, and thus reinforce, racial and hegemonic ideologies of the more recent and dominant western society in North America, which tend to emphasize the natural "rightness" of the legacy of the colonizer (L. Smith 1999; Wylie 1995). Although research has become sensitized to this ideological baggage, it has been pointed out that this on its own does not preclude the continued use of deterministic narratives (Rubertone 2000; White 1998). The study of Aboriginal history has struggled to find a relevancy free of the imperialist baggage that the European context has created (J. Cruikshank 2002; Fixico 1997). To understand how this baggage has shaped historical research, I will now look at the history of creating European-Native histories in North America.

Ethnohistory, Anthropological History or New Indian History. I do not make a distinction here between studies undertaken by anthropologists or historians of the "contact" era in North America. This kind of work has increasingly been of a common methodological and conceptual frame, collectively labeled "ethnohistory" (Faubion 1993; Krech 1991). This less than distinct research orientation and more an analytical approach and particularistic perspective arose from research in the postwar era tied to land claims research (Washburn and Trigger 1996). The formal, legal need for these studies privileged historic documentary sources over informant-based ethnographic data, forcing anthropologists into State archives to build cases to substantiate, or refute, First Nations' disputes with the State (Krech 1991:347).

The reliance on written records to document the impact of contact and colonialism meant that some portion of ethnohistorical research largely adopted the conventions of standard historical research. This form of history typically was assumed to be an objective exercise: revealing fixed "truths" by the act of uncovering data from archives and presenting that data within a deterministic narrative offered up by the historian. But while that kind of conventional approach still obviously requires the evaluative source critique expected of any historical research, ethnohistory also has to somehow negotiate the fact that information in written documents was recorded by individual Europeans. It encompassed their personal reactions and was based on their imperfect knowledge of the meanings of Indigenous behaviors and ways of life (Borofsky 2000; Sahlins 1985).

This is a critical challenge, since "truthfulness" is not the only issue with the documentary records from colonial powers. Indeed, the act of creating and archiving documents represents the preservation of an official record of the colonial enterprise (Comaroff and Comaroff 1992:34), which ultimately serves as the basis for the historical accounting of that colonial power. But, as this is only one dimension of the totality of the past, the ethnohistorian presumably also needs to listen for the omissions or "silences" in that record, which encompass alternate, unrecorded Indigenous experiences of that same past (Trouillot 1995; see also, Fogelson 1989; Mann 1999). This is no easy task for those attempting to tell histories of the Other from the documents of colonizers, especially when following the conventions and assumptions of narrative history. Consequently, for too many studies of Indigenous people in contact with Europeans, the resulting constructions situate Aboriginal history as response to European history.

To illustrate this point, an area in which the unreflexive acceptance of the messaging in written records has affected ethnohistoric interpretations in northeastern North America is the concept of dependency. Dependency in the context of European colonialism has meant a direct Native reliance on European powers for sustenance and supplies, and ultimately as the motivation for historically recorded behaviors such as warfare, abandoned lifeways, and so on. This idea was particularly common in the economic-materialist perspectives in fur trade studies, which have operated almost as a "subdiscipline" of ethnohistory (Albers 2002:119).

For some, dependency emerged from the imposition of European mercantile institutions and forces, something beyond Native power to control (e.g., Albers 2002:120; Wolf 1982:175). More common in the literature, however, is a kind of Native antiagency, a material determinism that saw rapid change and quick dependency due exclusively to an obsessive desire on the part of Native people for trade goods—what has been characterized as a "trade good junkies" mentality (Branstner 1991:208, 1992:187–188). As Branstner notes, fur trade studies attribute several dire consequences to this uncontrollable desire for goods, including a rapid decline in Native abilities to maintain traditional subsistence practices and mobility, leading to a sedentary lifestyle and reliance on Europeans for food (e.g., Bishop 1984; Ray 1988). Dependency was also seen as triggering a shift from egalitarian order and communal structure to mercantile behavior, materialistic attitudes and wealth accumulation; individual ownership of land; and differential social status, all leading to internal factionalism and ultimately, a disintegration of social order (e.g., Yerbury 1986). White (1983) also suggested that a reliance on European items led to changes in subsistence that in turn led to dependence on those goods.

Krech (1988) pointed out that dependency was rarely defined in fur trade literature (see also White 1991:482–485). He saw less scholarly analysis in the sweeping generalizations and more repetition of earlier Victorian sensibilities toward Indigenous peoples still living on the land (Krech 1988:63). Of course, these sensibilities also permeated the written records of trading post personnel, which were the primary source material for fur trade researchers advocating dependency. Historical accounts of starving Natives, of "lazy" families more content to stay by the post, preferring to drink and beg for food than go out and hunt, reflect the views of an enclave of mostly men at fixed places describing their experiences and the relative success and failure of their efforts. What occurred beyond their pen or beyond their care or capacity to understand cultural difference are some of those "nonevents" of the past so relevant to Indigenous-lived histories (Fogelson 1989).

For example, strong critical analyses suggest that European descriptions of Native starvation, poverty and alcoholism may be less an accurate reflection of dire circumstances and more a misreading of formalized interactions, speech conventions and behavioral variability within communities (e.g., Black-Rogers 1986; Vibert 1997; Wagner 1998). Recorded observations also indiscriminately captured or overlooked the vagaries, season to season, of the availability of game, the variable skills or emphases of hunters at a given time, and other specific contingencies that were much more transitory than the recorded permanence of historic observations can allow for. While these other realities need to be accounted for, it is easy to see how, with unreflexive assumptions about the inevitability of dependency and European influence, historic references to game depletion and starvation would be expected in the record, and when found, simply confirm the assumptions behind those expectations.

Krech (1988:64–65) suggested researchers needed to clearly define what they meant when using terms like dependency, and suggested there are qualitative and quantitative differences in the historic record between dependence as economic reliance, and dependency as a loss of political, social and economic autonomy; the latter being the dependency envisioned in the generalizations mentioned above.

While I concur with those qualifications, more generally I still wonder what was achieved by debating the year or generation when a family or community became dependent, or how many separate references in documentary sources were needed for a scholar to confirm dependency? And could there be no going back the following year? Just how do these kinds of debate advance the ethnohistorical aim of understanding the history of Native-lived experiences? To me, the insidious element of dependency as even a topic of research or concept in the histories written about Native-lived pasts is not even the materialist valuation ascribed to "independence" and "dependence." Rather it is that the discussion entirely framed any consideration of Native peoples within the Eurocentric history of capitalist endeavors. Their history, then, becomes something only about when, or whether or not, one or more aspects of the European experience in North America interrupted or extinguished traditional values. It also made victims of Native people, because they are presented as trapped in a very small world of either seeking commodities for trade accommodated within "normal" lifeways, or being obsessed with the capitalist pursuit. There was no capacity, regardless of where food or supplies came from, to consider the multitude of complex human behaviors going on within and between communities, and the histories of these people that occurred beyond the mercantile dimension. In this way, Natives could only ever be cardboard backdrops in a play about European economic interests, either depicted as cringing or defiant, but entirely in someone else's story.

Of course, I recognize that the concept of dependency as a viable dimension of Indigenous histories has declined as ethnohistoric work has sought to leave behind the implicit baggage of acculturation and dependency. Moreover, revisions to Aboriginal histories began to emerge with the efforts of researchers such as Merrell (1989a) and White (1991), who offered distinct interpretations of the impact of Aboriginal-European contact in the Eastern Woodlands, resituating the narrative to more directly reflect Native-specific experiences, aims and agency. White, for example, conceived of a temporally, ideologically and spatially distinct "Middle Ground" within the Great Lakes area, during which neither Aboriginal or European held dominance. As such an accommodation had to emerge where people could bridge each other's differences and imperfect knowledge to find a common ground from which to interact. Merrell offered an even more Native-centered accounting of contact, with communities creatively adapting to European expansion and disruption by creating distinct, physically separate Native "New Worlds," a strategy of holding on to identity and tradition in the face of rapid change.

These studies were part of a major catalyst for revising Native North American history, resituating Aboriginal nations on an equal footing with European colonial powers in contact histories, and emphasizing an Indigenous agency (Albers 2002:120; see also, Cobb 2005; Hauptman 1995). There was a sense, particularly in American historiography, that a "New

Indian History" had emerged, one that brought a relevance to the study and recovered it from the margins (Axtell 1997; Fixico 1997; Hagan 1997).

Yet there was still much in revisionist approaches that continued to rely on the central master narrative of contact, decline and obscurity. For example, Merrell (1989a:556) referring to the Catawba peoples as either "clinging to their cultural identity," or observing that "the deck was stacked against them. They played the hand dealt them well enough to survive, but they could never win." Likewise, White (1991:518–523) saw the Middle Ground yielding to assimilation and otherness by the early 19th century. Elsewhere, Osborne and Ripmeester (1997:269) characterized the relationship of Ojibwa to Euro-Canadians as one of "parasitic dependency."

The continued use of this kind of language in historical research has proven difficult to overcome. Notably, Morantz castigated fur trade researchers and others for the use of value-laden language as she convincingly challenged the assumption of instant dependency: "Yet what is disturbing in present-day native histories is the lack of attention to the influence of certain terminology that subtly affects the reader's view of Indians, just as 'savage' used to do" (1992:187). But despite this critique, in the same article she offers statements such as "Dependency was the *pitiful* path towards which *all* Indian societies were headed, but it is not the subarctic fur trade alone that *propelled* them to this *end*" (Morantz 1992:186, emphasis added). This is a stark demonstration of how embedded the judgmental language of negative master narratives, and the assumptions reflected in that language, can be, even when trying to overcome it.

The use of such language echoes earlier acculturation sensibilities, reaffirming the ultimate conclusion those studies reached: that the final chapter remains one of Native people being overwhelmed and lost in a European/American/Canadian national history. And despite pleas for a broader relevance to "Native history" within history proper (e.g., Merrell 1989b; Richter 1993), the continued implicit support of a negative master narrative means the moral of the story is already known; any retelling or minor retooling of limited interest beyond the specialist field.

I do not want to imply here that I am dismissing out of hand all ethnohistorical efforts in the Northeast as parochial or imperialist, nor denying that significant advances in scholarship and critical analysis have occurred and are occurring. Indeed, while White's Middle Ground continues to influence thinking (e.g., Gosden 2004), it is also true that many have moved away from the tropes in contact = conquest narratives (e.g., compare Richter 1992 to Richter 2001). Moreover, the canon of ethnohistorical work has contributed meaningfully to a broader understanding of the history of interaction between Indigenous nations and European nations. The trend in this research over the last two decades represents a strong move toward the kind of distinctive blending of anthropology and history that ethnohistorical approaches are striving for. Nevertheless, it is also fair to say that the blending of history into anthropology is ongoing, and this work, under the title ethnohistory, anthropological history, New Indian History or some other, is still working its way through a slowly moving reflexive critique. As such, current thinking is more a point along this transition than a completed realignment (Cobb 2005; Deloria 2002; Meyer and Klein 1998; White 1998).

So the internal, critical revision that arises from an overtly theoretical discourse has begun to penetrate the ethnohistoric enterprise. As it has in the fields of history, anthropology and archaeology more generally, the manifestation of this revision in ethnohistory will redress any marginalization through reflexivity, making overt embedded assumptions, exposing the artifice of scholar and subject, expunging otherness from narratives (e.g., Borofsky 2000; Dirlik 2000), and ultimately making "ethnohistory" as a categorization—and research ghetto—irrelevant to the anthropological history of North America. Archaeology can play a critical role in furthering this direction.

Archaeologically Imagining the Past

The theoretical debate in archaeology encompasses the same reflexive critique that has consumed the other historically oriented social sciences. Archaeology, too, has had to negotiate the past as foreign, subjective, and constructed in the present and unhistoricized. The ebb and flow of various theoretical strands in recent archaeological debates reflect the struggle to come to terms with how archaeologists construct the past from fragments, and whether or not to accept archaeology as historicized (e.g., Hodder 1986; Trigger 1989a, 1989b; Wylie 2002).

As with history, archaeology must also contend with the fact that it inherently is the act/art of selective emphasis on limited available material traces—artifacts, features and contexts—making it a construction of a collage of fragmented and contestable meanings rather than a reconstruction of a singular truth. The resulting interpretations are thus the product of a contemporary practice of selecting particular stories from a record that can accommodate many differing interpretations and emphases (Hodder 1986; Wylie 1993), and situates archaeologist, archaeological methods and narrative presentation as essential elements in the story being told. The relativity implicit in this view of archaeology can leave some breathless, but also implicit here is the need for constant revising of interpretations based on constantly refined understandings of the archaeological record. Archaeological "progress," then, is a continual hermeneutic spiral (Hodder 1991, 1999), building an interpretive corpus on top of the accumulated record that counters "just so" story making (Trigger 2006).

Recently, there has been a coming together of various theoretical strands that advances reflexivity and archaeology as history alongside the cultural historical need for classifying and ordering data, and the processualist demand for rigorous data analysis. This intellectual legacy of the immediate past half century is described as the emergence of either a new conceptual paradigm or a kind of interpretive middle ground—an eclectic pragmatism that welcomes pluralism (e.g., Duke 1995; Pauketat 2001; Trigger 2006). As part of this pluralism, archaeologists from all intellectual stripes now seek historical perspective in their interpretations (Hodder 2001), finding a more nuanced understanding of the past by acknowledging the historical context within which social processes—embedded in the material traces under investigation—operated. To get to this understanding, archaeologists have turned to several conceptual and analytical tools to enhance a "historicization" of archaeology (e.g., Last 1995).

Archaeological History

An overt embracing of archaeology as history has arisen from the common conceptual ground that archaeologists have found with the French Annales school of history, most prominently represented by Braudel (1972, 1980). Annales historians have sought a multidisciplinary, data-rich approach to the examination of the broad economic, environmental and social factors that shape history, leading to the development of extensive ethnographic social histories over relatively deep time depths.

Of particular interest to archaeologists has been Braudel's multiscalar conception of time, specifically the idea that different historical processes operate along differing temporal rhythms (Braudel 1972:20–21; see also Bintliff 1991; Hodder 1987; Knapp 1992), each characterized by particular sociocultural processes that shape the historical narrative differently (M. Smith 1992:25). This includes time as event: a short duration dominated by personal and political processes. Of medium duration is time as conjuncture, which is dominated by economic, nationalist and societal processes. Then there is time as *longue durée* or long-term, an almost unchanging duration over centuries, dominated by environmental processes and structures that are largely invisible in the shorter rhythms of time, but still constrain and shape change at those levels. It is the long-term that is privileged in Braudel's work, while events are considered almost epiphenomenal, mere foam on the sea that is the deep history of the long-term (Braudel 1980; Last 1995:142).

With its access to the momentary acts that cause archaeological traces, to the palimpsest of actions and motivations captured in a site occupied for decades or centuries, and to the long-term, ancient patterns those traces collectively create within the archaeological record, Braudel's conceptual framework fits well within archaeological perceptions of the past (Duke 1992:101). As well, the differing scales of change through time implied in Braudel's hierarchy encourage multiscalar analyses—change evident at the short or medium term can take on a different meaning when a longer context is considered. These scales of time thus operate along a continuum, providing "a heuristic framework in which to conceptualize time and change in . . . society" (Knapp 1992:10).

Annales studies also underscore the important role of narrative and a historical imagination that negotiates between lived reality and our representations of that reality (Ricoeur 1984, 1989). So narrative is recognized as the "natural" part of understanding the past, albeit as the constructionist and ideological presentation the reflexive critique has noted (Last 1995:147).

While Braudel's brand in particular of the Annales approach has been criticized for undervaluing the importance of events and underplaying the importance of the ideational, subsequent Annales work has emphasized events and *mentalité*, or the ideational (Burke 1990). This creates a more interactive tension between long-term structures and events (Last 1995:143), allowing human action a greater role in affecting structural change (Duke 1992:101). This also more closely situates Annales approaches with archaeology, which continually negotiates between the particular instances of site formation and material deposition, and the long-term human history that record reveals.

While archaeological exploration of Annales thinking has been less the gaining of a theoretical orientation and more a conceptual methodology or analytical tool, its focus on time and the tension between event and structure—agency and process—has in turn increased the profile of other conceptions at play in constructing archaeological histories. Notably, archaeological explorations of Annales thinking link closely with the concept of agency by seeking a more dynamic understanding of the processes of agency within an historicized context, tying long-term multiscalar analyses with the active social processes in which all individuals and groups participated (Dobres and Robb 2000:7). Of particular emphasis has been the effort to recognize how "in-time" historical context shaped, and was shaped by, the negotiation of daily life. This conception of the past is seen as self-referential and relative, based on the specific historical contexts in which individuals and groups all lived. From this perspective, archaeological data are no longer just static, a-historical remnants of the cultural systems of past human behavior, since the materiality of the past is seen to have significance not so much in its form, but in the diverse contexts it operated in as *part* of the social processes and practices existing in that historical reality (Barrett 2001:157; see also, Pauketat 2003). Thus, agency arises from daily living, where cultural categories, values, and meanings are continually negotiated, reproduced, transformed and ultimately infused into the archaeological record (Deitler and Herbich 1998:246–247).

Much of the discussion of agency in archaeology relies on Bourdieu's (1977, 1990) practice theory and construction of habitus, and Giddens's (1982, 1984) notion of practice in maintaining and transforming social structures. Bourdieu provides a framework for understanding the world as lived through the concept of habitus, which consists of the durable dispositions people have: those perceptions of themselves and the way the world works around them—their ways of knowing and doing (Hodder 1986:70–76; S. Jones 1997:88–89). These dispositions are a set of less-than-rules that operate unarticulated and underneath daily living, and represent the conventions and unexamined assumptions of how the world is ordered. They are ultimately passed on between generations through enculturation. Dispositions structure new experiences based on knowledge gained from past experience, with all the embedded inequities or counter-intuitive practices such as class, gender, divisions of labor and authority that are naturalized into these perceptions of the "way things are." As such, dispositions create "tendencies" (culturally perceived limits) to possible patterns of choice. But dispositions are also interactive with lived experience. Indeed, daily practices and dispositions (action and structure) are in constant negotiation, continuously revising these referents that make "sense" of the lived world. Unpredictable circumstances, surroundings and participants can all cause the implicit to become explicit and open to analysis and discussion, which can trigger a reinforcement of the existing habitus (orthodoxy), or greater, paradigmatic revision (heterodoxy).

Giddens (1982:36–37) contributes to this conceptual framing by seeing structure and agency in an interconnected, ongoing process of producing and maintaining each other. Here structures are both the medium and outcome of practices that make up the social system. Thus, agency is more the continuous *process* of practices than it is the active participation in culture of individual agents.

The ideas of these two theorists have frequently found their way into interpretive archaeology that examines social process, power, identity and gender. But it is in the area of material culture where the framing of agency through practice is emphasized (e.g., Deitler and Herbich 1998; Dobres 2000). Here material culture is conceived of as technology operating through a sequence of dynamic processes reflecting culturally and historically specific contexts of interaction, meaning-making, and choice (Dobres and Hoffman 1994:215; Deitler and Herbich 1998:238). Each of these processes inter-sects various dimensions of social action, and individuals who act on their imperfect knowledge of the world make choices and mediate expectation, understanding, opposition, and alternative (Dobres and Hoffman 1994:223). Moreover, there is a temporal dimension here, both in terms of maintain-ing practices between generations (enculturating the young in ownership of knowledge, material, methods, one's lot in life), and in the "drift" of dispo-sitions, either through the ongoing act of revision or through heterodox or orthodox alterations to the habitus.

The importance of this conceptual framework is significant for archaeol-ogy. A ceramic pot becomes something more than an object to be described. It is the recovered medium through which a range of social actions are nego-tiated and played out, representing all the social dimensions touched upon when harvesting clay, manufacturing and designing, and purchasing or trad-ing, as well as in terms of function, domestic use, cuisine, and trash dis-posal. All the people encountered along that sequence of social planes shape and are shaped by the choices available in the pot itself. Here, then, is the unique purview and potential of archaeology: multiscalar investigations of daily lived experience getting at and beyond historical otherness and "into" the historical context of the people whose remains are being examined, so as to, for example, know things such as "what hunter-gatherers were like in a world of hunter-gatherers" (Sassaman 2000:164).

This conceptual approach to archaeology can also bridge the chasm between precontact (or anthropological) and postcontact (or historical) archaeology (e.g., Lightfoot 1995; Williamson 2004) by focusing on those social material dimensions of lived life (e.g., settlement-subsistence, material culture process and enculturation) that remain accessible with or without documents. The main difference between these "pre" and "post" facets of archaeology then becomes a methodological issue, not a theoretical one (e.g., Small 1999; Thurston 1997), since the theoretical issues of seeking to under-stand the past agency and historical structure of the world those actors lived in, and the role of the archaeologist in constructing that understanding, are the same (e.g., Paynter 2000a:23). In this way, too, "historic" archaeology becomes demonstrably something other than a "handmaiden" to history, enjoying the same unique access to lived experience through the remnants of daily life that the rest of a more pluralistic, precontact archaeology does (Funari et al. 1999; Little 1994).

Eliminating the divide between pre- and postcontact archaeologies is critical for allowing the examination of contact and subsequent processes of colonialism beyond the context of specific historic events, and free of the generalizing and essentialist assumptions of negativist master narratives. This reflects the utility of long-term perspectives to strip away the particular from longer rhythms of time, providing an Indigenous context from which to explore contact. This is history exclusively through the perspective of archaeology, as anthropological and historical scholarship cannot reach beyond those written records, or can do so only more "imperfectly" than archaeology. Critically, then, it is the exclusive purview of archaeology not only to know of the history of hunter-gatherers in a world only of hunter-gatherers but also to know of the connected "pre" and "post" histories of the global, anticolonial, other-European past. It is only within this deeper temporal context that a more pluralistic, multiscalar and reflexive attempt to understand the last 500 years can emerge.

Archaeologies of Contact/Colonialism

In ethnohistory, some researchers have suggested archaeology is too limited to grasp the complex, social dimensions historical research has access to (e.g., Axtell 2001; Richter 1993). There is also a perception that archaeology is largely about the theft of Indigenous culture, which compromises the legitimacy of archaeological findings (e.g., Fixico 1997; Thornton 1998). Despite this, others have recognized that recent theoretical advances in archaeology provide much more meaningful interpretive links between material record and social organization or group worldview than previous, descriptive cultural histories could ever have allowed (Albers 2002; Krech 1991; Meyer and Klein 1998). There is also a growing awareness of the complexity and depth to the archaeological histories in the millennia before Europeans arrived (e.g., Calloway 2003; Richter 2001; Salisbury 1996), something historians had been largely unaware of previously.

While anthropology has embraced historical perspective, there has been a reluctance to recognize archaeology as an important added dimension to diachronic studies, despite acknowledging the limitations to how far in time anthropology can reach back (Silverman and Gulliver 1992:39), or that long-term history is not "easily accessible for histories of non-literate peoples" (Ohnuki-Tierney 1990:3). This failure to recognize the use of archaeology to reach back and provide histories of, in particular, nonliterate peoples in a time before contact or colonialism is ubiquitous within much of the reflexive writing in historical anthropology.

But if some historians and anthropologists were slow to accept the merit of archaeology, archaeologists have also been slow to act on the potential of their work within the realm of contact and colonialism. Previously, archaeologists tended to buy into conventional historical narratives for the contact era, by looking at the archaeological record for evidence to confirm rapid change associated with a desire for European goods. These expectations were reinforced by assumptions that the archaeology of Indigenous groups "ended" at the culmination of early contact (Rubertone 2000), which tended to mean that historical archaeology in North America was interested in studying Native cultures only "when their basic cultural and ecological patterns were altered by contact and when this was displayed in archaeological data" (Schuyler 1978:28). As Rubertone (1996, 2000:429) notes, this view relegated archaeological contributions to confirmatory footnotes in the last chapter of historic Native dependency narratives.

This "handmaiden to history" perspective was augmented by the fact that past, cultural historical archaeology, acclimatized to a specific range of material remains expected on precontact sites, associated the "sudden" appearance of a wide range of European-made items, distinctive and colorful, with dramatic change. After all, for culture historians, material culture change in the Great Lakes of a more limited nature, such as altered artifact decoration or new tool forms, had been interpreted as signaling massive population migrations or militaristic ethnic cleansing. The logic thus follows that the relatively sudden appearance of European-manufactured items on Native sites was presumably as dramatic for those inhabitants as it certainly had been for the archaeologists who rediscovered them.

In recent years, more complex interpretations of the archaeological record from the last 500 years have emerged. Attempts have been made to overhaul material measurements of change arising from Quimby's acculturative trait lists (e.g., Bamforth 1993; Ramenofsky 1998; J. D. Rogers 1990). Others have argued that Indigenous interests in and consumption of European goods was selective, driven by Native-centric logic and needs, and that these items, once accepted, operated inside preexisting Native conceptions of the material world (e.g., Hamell 1987; Miller and Hamell 1986; Trigger 1991). However, some of these approaches still conveyed a sense of Indigenous groups mesmerized by European objects, ascribing them greater meaning and value than Indigenous analogues, albeit based on a Native-constructed habitus. As a result, others have questioned using trait lists altogether, cautioning that they risk revitalizing acculturation notions of Native passivity and dependency (e.g., Fowler 1987), or that they still conceptually imply a unidirectional path of change without choice or alternatives (e.g., Rubertone 2001), or assume Natives were consuming European goods *and* the cultural values embedded in those objects (e.g., Cusick 1998; Upton 1996).

That being said, some authors of revised material culture studies clearly are revisionist in their thinking and offer more nuanced understandings of what change in material culture does, and does not, reflect (e.g., Farnsworth 1992; Hoover 1992; J. D. Rogers 1990). Indeed, Rogers' work is often cited as groundbreaking (e.g., Cusick 1998; Rubertone 2000). He argued that trait lists are of little utility since trade goods, as with all artifact classes, are not randomly distributed across sites, which suggests differential cultural processes create differing archaeological contexts, and thus contextually variable meanings will be associated with those differences (J. D. Rogers 1990:100–101). Repeating patterns in each context thus reveal temporally discrete meanings and reflections of agency, rather than a simple presence-absence of directed acculturation.

Spector (1993) similarly eschews categorizing European-manufactured items as distinct classes of artifact, or assuming that their value and meaning came to Native people solely from the fact that those items were European-derived materials. Rather, she argues meaning is accessed through a consideration of these objects within holistic analyses of the material assemblage used by Native people day to day. This rejects outright the notion that European-imbedded cultural meanings are somehow "naturally" transferred intact with the artifacts themselves, and recognizes that these items, found within Native spheres of life and livelihood, were understood by Native peoples within that context and their worldview, and not foreign to it.

From these revisionist perspectives, trade goods thus are less agents of immediate change and more innovations to existing material culture. These enhancements may have assisted subsistence or augmented artistic and symbolic expression, and may even have encouraged change to facilitate continued access to these goods. But as cosmologies, foodways and subsistence are also inherently and strategically conservative, adopted innovations and enhanced economic strategies also reflect limited accommodation—change *and* continuity—rather than wholesale modification and abandonment of the past, something Nassaney and Johnson (2000:15) point out is often unaccounted for in conventional acculturation studies of Native-European contact.

In effect, these perspectives achieve an "inside" context to the historically lived experience of Native people. Rubertone (2001:xiv–xv) sees such interpretations as a kind of cultural translation, using all threads (historical, archaeological and memory) available from the past to weave an understanding of particular peoples at particular times. She suggests (2001:189) that there are multiple histories of the colonial experience to tell, and that although they will conflict with each other, in the end, they are "truer" to individual lived experiences than any master narrative that inevitably favors the colonizers. As Rubertone (2000:432) notes, these transformative processes more significantly reflect Native-centric beliefs, motives and behaviors, and so situate archaeology as both contributor and challenger to historical interpretation. The results provide more robust interpretations of the past, emphasizing a temporally deep context for contact and a more nuanced understanding of colonialism; and both from the perspective of the Indigenous (Lightfoot 2006). The interpretive results, in turn, have proven "profound" (Rubertone 2000:431) for archaeology and for understanding the last half millennium.

Archaeological "Contacts"

The emphasis in these revisionist studies on internal processes governing the selection, use and disposal of exchanged goods is not new; archaeologists continually grapple with and interpret these processes of interaction throughout the archaeological record. Indeed, the conventional focus of acculturation— European contact as the catalyst for change within Indigenous cultures—is a narrow understanding of interaction. What archaeology shows, in either Old or New Worlds and in either the recent or distant past, is that human populations were constantly "in contact" with foreign (external) peoples, their ideas and material culture. Moreover, archaeology clearly reveals that external influences are manifested differently within communities: selectively rejected or accepted, incorporated and internalized (e.g., Schortman and Urban 1998). This recognizes the porous and fluid nonboundary state of "cultures" (if not a demonstration of the real lack of utility the concept has for understanding human behavior), and the basic interconnectedness of communities over wide geographies.

If we thus accept there is a kind of "archaeological law"—i.e., that external contact and change was/is a constant of human existence—then there needs to be a conceptual shift in the study of European-Native interaction in North America. Seeking unidirectional evidence of acculturative change or dependency triggered by the sudden arrival of Europeans, along with the assumptions that Indigenous groups passively accepted—or actively hungered for—the ideological and material manifestations of dominant societies, becomes moot (Williamson 2004). Instead, shifting conceptions means focusing on the complex internal processes of identity maintenance and revision manifest through the acceptance and rejection of external innovations (ideological or material) reconstituted within local actions and beliefs—processes that are found within all peoples at all times.

This perspective invites expanding the temporal and geographic range of contact and colonialism from that conventionally examined in acculturation work. Rather than assuming contact must be explained within the rise of European imperialism and a capitalist world economy, archaeologists can also examine global patterns from other periods of contact and colonialism (Gosden 2004; Lyons and Papadopoulos 2002; Stein 2005) in comparison with patterns detailed from the last half millennium. These broader contexts consistently confirm Cusick's point (1998:140) that contact is structured but not deterministic, shaped by historical contingencies and the particular people and time under study.

Expanding on this idea, Alexander (1998:482–487) points to broad regularities in the studies presented in Cusick's volume as reflecting a continuum of contact histories. At one end of this continuum is "Symmetrical Exchange"—the kind of interregional interaction Jamieson (1999), Nassaney and Sassaman (1995) and others have discussed for precontact North America. These are networks of interaction extending across geographic, national and linguistic boundaries, connecting communities along commonly understood economic, social and ritual domains (Alexander 1998:486).

Further along the continuum are contexts referred to as "Cultural Entanglement"—contact between colonial states and hinterlands or nondirected contact between distant groups or nations (Alexander 1998). Here interaction leading to change is innovative, selective, and follows situation-specific logic. This interaction may serve as a precursor to colonialism, or not, and can be sustained in its own right for centuries or millennia. The first few centuries of European contact in the Northeast can be characterized this way, for example (Wagner 1998, 2001).

At the far end of this continuum are contexts of formalized colonialism—"Asymmetrical Interaction"—where economic and power differences are extreme between colonizers and colonized (Alexander 1998:482). Here is the active, coercive force of formal colonialism, often imposed over great distances and manifested through local colonizer populations facilitating an extractive economy that benefits the core at the expense of the periphery. Indigenous economies are heavily modified and labor structures altered, affecting social organization. Also operating at this end of the continuum are myriad forms of resistance, from conflict and struggle against coercive power, to a range of more subtle forms of defiance and imaginings of a hopeful future shaping the daily lived experience of the colonized (Given 2004; Scott 1990). I would also suggest that later stages of colonial asymmetries in some contexts become qualitatively different, characterized by institutionalized inequality, social experimentation, and marginalization of Indigenous populations in favor of now dominant populations racially or culturally recognized as being of the colonizer: in effect a resituating of "enclave" from the colonizer to the Indigenous.

Conceiving of contact as continuum, attuned to place, time, local agency and specific historical context, but also contextualized within the deeper time depth only archaeology can access, is a critical revision to conventional notions of European-Indigenous histories. It also implies that "contact", as a qualitative term or category of experience, will be an important social process but only one of several in understanding human historical trajectories. In this sense "contact" also becomes meaningless as a descriptor for any given period of the past. What becomes more important is to conceive of change and continuity as happening continuously within the negotiated planes of social processes encountered daily. So experiences of "first contact" are removed from the novelty of the written record of Europeans' experiences, and placed within the Indigenous structures and agency of individual and group interaction with the external.

The critical point I take away from researchers like Alexander, as well as Silliman (2005), is that histories of interaction are a continuum of contexts and recursive social processes. So for me, being able to conceptualize contact as interaction, and interaction as social process, eliminates the normative and essentialist baggage of "cultures in contact." This ultimately means that the Native-lived history of the last half millennium for the lower Great Lakes can be characterized as continuing symmetrical exchange between local Aboriginal communities and foreign Aboriginal and European groups through much of the 16th and early 17th centuries. Entanglement, which I take to mean the existence of a colonizer with an imperial, transregional economic agenda within the historic theatre of the Northeast, characterized the late 17th and much of the 18th centuries, connected to the structures and processes that had emerged over the previous couple of centuries.

However, colonialism, as a distinct quality of Great Lakes history, did not manifest itself until late in the 18th century, and then peripherally, spreading as a revising set of dispositions manifest both as intangible concepts and as real impacts experienced in the everyday. Indeed, as the context that touched on and began to constrain the daily lived experiences of Native people, colonialism did not fully emerge until the Colonial state really began to *ignore* the autonomy of Aboriginal nations through the callous and indifferent acts of transforming the region into a world of and for the colonizer. Importantly, thinking of the archaeological history of Native-lived colonialisms in this way thus becomes an exercise in understanding Native people negotiating social processes and the external forces impinging on those processes *as* a continuation of their own deep histories, albeit increasingly as the means of maintaining a coherency in the face of that emergent colonialism (e.g., Given 2004; Williamson 2004).

Archaeologically Being in *Their* Time

The conceptual shift in archaeology toward context specific, multiscalar archaeological histories of lived life creates opportunities to illustrate the critical value archaeological evidence brings in understanding Indigenous experiences (e.g., Rogers 1990; Rubertone 2001; Spector 1993; Wagner 2001). From this orientation, then, archaeology connects the threads of evidence found in the material record to those social dimensions of life and worldviews nonarchaeologists believe we cannot access. This is certainly the case when examining material culture not as static objects but as the traces of negotiated social planes arising from the internalized processes of maintenance and revision to habitus. These planes encompass processes of enculturation that order the world between generations, manage labor and gender dynamics within and outside the house, and define perceived limits to choice, future goals and the "achievability" of these, even in the face of hegemonic power.

   Another critical, archaeological way of understanding that allows access to these deeper social processes arises from constructions of settlement and subsistence. This is the world negotiated every day, the stuff of the prosaic and mundane and the ordering of domestic needs, where nonetheless social meanings and structures operate (e.g., Hodder 1998, 2004; J. Thomas 1996). Settlement-subsistence activities reflect a wide array of decision-making strategies and tensions that are all defined and negotiated around socially constrained options—or dispositions—informed by knowing the past, experiencing the present, and assuming the future (e.g., Binford 1980; Jochim 1991; Kelly 1992). On top of this is layered a host of ecological realities, such as landscape, climate, seasons, and resource abundance that are reflected in the who, what, where and when, for example, of scheduling farming-related tasks during fish or game harvest times. The myriad factors accounted for in subsistence decisions become translated as social choices or priorities that are weighed differently from community to community, as well as within the household (e.g., K. Jordan 2002:68–69; Kent 1989). Ultimately, it is this prior knowing subsumed in daily decision-making that shapes, and is itself shaped by, an intimately understood heritage of place and community that integrates economic, social and ritual dimensions of human experience, and contributes so greatly to defining identity and the world beyond the edge of the village, camp or cabin (Evans 2003; Rival 2002).

Indeed, more than any consideration of an artifact's utility, decisions around subsistence scheduling, whether or not to relocate settlement or to use differing house forms, to disperse or congregate, seasonally or annually, will rely on set dispositions that are resistant to the vagaries of the immediate, and shape responses to the immediate (e.g., Sassaman 2001:226–227). In other words, the social structures and processes developed over generations of experience constitute a historically informed knowledge base that has "enhanced selective value" (Trigger 2003:12) over the new or different. Therefore, an important way for archaeologists to examine change and continuity over the last 500 years is to pay close attention to shifts in settlement-subsistence, as these can better offer insight into deeper social change or continuity than the surficial changes seen in material assemblages (Prince 2002).

But despite an enhanced selective value for the known over the new, it is important to recognize that scheduling the annual seasonal round activities of subsistence and settlement needs also requires a historically informed flexibility to accommodate contingencies. This means that the social processes manifest in settlement-subsistence are constantly being revised. So, change *and* continuity exist constantly and in tandem. Significantly for distinguishing changing continuities from discontinuities over the last five hundred years, then, change as deleterious to cultural integrity is seen archaeologically only when it deviates from, and so is fundamentally inconsistent with, historic trajectories of behavior. Deleterious change does *not* arise if change represents continuous refinement of those trajectories. This is an important acknowledgement of complexity and fluidity operating in communities, and the nonlinear nature of changed continuities.

Getting at these trajectories as reflected in settlement-subsistence is truly the unique purview of archaeology. Moreover, beyond constructing meaningful settlement-subsistence patterns directly from archaeological data, archaeologists can also access comparable data from written records—a kind of archival excavation of historically documented data of archaeological relevance (e.g.,

Galloway 1992). For example, records written by trading post personnel or missionaries resident in a Native community are written from a fixed place, and so can offer insight on the daily, seasonal and yearly rhythms of people, hunting and farming activities, and other seasonally sensitive emphases of daily life. In other words, a written calendar tracking the social dispositions informing settlement and subsistence decision-making can be recovered, entirely compatible with archaeological data. Of course, historic observations also include observer biases. But if the point is to construct archaeological narratives to understand the historically lived experience of Native communities, who cares what an 18th-century priest or fur trader thought of or judged Native lifeways? An archaeological history brings with it the ability to negotiate around the narrative and observations of European "I-witnesses" (Dening 1994), the term Dening uses to both capture the notion of the subjective author and underscore the biases and personal perspectives that exist within the historic observations of European scribes of European-centric experiences of the past. To recover the *archaeologically* meaningful data from the written record, archaeological histories need to find and be interested in the observation of hunting, referenced to a particular date in time, and not the opinions of the recorder.

Importantly, combining archaeological and written records is not a negotiation of a middle ground where historical observation and material record must find accord (e.g., Cleland 2001a; Patterson 2000). I am not interested in making archaeology conform to historical understandings of the past but rather in understanding this past as an archaeological narrative of the individuals and communities that shaped the record—counter to, consistent with, or differently masking the narrative of the written past (Wylie 1999).

But while this kind of archaeological history may challenge conventional historical narratives of decline, dependency and cultural decimation, this in no way should negate the stark realities of the history of the last 500 years or downplay the trauma and drama of that history as experienced by Indigenous North Americans negotiating Europeans and their colonist progeny. I do not deny either the hardships or the systemic, institutional and cultural marginalization Aboriginal nations experienced and continue to negotiate in North America. Most assuredly, historic events in the Great Lakes, such as epidemics and warfare, were painful and horrific for the people who had to struggle to live through them. These facts of the past are not to be forgotten or glossed over.

But what those conventional historical narratives repeatedly failed to reconcile is the fact that the experiences of Aboriginal peoples have been more about survival and resistance than about declination and oblivion, a contemporary fact often denied in many of the conclusions reached in the acculturation-based histories of the last half millennium. This literature has offered such a deterministic narrative, one that takes past assumptions and biases and applies them to present research so that interpretations often can seem to be a simple connecting of the dots to cultural obscurity. The implication of the interpretive revisions offered in this study is a perspective that sees archaeology contributing significantly and meaningfully to a broader goal of seeking to understand the past as experienced by Native people. This is the real strength and potential of archaeology in a truly multidisciplinary approach to the histories of "Other" (Stahl 2000).

Indeed, I would argue that the importance of this archaeological perspective to reach beyond the constraints of historical records needs to be recognized broadly in the historically oriented social sciences. After all, the reflexive critique of archaeological constructions of the past mirrors the anthropological critique of making history, and the politics of historical authority in the present. Importantly, the historicizing of archaeology has engaged it in the present, made overt the political and power dimensions of the discipline, and opened it to the criticisms of its colonial past and present offered up by descendant populations and others (e.g., Wylie 1995). The ability to engage in the depth and daily lived breadth of the human past, while engaging the anthropological need to link the past with the present, is the ultimate potential—perhaps wider relevancy—that the enabling of archaeology as history brings.

3

Changing Continuities

OJIBWA TERRITORIAL COMMUNITIES IN
SOUTHWESTERN ONTARIO

When the Great Spirit made the white man and the Indian, he . . . placed the white man across the great waters, and there gave him his religion written in a book; he also made the white man to cultivate the earth, and raise cattle, etc.; but when the Great Spirit made the Indian, he placed him in this country, and gave him his way of worship written in his heart, which has been handed down from one generation to another; for his subsistence, he gave him the wild beasts of the forest, the fowls that fly in the air, the fish that swim in the waters, and the corn for his bread; and, before the white man came to this country the Indian did not know the use of iron, but for an axe he used a stone sharpened at one end, tied to a split stick; with this he cut his wood; and for his hoe he split the limb of a tree; he had also stone pots to cook with; these things answered his purpose, and he was contented and happy.

— Bear Creek Ojibwa Chief Canotung to Peter Jones, 1828

(P. Jones 1860:123–124)

Ancient Anishnabeg Archaeological Histories From Southwestern Ontario

LATE WOODLAND ARCHAEOLOGY IN SOUTHWESTERNMOST ONTARIO varied from that of areas further to the east, where the ancestral pattern was one of broadly developing Iroquoian systems of community organization and thought (see chap. 5). To the west, the Late Woodland Western Basin Tradition reflected a distinct archaeological suite of material culture use, settlement-subsistence organization and mortuary practices (Murphy and Ferris 1990; Watts 2006). These patterns reflected seasonally mobile communities operating across defined territorial ranges over the course of a year. Incorporation of cultigens occurred over a long period of time. When cultigens began to appear in quantity in the record after about AD 1000, it reflected less a shift and more an incorporation into, and a maintenance of a diversified and mobile subsistence strategy. Subsequently, shifts triggered by horticultural demands included situating warm-weather settlements in locales within close proximity to diversified environmental settings (e.g., Kenyon 1988). While this did give rise to more "organized" settlement (e.g., warm-weather groupings of longhouse-like dwellings), cold weather dispersal into smaller family groups is also evident (Murphy 1991).

This pattern may have created a seasonal underutilization of some areas, including the easterly frontier with adjacent Inter-Lakes Tradition peoples, facilitating a relatively benign co-utilization of the region with these groups (Ferris and Spence 1995:114–115). This also heightened an ongoing westward contraction of Western Basin communities and westward expansion for Inter-Lakes communities, which may have become less benign by the later 15th century (Lennox and Fitzgerald 1990; Murphy and Ferris 1990). At that point, there was a consolidation of Western Basin communities into larger aggregates, so that only a very few, large Western Basin sites have been documented in the region, all near the Detroit River and Lake St. Clair. These aggregated communities appear to have been warm-weather villages carrying out a mixed subsistence with a moderate focus on maize.

By the mid–16th century, there appears to have been no Western Basin sites in southwestern Ontario. Terminal Woodland trends at this time appeared to reflect less interaction to the east, and more with Fort Ancient, Upper Mississippian and Oneota archaeological traditions further to the south and west in the Great Lakes basin (e.g., Brose 1994; Drooker 1997; Schroeder 2004). These Terminal Western Basin manifestations were most likely the immediate ancestors of the "Gens de Feu" or Fire Nation Central Algonquians depicted in early-17th-century cartography, before further contractions away from the western end of Lake Erie occurred in the 1640s (Heidenreich 1987, 1988, 1990).

Though permanent settlement in southwesternmost Ontario was absent until the 18th century, given continued seasonal mobility, parts of the region likely continued to be utilized, as indicated by later 17th-century accounts of occupations noted on either side of the Detroit River (e.g., Lajeunesse 1960). Later, descendant Anishnabeg peoples such as the Potawatomi returned to ancestral Western Basin territory around western Lake Erie and southern Lake Huron, some eventually returning to southwestern Ontario during the 19th century, where they continued, and continue, to thrive as part of Anishnabeg communities such as at Bkejwanong (Walpole Island) (Clifton 1998; Ferris 1989).

Anishnabeg Ojibwa Ancestral Histories

While Anishnabeg communities of southwestern Ontario link back to ancient archaeological histories, these histories were also augmented in the 18th century by the movement into southern Ontario of Ojibwa peoples who, by the mid–18th century, had settled throughout the northern drainages of the lower Great Lakes (e.g., E. Rogers 1978, 1994; Schmalz 1991). These people were the descendants of Aboriginal communities that earlier had occupied the northeastern portion of Georgian Bay, the north shore of Lake Huron, and at least the eastern Lake Superior shoreline and associated drainages (e.g., Cleland 1992b; E. Rogers 1978). In 17th-century records, these communities were defined as seasonally mobile territorial groups associated with particular river drainages or stretches of shoreline (e.g., Raudot cited in Kinietz 1940:365–372; see also Albers and Kay 1987; Cleland 1992a). Subsistence was mainly based on hunting, fishing and collecting. Each territorial group was distinct, known by names such as the Saulteaux, Mississauga, Amikwa, Outchibous and Marameg (Heidenreich 1987; E. Rogers 1978).

By the end of the 17th century, many distinct groups had been subsumed into larger territorial communities, or were at least being referred to by these broader designations by European observers (notably Saulteur and Mississauga). Members of these broader groups extended seasonal and permanent use of the area north of Lakes Erie and Ontario that had been underutilized or subject to contested use as a result of the events of the mid-1600s. Whether this was due to successful warfare against the Iroquois (Schmalz 1984; D. Smith 1981), Iroquois indifference (Konrad 1981), or the result of a late 17th-century negotiated peace agreement between Aboriginal nations to commonly share a disputed territory (Aquila 1983; Brandão and Starna 1996; Lytwyn 1998), the consequence was that, a century later, the descendants of these Algonquian-speaking Anishnabeg had extended territorial communities across southern Ontario.

By the first decades of the 19th century, the terms Ojibwa or Chippewa had been commonly adopted by colonial authorities to refer to all southern Ontario communities descendant from north shore Great Lakes Anishnabeg peoples. Of course, the term Ojibwa, though self-referential at the time, nonetheless masked a great deal of group variation, distinct identities, and ancestries within and between communities (Cleland 1992b, 2001b; Peers 1994). For example, some Ojibwa communities represented descendants of Saulteur and Mississauga groups who had moved into the region at the start of the 18th century, while others were comprised of Ojibwa who had relocated in the 19th century from Lakes Huron or Superior.

Despite the reductionist mask a term like "Ojibwa" engenders, it will be used here because it so dominates the historical record, and was self-referential to the 19th-century communities examined in this chapter. As well, the designation "Ojibwa" in southern Ontario also denoted a distinctive form of "Aboriginality" perceived by the Europeans settling and imposing a colonial order onto the region in the 19th century. Specifically, and in contrast to other Native communities, the Ojibwa were seen as unsettled and nomadic, living primarily from the hunt. As well, the Ojibwa were described as a "nation of beggars and thieves" in both historic accounts (e.g., Jameson 1838; P. Jones 1860, 1861; Sabathy-Judd 1999) and in local histories (e.g., Goodspeed 1889; Hamil 1951). Typical is an opinion offered in the second annual report of the Missionary Society of the Methodist Church:

> In its various tribes, [the Ojibwa] are by far the most numerous. They spread out the whole length of the Province, extending also far to the north. Their wandering state and manner of life, have been supposed to be insurmountable obstacles in the way of their conversion; for they are everywhere at home, seldom long in one place, never erecting any permanent habitations; but residing in temporary huts, covered with matted flags, or with barks from the trunks of trees. (MSAR 1826:8)

In other words, as I argue below, the Ojibwa communities of southern Ontario maintained a traditional livelihood well into the 19th century, so their history though this period stands in stark contrast to the master narrative of decline, dependency and irrelevancy portrayed for the Aboriginal nations of the Northeast in past conventional, historical and anthropological literature.[1]

The Ojibwa in Southwestern Ontario

By 1800 the various regional communities of Anishnabeg collectively referred to as Ojibwa had been resident in southwestern Ontario and adjacent parts of Michigan for a century. This included a community of "Saulteurs and Mississauguez" that Cadillac reported as settling at the north end of Lake St. Clair in 1703 (Lajeunesse 1960:23), possibly on Harsen's Island (Charlevoix 1761, 2:40; Lajeunesse 1960:xliv, 25–26). Early-18th-century estimates suggest a population of three to five hundred for this group (Lajeunesse 1960:25). When settlement extended into the interior is not known, although a Thames River Ojibwa chief Seckas (Sekahos) contributed 170 warriors to Pontiac's siege camp at Detroit in 1763 (Quaife 1958:128–129; see also, Curnoe 1996:114).

This would suggest a total population of five to eight hundred individuals in the region, consistent with estimates for communities from this area in the late 18th century (Ferris 1989: tables 3.4, 3.7b).

But the term "southwestern Ontario Ojibwa" is also a misnomer, in that there was not just a single, generic Ojibwa presence in the region, and neither were these communities coincidentally restricted to contemporary provincial boundaries. In fact there were four to six territorial communities, each occupying distinct geographies associated with major drainages and lakeshores (fig. 3.1). And while there was a sense of ownership—the resources in a particular territory belonging to the community and representing a home range or defined extent of resource utilization—borders did not define autonomous or national boundaries, and were fluid. There are several recorded instances of mobility: individuals moving from one community to another (Jacobson 1895:21; Plain 1973), family movement (MPHSC, 20:617), or actual band movement (e.g., Graham 1975; Gulewitsch 1998). Concurrent with the notion of defined but open boundaries, fixed, permanent settlements (i.e., villages) did not exist. Certainly central places existed for each group, and these locations helped define the "heart" of a territorial range. But the Ojibwa settlement pattern was much more complex than any single, fixed locale on the land.

Territorial Communities

At 1800 these four to six Ojibwa territorial communities existed in differing forms (Ferris 1989; fig. 3.1). There were at least two large communities: one occupying the shore of Lake St. Clair and the St. Clair River, and another occupying the interior Thames River drainage. Another, smaller group is often referred to as the Bear Creek Ojibwa, residing along the interior drainage of the Sydenham River. There were also smaller communities along the Detroit River and at Point Pelee that likely were distinct (Leclair 1988). Another community stretched along the lower Lake Huron shore north of the St. Clair River, centered on Kettle Point and the mouth of the Ausable River, and perhaps as far north as the Maitland River (Gulewitsch 1995). Population estimates (see Ferris 1989: tables 3.1–3.9) for each group varied, but in general a territorial community ranged between 150 to 300 individuals. Within these territorial communities were smaller segments of 30 to 80 individuals, operating as "subterritorial" groups and comprised of interrelated family or clan lineages. The basic family unit was the extended family (nuclear unit plus unmarried children, elderly parents or close relations), ranging anywhere from 5 to 15 individuals (Ferris 1989).

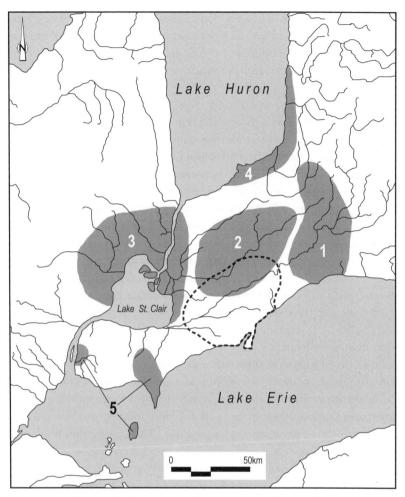

FIGURE 3.1. Estimated "boundaries" of southwestern Ontario Ojibwa territorial communities around 1800.

1 Thames River (Muncey)
2 Bear Creek (Sydenham River)
3 Lake St. Clair / St. Clair River
4 Kettle Point / Ausable River
5 Anderdon

Other Ojibwa communities (e.g., Black River/"Thumb" area of Michigan) are not represented. The dotted line below the Bear Creek territory is an approximation of the territorial extent for this group prior to relocating onto the Sydenham River.

Given seasonal mobility, full gatherings of a territorial community were restricted to a few occasions, such as during short-term, intensive resource harvests, or for social, religious or political events. More often, the dictates of seasonal mobility created multiple settlements across a territory, either as warm-weather base camps of several families (subgroup?), sugaring and winter hunting camps of one or a few families, or smaller and more informal hunting camps and overnight travel camps of one to a few individuals. It would be inaccurate to interpret this dispersed mobility as wandering or nomadic. Movement was directed and related to an intimate personal and community knowledge of the resources and landscape within a home territory (Ferris 1989).

Authority was maintained by informal consensus. While the concept of chiefs or principal men was favored by the British authorities for treaty negotiations and group representation, these chiefs did not function in the political sense of imposing direct authority over a community (contra Mainfort 1985). Rather, chiefs reflected lineal descent lines, and authority was earned through one's abilities, such as hunting and sharing, handling crises, making decisions, orating, or shamanistic ability. It is also clear that individuals were "chiefs" (representatives) of, and could speak for, smaller territorial subunits. For example, in an Ojibwa census from 1831 (PAC RG10 708: C13 140), 16 individuals were labeled chief (as opposed to 70 warriors, i.e., adult males) for the St. Clair Ojibwa (divided between Walpole Island and Sarnia), 10 for the Thames River Ojibwa (62 warriors), and 8 (12 warriors) for the Bear Creek Ojibwa. Given overall population (327 for the St. Clair Ojibwa, 238 for the Thames and 77 for the Bear Creek), this suggests leadership was ascribed to most male heads of households. Nonetheless, there also existed several higher-level chiefs who were acknowledged to be territorial leaders, although their ability to act on that authority lay solely on the credibility of the individual as accepted by the community at that moment.[2] Ability to influence others in the community was limited to informal encouragement, obligations and social coercion.

Territorial boundaries were not fixed and did change over time. A notable example is the Bear Creek Ojibwa on the Sydenham River. This group appears to have settled along that drainage only in the late 1780s or early 1790s; prior to that they occupied the lower Thames River drainage and seasonally exploited migratory bird and spring fish runs at Rondeau Bay on Lake Erie. However, in the 1780s increasing numbers of Euro-Canadian squatters began settling along the lower Thames. As well, in 1792 the Moravian Delaware settled further along the river (see chap. 4). Missionaries there noted Ojibwa traveling through the village on their way to the next river north, and also noted members of that community speaking of selling their land and leaving the Thames due to the numbers of people settling there (e.g., Sabathy-Judd 1999:97).

The founding chief of the Bear Creek community was Kitchimaqua (Big Bear—which is why the drainage they moved to was called "Bear Creek"), a signatory to a 1796 treaty (Curnoe 1996:48; Denke 1991:16). His son, Kitschi-Makongs (Great Lesser Bear, also known as Nabbawe), replaced Kitchimaqua and married the daughter of an Odawa chief (Onagan—Big Bowls) of the community that had just come from Sandusky Bay to resettle at St. Anne's Island of the Walpole Island delta (Curnoe 1996:74–75; Denke 1990:8, 1991:16, 1993:7). Nabbawe was replaced prior to 1820 by Canotung (Joseph Canotung), who signed land surrenders on behalf of the Bear Creek Ojibwa in the 1820s and remained chief after that group relocated to the Thames Ojibwa reserve community in 1832 (Curnoe 1996:18–19; P. Jones 1860, 1861). Population estimates for the Bear Creek Ojibwa ranged from 80 to 150 people.

The history of this community is intriguing and consistent with patterns of group mobility and community formation seen in southwestern Ontario earlier during the Late Woodland (i.e., territorial movement and overlap of archaeological traditions between ca. AD 1000 and 1550; see Ferris 2006; Ferris and Spence 1995). In this 19th-century instance, the Bear Creek Ojibwa had been a subgroup of the Thames River Ojibwa, large enough to maintain for itself a separate identity on the lower Thames, at least when the group moved away from encroaching settlement and onto the Sydenham. Once there, they operated as a largely autonomous group.[3] When Nabbawe, the early-19th-century Bear Creek chief, developed familial ties with the St. Anne's Odawa, he in effect secured access to the St. Clair fisheries for the Bear Creek group, and allowed those newly settled Odawa use of the upper Sydenham winter hunting grounds. Despite these connections, it was the Thames River Ojibwa at Muncey to which the Bear Creek community returned in the early 1830s, reflecting a deeper historic connection to that community than to the St. Clair group. However, Canotung and that group maintained a distinct identity within the larger Muncey group through the 19th century, in part contributing to community factionalism (e.g., Graham 1975; P. Jones 1861). This process of fissioning and fusing of distinct communities, and the ability to maintain greater than family and less than territorial community identity even when living in larger groups, speaks to the antiquity and significant strength and flexibility this social structure held for the Ojibwa and Aboriginal nations of the region.

Ojibwa Archaeological History At 1800

In this section I will integrate historic observation with archaeological evidence to provide a robust understanding of the archaeological history of Ojibwa lifeways during the late 18th and early 19th centuries within the western end of the north Erie peninsula.

Historical Data. There are a wide range of historic sources available for the late-18th and early-19th-century Ojibwa of southwestern Ontario. These include missionary accounts—diarists who lived among the Ojibwa (Dreyer 1997), or who lived adjacent to and interacted with Ojibwa communities (P. Jones 1860; Sabathy-Judd 1999). As well, British Indian Department records provide insight into the Ojibwa interaction with the emerging colonialist regime of the period, though these records are weak on insight into daily life. Another source is the personal accounts of travelers (e.g., Quaife 1958; Weld 1799) and others whose observations provide passing reflections of Ojibwa life. Collectively, these documents provide insight into settlement-subsistence, especially the scheduling of seasonal round activities, simply by tying observations of Ojibwa activity to the time of year those observations were made.

It is important to keep in mind, however, that the data extracted from these records of European observations reflect only what those observers could see, as well as their biases and preoccupations. It is likely that some Ojibwa activities were minimized or ignored in the records, while other aspects of Ojibwa settlement-subsistence may well have been unknown, particularly if such pursuits were conducted away from observers, or were too informal to take note of. As well, I acknowledge that the results extracted from these data, by virtue of the sources themselves, provide a compiled pattern for several distinct territorial communities covering a relatively long period of time, and so may mask shorter term trends and changes. Nonetheless, the archaeological "data" extracted from these European observations will provide insight into Ojibwa livelihood while minimizing the agenda-driven opinions that tend to accompany those data.

Archaeological Data. Given mobility within territorial communities, the potential for archaeological traces of seasonal Ojibwa settlement should be high. However, less than a handful of 18th- or 19th-century Ojibwa habitation sites or components have been documented in southern Ontario (Ferris et al. 1985; Riddell 1984; Ross 1998, 2004; Timmins 2003; Triggs 2004) or eastern Michigan (Beld 1990, 2002). In general, sites from this period are dif-

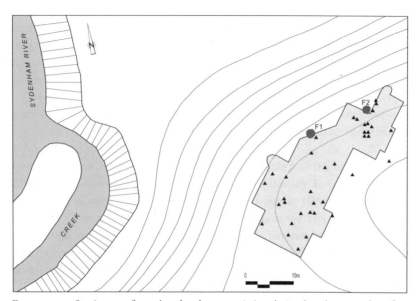

FIGURE 3.2. Setting, surface glass bead scatter (triangles), plough-exposed surface feature locations (F1 and F2), and excavation extent at the Bellamy site. Contours are at 50-cm intervals.

ficult to "see" archaeologically. Reasons for this are mostly related to changes in material culture through the 18th century, rather than the loss of a distinct Aboriginal archaeological expression. Principal artifact classes found on the ploughed fields of southern Ontario for earlier Aboriginal sites—ceramics and lithics—are mostly gone from material culture assemblages in the later 18th century. Moreover, other dominant artifact categories—fire-cracked rock and faunal remains—are ubiquitous for all sites of at least the Woodland period. As such, being able to distinguish one locale as having an 18th- or 19th-century Aboriginal component distinct from more ancient components is difficult if the odd kaolin pipe fragment or gunflint found among this material is assumed to be related to a Euro-Canadian component. As well, given seasonal mobility and territorial rather than fixed settlement, Ojibwa sites are relatively sparse deposits of material culture, difficult to spot without the aid of those other, albeit masking, components being present.

In the mid-1980s, an Ojibwa habitation located on the Sydenham River was excavated (Ferris 1989; Ferris et al. 1985). This locale, known as the Bellamy site, was first identified as a result of a late-period trade axe found by Stanley Wortner, and from 19th-century land surveyor's notes, which reported an old Indian clearing on adjacent river flats. The site is on a high sandy knoll overlooking these extensive river flats (fig. 3.2). Data from this site provide insight into the seasonal, community and material patterns for this period—a dataset left by the Ojibwa themselves to complement and contradict patterns recovered from the written record.

Ojibwa Subsistence in 1800

Subsistence at the start of the 19th century was a mobile strategy based on a diverse number of resource harvesting activities that ebbed and flowed over the course of a year. Social gatherings, participation in warfare, and even traveling to British posts to obtain annual gifts of allegiance all had to be accommodated within the annual cycle of subsistence activity scheduling. Also, exchange of surplus yields, gift-giving and asking for food were all part of the reciprocal social structure the Ojibwa constructed within their communities, and with Aboriginal and non-Aboriginal neighbors.

Figure 3.3 charts subsistence strategies mentioned in historical sources by month for southwestern Ontario Ojibwa, as extracted from records dating between the 1760s and 1830s (see Ferris 1989). The hunting graph illustrates the primacy of this activity and highlights three peak periods: autumn (October-November), midwinter (January), and midsummer (July). Deer dominate references to hunting from June to December. Bear and other mammals, such as raccoon and muskrat (all hunted in their dens), are noted as primarily winter game. References to less formal hunting also exist for every month.

Sugaring followed the winter hunt. This was an intensive, intermittent activity depending on weather conditions affecting flow of sap. Later on (i.e., late March or early April), boiling sap was a full-time activity, especially for women at the sugar camps. The importance of this food source is in both its timing—arriving when game was scarce and food supplies depleted—and its abundance, with surplus yields traded for food, liquor and goods.

Hunting references are at their lowest in April, a time when large numbers of people (i.e., multiple territorial groups) gathered at places like the St. Clair River rapids to jacklight, spear or net spring spawning fish runs (e.g., Quaife 1958:234). Harvesting fish during this period was highly intensive. Although the peak period ended by May, fishing continued as an informal activity throughout the summer and fall, and there may have been a smaller, intensive harvest of fish during fall runs on the St. Clair River.

By late May, subterritorial groups or families moved to summer base camps to plant corn and other cultivars (e.g., potatoes and squash). After planting,

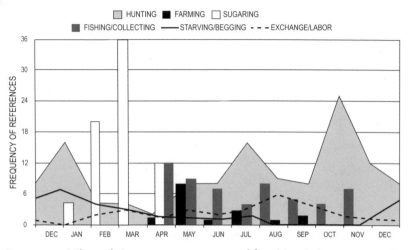

FIGURE 3.3. Ojibwa subsistence patterns constructed from historical sources. Monthly totals represent the number of occasions the activity was specifically referred to in historical accounts available between 1765 and 1840 (see Ferris 1989).

plots were only intermittently cared for through the summer. Nearby these camps, women, the elderly and children were all noted to be berry gathering in July through October, collecting nuts in September through November, and informally gathering grasses, herbs and roots throughout the period of camp use (e.g., P. Jones 1861:72).

An extensive faunal assemblage was recovered from the Bellamy site (Prevec 1985). Overall, seasonality as reflected in the assemblage indicates warm weather. Bones from immature deer and raccoons imply death during the early summer. A number of the bird species present, such as woodcock, wood duck, passenger pigeon, white-throated sparrow and a possible white-winged scoter, are all migratory. Many of the fish species present, such as lake sturgeon, bowfin and drum, are primarily lake-dwellers, and would not be expected inland along the Sydenham River. Presumably these remains were transported to summer base camps as foodstuffs generated from spring fishing activities.

White-tailed deer make up just over 61 percent of the identified mammal bone (Number of Identified Specimens Present [NISP] = 828); raccoon, 24 percent (NISP = 326); and grey squirrel, 5 percent (NISP = 63). Although representing 90 percent of identified mammal bone, these three species comprise only 15 percent of the 19 identified mammal species present at the site; in other words, there is both focus and diversity in the assemblage. This is also

the case for fish, with identified bone dominated by riverine species, including various catfish and bullhead species (31 percent, NISP = 47), drum (30
percent, NISP = 46), and bass (11 percent, NISP = 17). Collectively these
represent one-third of the 17 fish species identified. Of the 18 bird species
identified, duck (28 percent, NISP = 39) and pigeon (13 percent, NISP =
11) dominate. While many of these animal species are not accounted for in
historic records, which emphasized deer, bear and raccoon, these other species
are indicative of a diversified hunting regime and the augmentative role most
of these species played in contributing to the diet of the Bellamy occupants.[4]
Also represented were domestic species: pig (1 percent of identified mammals,
NISP = 11), chicken (8 percent of identified birds, NISP = 7), sheep (NISP
= 3), and cat (NISP = 1). The sheep bones were found on the site surface,
while the other remains are all from a privy dating late in the occupation (ca.
1820s–1830s). These may represent exchanged meat or opportunistic taking
of livestock once settlers began to move into the drainage.[5]

A single beaver bone was recovered, as well as 23 muskrat bones. Given
seasonal subsistence emphases and the distribution of bones across the Bellamy site, fur-bearing animals such as raccoon and muskrat appear to have
been harvested at this site as food, along with the deer and other food source
animals, though skins were also collected and processed (see settlement patterns, below). As such, the assemblage suggests very much the continuation
of a traditional subsistence regime, with no indication of overhunting to generate pelts and skins for trade. This is contrary to some interpretations others
have offered for similar faunal assemblages from late-18th- or early-19th-cen-
tury Central Algonquian Anishnabeg sites. For example, from the Potawatomi Windrose site in Illinois, with a high deer (52 percent) and raccoon (35
percent) assemblage and very diverse mammal, fish and bird representation,
the following conclusion was drawn: "Considered as an assemblage, animal
remains from the Windrose site suggest that the inhabitants participated in
the fur trade economy of the Kankakee River valley by exploiting second-
line fur-bearing animals such as raccoon and white-tailed deer. Their daily
dietary needs were met by local aquatic animals, especially fish and turtles"
(Martin 1996:487).

While admittedly a much higher number of turtle bones are present at
Windrose, seemingly due to the site being located close to a marshy setting,
it seems counterintuitive not to allow that at least the meat of raccoons and
deer was also being consumed by those inhabitants, as was certainly the case
for the southwestern Ontario Ojibwa. There is no need to invent a differing
pattern suggestive of subsistence alterations to accommodate fur trade economies, when it appears readily evident that any servicing of external exchange

with Europeans or other Aboriginals was met entirely within traditional harvest yields.

Moreover, there were *no* references to trapping or trading in furs in the documentation reviewed, which suggests that either fur-bearing animals were not abundant in the region (but note that species harvested for meat included raccoon, beaver, otter and muskrat), or that trapping and trading was not an activity of any "notable" significance from the perspective of European observers. Indeed, trading in deerskins, a more abundant and available resource to the deer-hunting Ojibwa of this region, happened only when there was a large harvest, and meat was the item desired, not skins. There simply is no written data suggesting the Ojibwa, well over a century after the emergence of a "fur trade economy" as conventional histories characterize the period, had altered subsistence to create large yields of pelts specifically to trade with Europeans.

Indeed, similar patterns of game harvests and opportunistic capture of a wide variety of species, along with an absence of overabundance of fur-bearing species, and notably small frequencies of domesticates, is seen on other Ojibwa (e.g., Martin and Richmond 1990, 2002; Ross 2004), Odawa (Stothers and Abel 1989), Kickapoo (Parmalee and Klippel 1983), Potawatomi (Martin 1996, 2001), and Winnebago sites (Richards 1993; Spector 1975).

Floral data (Macaulay 1988; Murphy 1985) included quantities of raspberry/blackberry seeds, a food gathered and dried midsummer. Grape seeds are indicative of late-summer or early-fall harvest. A quantity of black walnut suggests an autumn use of the site. The cultigens recovered at Bellamy included traditional 8- and 10-rowed flint maize. Beans and sunflowers are marginally present. No European introduced fruits or grains were identified, which is similar to other analyses done for 19th-century Central Algonquian Anishnabeg sites (e.g., Bonhage-Freund et al. 2002; Parker and Newsom 2001).

Ojibwa Mobility and Settlement at 1800

A critical element of Ojibwa subsistence was mobility, as activities and time of year warranted. Groups, families, or individuals moved within the territorial community, or home range, though travel further afield for subsistence and social or economic reasons also occurred. Historic records provide numerous accounts of formal group mobility (e.g., moving to sugaring camps, winter hunting territories, long distance travel), and convey a sense of constant informal movement all year long (e.g., an individual or family passing by, social visits, a hunter trading a shank of deer meat).

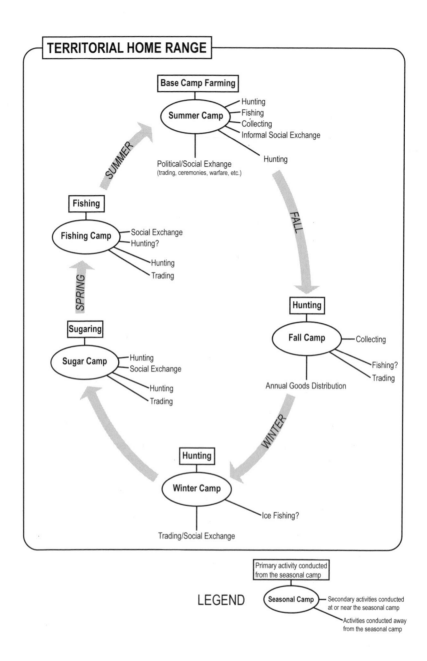

FIGURE 3.4. A representation of the Ojibwa seasonal round and mobility over a community's territorial home range around 1800.

Mobility. In general, the Ojibwa traveled between four or five settlement camps at different locales within the community's home range over the course of a year (fig. 3.4; see also Ferris 1989:171–183). Sugar camps were set up by late January and occupied by a number of families gathered together from more dispersed winter hunting camps. Occasionally sugar camps were established in close proximity to each other. The community at a camp likely would have comprised the majority of a subgroup within the territorial community. These camps were typically in the interior, along secondary creeks and river drainages. Informal socializing, and brief trips to other camps, were frequently reported, and included drinking parties, dances, and feasts.

By early April, sugar camps dispersed and individual families would make their way to spring fishing camps. Some camps were made up of a few families, while others were clearly interterritorial gathering places. Accounts indicate that people came and went over the duration of the spawning run, and others would come to visit, creating a very fluid population at these camps (e.g., Quaife 1958).

By the end of the spawning runs, territorial subgroups moved to the interior along major river drainages to summer base camps. These locales, like sugar and fish camps, would have been resettled regularly. These were arrived at by mid-May, with most of the group present during the initial phase of clearing and preparing fields for planting.[6] When cached and not taken off-season as food, seed corn would have been left for the next spring's planting. Apaquois[7] or wigwams were constructed, or standing frames repaired and covered. Smaller camps consisting of a single family were also known.

After this initial period of intense activity at the camp, the community would begin to disperse, with a few residents remaining behind to fish, hunt, collect, maintain material culture or travel short distances (i.e., a day or two) to other settlements. The only members of the community who stayed at the camp through the summer were the elderly, and less regularly women and young children. As well, people would return to the summer base camp off and on over the rest of the season. By late September, most of the base camp would reunite to harvest the garden plots and perhaps begin fall hunting.

From summer base camps or from smaller family hunting camps, the Ojibwa conducted a late fall hunt in October-November. Then families would disperse into the interior to winter hunting areas, or travel further afield to overwinter with other groups.[8] Winter camps were less locales that were returned to each year, and more general vicinities where access to game was relatively reliable. Depending on how hard a winter was or how available winter game was, families would remain in one area through the winter, relocate their camp, or join up with other community winter camps. Off-season camps might also be visited, in part to recover cached food supplies. Lastly, short-term, temporary camps were used frequently throughout the year, particularly during periods of regular mobility (e.g., during the hunting season).

Subsistence strategies over the course of a year's seasonal round emphasized a maximization of all available resources. For this to be successful, the pattern of seasonal mobility practiced by the Ojibwa had to be intimately connected to detailed knowledge of the territorial landscape in which they resided, and clearly informed by recursive, historically known, successful patterns of behavior—a quintessential characteristic of seasonally mobile hunters and foragers (e.g., K. Morrison 2002; Rival 2002). While clearly flexible enough to adjust to seasonal vagaries, new technologies and lived experience, this way of ordering life was also resistant to change; in the Ojibwa example, despite being surrounded by alternative Native and Euro-Canadian ways of living life.

Settlement. Settlement patterns at seasonal camps varied based on the duration of occupation, subsistence activity foci, group make-up, and weather. Residential dwellings were generally one to two family structures, such as apaquois/wigwams or circular tepees, or smaller, more temporary pole structures. A planked or hewn shanty was also used, but log cabins were not in use at the start of the 19th century. For locales that served as relatively "fixed" habitations from year to year (e.g., sugar camps, large fishing camps tied to recurring fish runs, and summer base camps), bark, mat or hide coverings were removed from dwellings, but the pole structures were left until revisited later in the season or the following year, often noted by European travelers as structural "skeletons abandoned" on the landscape (e.g., Denke 1991, 1993, 1994, 1996).

The rituals of daily living—cooking, eating, shelter maintenance, processing game, storing food, making things, disposal, and so on—were undertaken to differing intensities in and out of dwellings. As well, the extent of outside activity areas at a settlement depended on the primary function of the camp (e.g., boiling sugar, processing meat or skins, making tools), and seasonally what ceremonies, feasts or social events occurred there.

The layout, structures, and nature of the settlement patterns at Ojibwa summer base camps is captured in writing by the missionary Denke, who traveled to the Bear Creek Ojibwa summer base camp known as Kitigen in 1801:[9]

About 2 o'clock we reached the Indian 'town'. The settlement consists of seven houses of which two are built a short way down the river. They stand very irregularly and in a cluster so close together that only a small passage is between them. Two of them are from hewn, thin timber, the

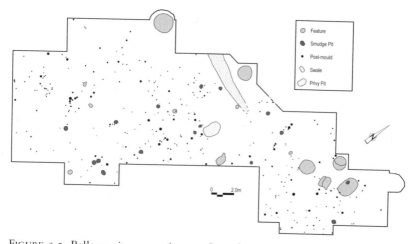

FIGURE 3.5. Bellamy site excavations, 1984 and 1985 results. Removed from this map are Late Woodland features and recent disturbances.

rest have a house like a framework of poles covered with bark. In the middle of the house, the fire is made. They do not have floor or plank beds but sit and lie on the ground. In such a house, 5 or 6 families often live together. They have no doors at their houses but an old hide or a piece of bark is hanging before the small opening instead. Under the roof, there are poles on which the fresh meat, intestines, etc. are dried. Near the 'town', because the river makes a bend there, is a small 'bottom' where they make their plantations. (Denke 1996:4–6)

This vivid image is reflected in the settlement patterns documented at the Bellamy site, where excavations revealed discrete activity areas represented by differing feature types and concentrations (fig. 3.5). A storage/caching area along the edge of the slope is indicated by a number of large, circular-to-oval pits with basin-shaped profiles, at least three of which were inter-sected by later pits, while two exhibited heavy mottling, a distinctive water "swirled" soil matrix effect, and inverted lenses of pit fill and subsoil. In one instance, an intersecting feature was bark lined. Similar artifact assemblages from these two features indicate that their use, infilling and later intersecting all would have occurred in a short period of time.

Denke noted in 1801 (1996:4) "If they are going hunting from home and leave behind a small corn-supply, they have the habit to keep it in under-ground pits lined with bark." Denke (1991:11) also noted in February of 1806 that summer base camps like Kitigen were places people would go to get cached seed corn as a winter food supply. Digging out a storage feature in winter conditions would cause the distinctive mottled soil matrix seen at Bellamy. Clearly, a primary function of the large features at Bellamy was to serve as cache pits for food supplies. This was an important dimension of managing surpluses and minimizing transport within mobile seasonal rounds, and an important source of food to tap into during times of the year when food supplies were otherwise scarce (Dunham 2000). Caches at such sites also served as conceptual placeholders for imagining oneself and one's family within the communal home range, and especially for anticipating future mobility (see also, Kent and Vierich 1989). The act of deciding what to leave where and what to bring in effect constrained and shaped travel plans over the course of a year. This underscores a highly planned and mapped concept of mobility onto territory.

Large storage pits have been documented for other 17th–20th-century Central Algonquian Anishnabeg sites (e.g., Behm 1998; Conway 1980; Dunham 2000; Parmalee and Klippel 1983; Richards 1993; Spector 1975; Wittry 1963), archaeologically a reflection of the need to cache food and supplies within the seasonally mobile subsistence regimes these groups all followed. This distinctive archaeological feature is also found in southwestern Ontario on Western Basin Late Woodland habitations, and is particularly prevalent at locales associated with seasonally limited occupations and the harvest of seasonally abundant resources (e.g., Ferris 1990; Kenyon et al. 1988; Lennox 1982; Watts 1997).

At Bellamy, most cache pits were largely devoid of artifacts. This fact, along with high artifact frequencies in the ploughzone and a high percentage (15 percent) of post moulds found to contain faunal remains, metal artifacts and glass beads,[10] suggests waste at these seasonally occupied sites was not managed in a manner similar to that seen in village communities (i.e., middens). This was suggested by Denke (1996:4) when visiting the summer base camp on the Sydenham River in 1801: "For the most part of the year, they [the Ojibwa] live on fish whose bones and other offal get thrown close to the houses and cause an evil odour." Disposal at such camps, then, was to one side, rather than set aside.

A frequent task carried out at Bellamy is represented by a series of small circular-to-oval pits, whose fill tended to be composed of carbonized plant remains and ringed by a small layer of fire-reddened soil. The carbonized material in these pits consisted of outer bark from trees or maize cob and stock fragments (Macauley 1988). These pits were found across the site, and exhibited little variability in plan (20–30 cm) or profile (> 10 cm). Binford (1967) has described similar features as smudge pits: the use of bark,

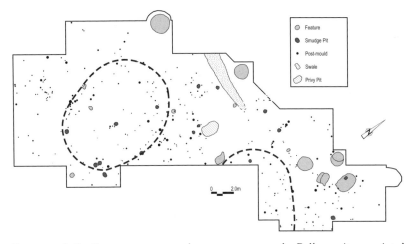

FIGURE 3.6. Outlines encompass settlement patterns at the Bellamy site associated with apaquois/wigwam structures identified after excavations.

corncobs or other green plant material providing a slow-burning agent generating a great deal of smoke. These pits were used to tan hides by attaching them to a cone-shaped scaffolding placed over the pit, which then filtered the smoke through the hide (see also, Densmore 1979:164–165, Plate 75). Similar pits have been found on other Central Algonquian Anishnabeg sites (e.g., Spector 1975; Wittry 1963), and on Western Basin Late Woodland sites (e.g., Kenyon 1988).

Excavations at Bellamy uncovered apaquois/wigwam structural patterns. A completely exposed structure was documented in the center of the excavations, and a second structure was partially revealed to the northeast (fig. 3.6). The fully exposed structure is oval, measures 9 by 7 m, and appears to have an internal support row along its eastern side. It dates later than some of the occupation at Bellamy, as several of the wall posts intersect pits. The interior floor of the structure is "clean" of features or posts, although a small hearth is located just south of the center of the structure. The clustering of posts along the exterior wall of the structure suggests that the north and perhaps east walls underwent fairly substantial repairs, and thus were used on more than one occasion. However, the east row may also have served to create a bench, perhaps used as a sleeping platform, reportedly a common feature in warm-weather structures (e.g., Weld 1799:241). Other archaeologically documented examples of this kind of structure are rare (Beld 1990:46–49; Triggs 2004). Late Woodland examples have also been documented (e.g., Brose 1970; Ferris 1990; Murphy 1991).

Densmore (1979:25–28) indicates that Ojibwa apaquois/wigwams were typically dome-roofed oval structures with a single entrance. Both winter and summer structures were constructed from a number of small saplings, perhaps 12 to 14 ft long, placed relatively deep into the ground and bent over, forming the domed roof (P. Jones 1861:72). Normally, a wigwam would take one to three days to build, although temporary houses—described as looking like a sugar loaf and built of twenty saplings—could be put up in a few hours (Rutherfurd in Quaife 1958:238–239). Depending on size and occupants, wigwams had one or more hearths, or the hearth was outside the cabin (Quaife 1958:240).

Architectural evidence from the material culture recovered at Bellamy includes hand-wrought and machine-cut nails,[11] a metal key, a door hinge, and six fragments of brick. As well, nine flat glass fragments, a furniture tack, and a cast-iron woodstove vent door were also recovered from feature and ploughzone contexts. These findings suggest the last period of occupation (ca. 1820s–1830s) was perhaps characterized by the use of a structure more substantial than an apaquois/wigwam. But no evidence of a cellar or foundation was found, suggesting this was likely not a log cabin, but perhaps a hewn-board shanty.

Associated with the last period of occupation was a formal privy pit (fig. 3.5) located just north of the apaquois/wigwam. It exhibits an oval plan and two separate pit profiles. The assemblage from this feature is consistent with the rest of the site, but also contains the majority of post-1820 material on the site. I believe the privy is associated with the period either just before the Bear Creek Ojibwa relocated to the Thames, or just after, when a few families still remained along the Sydenham until a large influx of Euro-Canadian settlers moved in over the 1830s. It is not possible to tell if this part of the occupation was a resettlement of Bellamy after a hiatus, though I suspect the site was continuously occupied from the late 18th century to the early 1830s, and that periods of nonuse for one or several years likely occurred.

While use of a formal privy speaks to the adoption of an European innovation, that the privy was used during the last part of this site's occupation at a time when non-Aboriginal settlement had risen dramatically in the vicinity also speaks to the adoption of notions of "privacy," and to the changing landscape and face of the neighborhood at that time.

Ojibwa Exchange and Material Culture at 1800

The scheduling of Ojibwa subsistence activities also generated seasonal patterns for interaction (fig. 3.3). Exchange with other Aboriginal communities, such as with the Delaware, or at European settlements in the area, was an important aspect of Ojibwa subsistence. Trading for corn, bread, butter, salt and liquor occurred regularly, reflecting the importance of these "scarce" resources to the Ojibwa (Ferris 1989). In fact, the frequent references to trading for corn (even for seed corn in May) implies that corn was available to the Ojibwa from their own supply only during the months immediately after the harvest. The Ojibwa typically traded meat, skins, bear fat and sugar for these goods. Occasionally someone might also exchange their labor for goods. Also, the annual distribution of largely utilitarian goods and objects of personal adornment as gifts of allegiance from the British Indian Department, which, by the 1790s, usually occurred in the autumn at Amherstburg, was also accommodated within other scheduled activities. These large gatherings of people from many Aboriginal nations also served as important meetings to discuss various social, political and military matters, and were opportunities to reinforce social connections at a broad regional scale.

Smaller gatherings, either of members from a territorial community or between communities, would occur at both fixed times of the year and by happenstance as events warranted. This included ritualized occasions of begging for food at places like the Delaware settlement on the New Year, to reinforce reciprocal social ties with that community, while feasts for the Ojibwa gathered together for the purpose occurred nearby (e.g., Sabathy-Judd 1999).

The material culture recovered from Bellamy was limited and generally obtained through trade and exchange, mostly from the British Indian Department during gifts of allegiance distributions. The site assemblage included a number of silver trade goods, including nine ring or ribbon brooch fragments, four earbobs, a hand-rolled strip of silver made into a bead, and a silver ring (fig. 3.7a–c). The latter is marked by a zigzag spiral motif popular among Great Lakes Algonquian groups (Phillips 1984). Silver trade items used by the British Indian Department were manufactured in England, with additional centers in Quebec and Montreal (Fredrickson 1980), and they are ubiquitous on Aboriginal sites between the mid–18th century and the 1830s (e.g., Quimby 1966).

Additional ornamental items from British supplies included 466 glass beads, most (n = 382) from soil samples of either pit fill or ploughzone. Beads were often the only artifact category present in pits and posts, and their ubiquity in the ploughzone samples attests to storage difficulties, ubiquity in fashions, and their complete dispersal over the entire living area of the site. Very small, white subcylindrical beads (IIa13/14) dominated (69 percent) the assemblage, and were used in embroidery work (Karklins 1992). A further 19

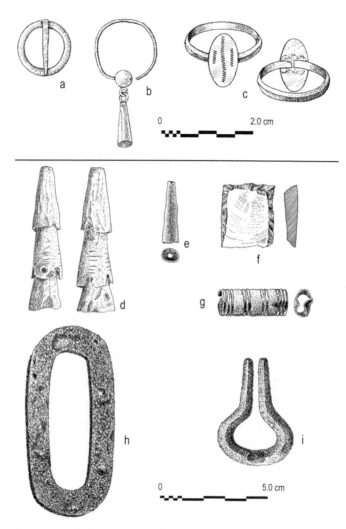

FIGURE 3.7. Artifacts from the Bellamy site:
a   silver broach
b   silver earbob
c   silver finger ring
d   bone cup and pin pieces
e   brass tinkling cone
f   spall gunflint
g   ferrule from a musket
h   iron firesteel
i   mouth harp.
(Illustrations by Thomas Kenyon)

percent of the assemblage consisted of white, blue or black glass tubulars, or "imitation" wampum (Ia5/2/18), while 8 percent were machine-made shell wampum (purple). The characteristics of the Bellamy assemblage suggest a date range between the 1780s and 1830s.[12] Similar bead assemblages have been found on sites throughout the Great Lakes, including within Wray's "Early Reservation Era" of 1779–1820 (1983; see also, Beld 1990, 2002; Berkson 1992; Cleland 1972; Herrick 1958; Martin and Mainfort 1985; Spector 1975; Wagner 2001).

Other goods likely derived from the Indian Department included fire-arms-related objects from a musket: a brass ferrule used to hold the ramrod (fig. 3.7g) and two gun springs, which were part of a gunlock's firing mechanism. Also found were sixty-six pieces of shot (35.55 g), five musketballs and sixty-four pieces of small lead wasting (17.74 g) generated during musketball manufacture. As well, sixteen spall gunflints (fig. 3.7f) were recovered along with a blade flint from the privy. Most gunflints exhibit extensive use and some were battered to small nubbins, likely reduced through use with a firesteel (fig. 3.7h) to make fires. The lack of blade gunflints is significant since spall varieties date earlier and were generally replaced by the blade type by the second decade of the 19th century (e.g., Hamilton 1980; Oerichbauer 1982:197; Witthoft 1967). British blade varieties continued to be used until the 1830s, when percussion mechanism rifles replaced muskets. Despite extensive soil flotation, no percussion caps associated with this later gun type were recovered.

Small fragments of iron (n = 24) and brass (n = 36) were recovered. All the brass objects exhibit evidence of cutting. Some were used to make tinkling cones (fig. 3.7e), and one long thin piece was rolled into a possible finger ring.

Evidence of European clothing (perhaps chief's or hunting coats) is indicated through the recovery of four metal coat buttons, one of which was a "cut-out" made from sheet metal with a shank attached—a manufacturing practice largely discontinued after the first decade of the 19th century (Ferris 1984). Also on British trade lists and found at Bellamy were wire-topped pins, two sets of metal scissors, a hawkbell, a mouth harp (fig. 3.7i), and nine fragments of kaolin smoking pipes.

Artifacts indicative of traditional Indigenous manufacture include a polished stone fragment that may have been part of a stone pipe. Stone pipes have been found on Michigan Ojibwa sites from the 19th century (Beld 2002). A number of bone artifacts were recovered, including two bone needles, one awl tip, and a polished bone fragment, which may have been used as an eyed sewing device for piercing hides. A bird bone tubular bead was also found and, notably, six deer toe bones carved into a conical shape and consistent with the Algonquian cup-and-pin game (Guilday 1963). A polished and grooved deer metacarpal was also found and may have been used as the pin for the game. Three of the cup specimens were found nestled together (fig. 3.7d), reflecting the aim of the game, which was to stack as many cups as possible onto the pin (Culin 1975:534; Densmore 1979:117–118). Other bone cups have been found at Ojibwa sites (Beld 2002:66; Wright 1967:94–95), a Kickapoo site in Illinois (Parmalee and Klippel 1983:274), and a Mesquakie site in Wisconsin (Wittry 1963:16). Two whetstones were recovered, as well as a long (15 × 3 cm) piece of slate from the privy, roughly knapped along both edges, smoothed and with a circular groove on one side. This object may have been a whetstone, though it likely served multiple functions of an idiosyncratic, personal nature. A second, flaked stone tool—an abrader—was also recovered from a storage pit.

A small assemblage of European ceramics was recovered, mostly from the privy and from a cache pit next to it. These sherds all date to the late 1820s–1830s. Their limtited quantity reflects the use of ceramics only after dry goods were readily available locally, which corresponds with ceramics appearing on other Algonquian Anishnabeg sites (e.g., Berkson 1992; Martin and Mainfort 1985).

Discussion

Both archaeological data and historical descriptions suggest Bellamy was an Ojibwa summer base camp. Denke suggested that Kitigen was home to a population of thirty, represented by seven houses. This implies that summer base camps were multi-family occupations consisting of a specific subgroup of the territorial community, perhaps representing between one-third and one-sixth of the total territorial population. Assuming that single fire apaquois/wigwams were occupied by one or two families, and that average family size was around six or seven individuals—as implied by the 1798 and 1799 counts of the Odawa residing at St. Anne's Island (MPHSC 20:564, 617–618, 641–642)—then it could be suggested that the population of Bellamy ranged between twenty and thirty, or two to four families.

But all indications are that a "population" estimate for a summer base camp is of limited use, given the very fluid and fluctuating nature of residents and visitors present at the camp in a given year. Bellamy was likely one of perhaps three or four similar camps established by the Bear Creek Ojibwa along the Sydenham during the summer. Likewise, residents at any of these camps may also have established smaller, individual family camps up- or downstream (as the Ojibwa Siskoba did by occupying the abandoned Denke cabin in 1806; Curnoe 1996; Sabathy-Judd 1999). From limited surveys, surface-collected artifact assemblages at two other locales have turned up spall gunflints and a catlinite bead (e.g., Kenyon 1987a). As these date earlier than the beginning of European settlement on the Sydenham, they likely were discarded or lost by Ojibwa, and represent, in light of the difficulty identifying such sites on cultivated fields, tantalizing hints of other habitation sites.

The settlement-subsistence patterns confirm that Ojibwa livelihood had accommodated but not been greatly altered by the presence of more settled Native communities and European settlements, or access to European-made items. Not only are the southwestern Ontario Ojibwa patterns consistent with both broad 18th-century patterns in the Great Lakes and with the Western Basin Late Woodland record for groups not heavily focused on surplus yield agriculture, but they also reflect general similarities to patterns documented for ancestral Ojibwa on the north shore of Lakes Huron and Superior. These are characterized by a seasonal coalescence and dispersal pattern centered on periods of abundance (e.g., Cleland 1992a; Heidenreich 1987; Kinietz 1940).

In short, the historic and archaeological data affirm that traditional livelihood, settlement, and social organization remained largely intact through the early 19th century, although material culture had significantly changed. Objects of clay were absent, and lithic industries appear to have been reduced to a few idiosyncratic stone objects. Traditional architecture was still in use, and if we assume that most of the architectural hardware recovered was associated with the last period of site occupation, then traditional house forms were still being constructed with limited aid of items such as nails. Given this, it appears that European goods *assisted* in improving traditional methods of Ojibwa livelihood; however, they do not appear to have *altered* settlement-subsistence.

This stands in contrast to the conventional assumptions that populate past anthropological and historical interpretations of Central Great Lakes Algonquian-speaking Anishnabeg from this time, especially assumptions about changes to social organization, settlement, subsistence and material accumulation being triggered by Aboriginal communities responding to European-induced fur trade realities (e.g., Bishop 1974; Hickerson 1970; Mainfort 1979, 1985, 1996). Of course, some of the data presented here (e.g., use of mass-produced European trade goods, assumptions of deer procurement as evidence of hide trade, use of a privy, historic references to hunger) could be selectively read as evidence of cultural decline or significant change due to European impacts. But this would be both selective and surficial, failing to consider more holistically how material change operated within daily lived experiences, and was self-referentially understood by the individuals participating in and experiencing those changes (Spector 1993).

Indeed, in terms of mapping complex cultural processes at play, the holistic, internal patterns to the Ojibwa data presented here reflect only what J. D. Rogers (1990:105–107) calls processes of "Maintenance" (the use of European analogues with Native counterparts, such as the use of glass and bone beads), "Replacement" (replacing Native analogues by European counterparts, such as the use of muskets), and "Adoption" (incorporation of European-made artifact classes into existing contexts, such as domestic use, burial or ritual). According to Rogers, none of these processes are a reflection of cultural stress. Rather, they are evidence of little change, or change only where the artifact system allows for it, such as that arising from innovation or technical improvement. This indicates the group associated with such an artifact system is maintaining cultural coherency (see also, Prince 2002; Rubertone 2001). So, the Ojibwa archaeological history at 1800 reflects only latent, surficial changes to material life—a coherent balance of adaptive accommodation and innovation while maintaining historically known lifeways and sense of self.

As with hunting-gathering communities elsewhere in place and time, the Ojibwa were clearly conservative to change beyond innovative adaptation, reluctant to abandon a historically constructed sense of self that came from the seasonal scheduling of livelihood and daily life. For the Ojibwa, mobility and hunting were as much dimensions of self-identity as language and belief systems (see Ferris 1989; note examples to this in Britain 1839; Canada 1844–45; P. Jones 1861; Sabathy-Judd 1999). Indeed, daily living was identity experienced across and read into the landscape of mobility, and reinforced as distinct when compared with other, more settled Native and non-Native communities. This worldview is also reflected in Ojibwa responses to the changes that occurred in the region subsequently through the first half of the 19th century, which are reviewed next.

Colonialism and Changing Continuities Post-1800

In 1800 the Ojibwa of southwestern Ontario were experiencing a "cultural zenith" of sorts. They utilized an abundant and diverse environment, maintained relatively easy access to manufactured goods, and held a strong position in the alliance of western Aboriginal nations and the British Crown. However, over the 19th century the Ojibwa shifted from seasonally mobile hunters to fixed communities of small plot farmers, augmented by continued exploitation of seasonally abundant resources such as fish and maple sugar. The underlying causes of this shift, when two hundred years of association with Europeans had previously failed to alter Ojibwa livelihood, are considered here.

Catastrophic Bureaucracy

The emergence of a British-imposed colonialism in southern Ontario began to be evident by the late 18th century. Unlike other regions of North America, colonialism imposed here was not overtly coercive, but rather a more subtle and insidious undermining of Aboriginal sovereignty that emerged from the attitudes, prejudices and assumptions—in other words, dispositions—of British society in the 19th century, and made manifest through State policies and bureaucracy (e.g., Allen 1993; Coates 2004; Tobias 1983). The colonial State's administration of its relationship with Indigenous groups operated as a kind of "catastrophic bureaucracy"—a term I use here less to convey impact of colonizer action, and more to describe the "quality" of bureaucratic culture. Catastrophic bureaucracy encompasses various State actions of good intent, self-serving interest, incompetence, indifference, racial bias, strategic disruption of sovereignty, neglect and deceit, all arising from the apparatus and populace of the colonial power of the day (British then Canadian) and imposed onto the daily lived life of Aboriginal communities.

By the early 19th century, the interests and focus of the colonialist state had shifted precipitously from the administration of a frontier and an extractive economy, to the administration of a colonial settlement. Consequently, an impetus of British policy in Upper Canada over the next few decades was to encourage occupation of the region by immigrants from the British Isles (Surtees 1982, 1983; Wood 2000). Procuring land through settlement protected against American imperial interests and helped secure sovereignty (Surtees 1994). Thus, a series of negotiations and land treaties were initiated, and by 1827 all of southwestern Ontario had been surrendered through treaties to the British Crown (fig. 3.8; Jacobs 1983).

Though these treaties were a "Nation-to-Nation" form of sovereign negotiation, British administrative policy nonetheless reflected a pursuit of blatant self-interest, one that had first emerged in the last three decades of the 18th century. Significantly, corporate attitudes toward the Crown's Aboriginal allies shifted, and language and policy post–War of 1812 reflect a notion

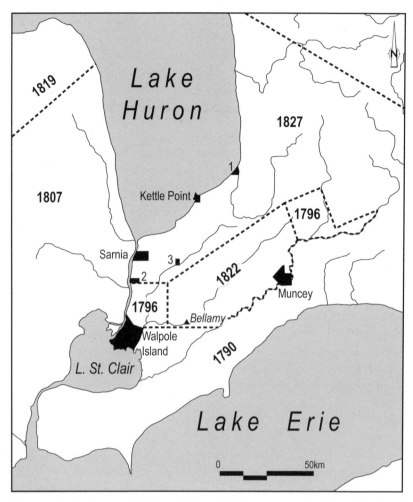

FIGURE 3.8. Land surrender boundaries and Ojibwa reserve locations. Numbered areas are reserves that no longer exist.

1   Au Sauble
2   Moore (Lower Reserve)
3   Enniskillen.

of "wardship," coupled with a bureaucratic obsession for economic restraint on such "programs" (e.g., Allen 1993; Coates 2004:181; Surtees 1969). Feeding this desire for decreased costs was the decision to pay for surrendered lands through annual issues of supplies, rather than providing one-time cash payments (Surtees 1983:70).

British administrative policy encompassed the Crown's changed view that Native communities had somehow become wards of the colonial state, whose welfare and future had to be managed by the British bureaucracy (Tobias 1983). Policies that sought to bring "civilization" and "protection" to Native people by the Crown became entangled with a Native reserve policy that arose by the 1830s (Surtees 1969). Reserves had been intended to be land set aside for the exclusive use by Native communities, who would also maintain continuing access to surrendered lands in order to hunt, fish and sugar. But seasonal mobility from fixed community reserves also was seen by Indian Department agents and missionaries as inhibiting the development of a more "civilized, Christian" Native culture (Britain 1839; Canada 1844–45, 1847).

By the 1830s, the Indian Department had embarked on an active policy of "aiding" civilizing efforts, by making Native families productive farmers within isolated communities administered by Indian Department officials. This redirection of policy occurred in concert with a reorganization of the Indian Department, which in 1830 ceased to be a branch of the military and became part of the public service (Allen 1975:91). The specific policies of Native civilization to be followed included gathering Native peoples together on reserves; encouraging cultivation of the land; providing for religious, educational, and agricultural instruction; and supplying communities with houses, rations, seed and farming equipment—all to be paid from the group's own annuities for signing land surrenders (Surtees 1969:92).

These policies came from within the colonialist administration and were imposed without consultation—Aboriginal sovereignty was irrelevant in the minds of bureaucrats who began to view themselves less as serving allies and more as managing a kind of past obligation increasingly seen as marginal to the affairs of the emerging colonial state. It would be wrong, however, to imply that the history of the colonial encounter during this period was solely one of misplaced good intentions and benign neglect. Clearly other motives were also driving colonial agendas. For example, the reserve policy was less for "protection" of the Native people and more for "moving them out of the way" to allow for colonial settlement.[13] Indeed, pressure for land was so great that there were frequent misrepresentations in negotiations, manipulation of treaty commitments and revised notions of obligations entered into, all undermining Aboriginal sovereignty (e.g., D. Smith 1981).

Native communities did not fail to recognize the other agendas at play in colonial governtment actions, and there are frequent accounts of Native leaders complaining to colonial authorities and hiring legal counsel to object to loss of land, accounting irregularities, the Crown's failure to live up to their treaty commitments or payments, etc. (e.g., Gulewitsch 1998). Native individuals voiced constant objections to the way the agents "administered" communities, land rights and financial matters. And these communities struggled continually to protect land, resources and money from acts of fraud, mismanagement and corruption committed by the very colonial agents assigned to protect those interests (e.g., Leighton 1981; Telford 1998).

The colonialist bureaucracy mostly ignored such protests, an indifference consistent with the paternalistic understanding of the empire toward what was clearly thought of as the Indigenous social detritus of empire building. Commonplace through the 19th and 20th centuries were neglect, fraud and embezzlement; self-serving agendas of the state; administrative decision-making based on racial stereotypes and Spencerian notions of cultural difference; and initiatives that undermined the stated aims of colonial policy toward Aboriginal nations. This forced communities to continually confront and negotiate this catastrophic bureaucracy, which denied them sovereignty within the emerging nation state of Canada.

Despite this chronic catastrophic bureaucracy imposed onto the daily life of Indigenous communities, the operational aims of the Indian Department to "civilize" mostly failed to affect change for the Ojibwa prior to the mid-1800s, partly because these policies did not directly interfere with existing settlement-subsistence strategies. The signing of treaties and surrender of territory did not immediately impede Ojibwa use of land. Although "reserve" areas were established, they were normally locales understood by the British Crown as centers where large seasonal gatherings occurred (e.g., spring fish harvest locales). Moreover, being based at a reserve did not translate into an abandonment of mobility. Reports of groups continuing to travel from reserves to hunting territories and maintaining a traditional seasonal round continued for all southwestern Ontario Ojibwa groups into the 1850s (Britain 1839; Canada 1844–45, 1847; P. Jones 1860; Slight 1844). The real impact of catastrophic bureaucracy was more indirect, as an ancillary affliction felt only after the onslaught of a rapidly changing landscape took hold in the region.

The Changing Place of Southwestern Ontario

Change in Ojibwa settlement-subsistence did occur in the 19th century largely as a result of the increasing encroachment of Euro-Canadian settlement and land clearing in southwestern Ontario. This increased European occupation was a direct, unaccommodating competitor to Indigenous lifeways. The Ojibwa traveled across large stretches of land over the course of their annual seasonal round to harvest all necessary resources and maintain

TABLE 3.1 Population Increases in Southwestern Ontario, 1805–1861

County/Township Population	1805	1820	1830	1840	1851–52	1861
Essex	2,347	3,732	5,297	9,175	17,817	25,211
Kent	809	1,257	3,444	7,474	15,354	31,183
Lambton	—	—	2,339	4,572	10,815	24,916
Middlesex	—	8,061	11,882	26,482	32,862	48,736
Muncey[1]	—	—	497	2,446	6,771	9,320
Bear Creek[2]	—	—	1,083	1,687	1,990	1,885
Sarnia[3]	—	—	—	1,002	2,642	6,524
Walpole I[4]	—	—	1,374	2,389	4,184	9,557

Note: Ojibwa community numbers refer to *Euro-Canadian* populations in the townships surrounding each Ojibwa community. 1. Combined totals for the townships of Delaware, Caradoc, and Exfrid. 2. Combined totals for the townships of Zone and Dawn. 3. Combined totals for the townships of Moore and Sarnia (and the town of Sarnia in 1861). 4. Combined townships of Dover, Chatham, and Sombra

a relatively small population. This use of the landscape seemed "backwards" and "wasteful" to the European settler notions of mastering the land, clearing and ordering the landscape by way of agriculture, and generating high yields from every furrowed acre to support the emerging rural agricultural economy of the region (Johnson 1974, 1983; Wood 2000). The European settler also introduced substantial quantities of livestock, and brought with them relatively new notions of land ownership, which meant greater potential of conflict between settler and Native over the use of and access to property, rights to water and game, and so on. As settlement and clearing occurred in areas Native families and individuals traveled and hunted, the sense of an increasing European presence in the region was accentuated, especially during the early wave of immigration into the interior of southwestern Ontario in the 1820s and 1830s.

A sense of how dramatic change was in southwestern Ontario is reflected in Euro-Canadian population increases (Johnson 1974:28, 31). Table 3.1 shows the increase by county and for townships around Ojibwa communities from 1805 to 1861. Figures were obtained from Johnson (1974), Goodspeed (1889), Gourlay (1822), Harris and Wood (1993), Kenyon (1997), W. Smith (1846), Wood (2000), and abstracted census data (Canada 1853; 1863). All counties underwent phenomenal increases in population over this period. This occurred within a single generation, and the impact on people already present, Native or Euro-Canadian, had to have been substantial.

TABLE 3.2 Acreage of Cleared Land in Southwestern Ontario, 1842–1861

County/Township	1842	1851–52	1861
Kent	24,561	64,260	115,858
Walpole: Dover	2,432 (3.5%)	5,837 (8.5%)	9,814 (14.2%)
Walpole: Chatham	3,749 (4.1%)	7,240 (7.8%)	14,311 (15.5%)
Walpole: Sombra	1,589 (2.1%)	1,630 (2.1%)	8,187 (10.6%)
Lambton	7,741	34,497	96,092
Sarnia: Moore	1,901 (2.6%)	3,198 (4.3%)	10,998 (14.9%)
Sarnia: Sarnia Twp.	1,366 (2.9%)	2,301 (4.8%)	6,136 (12.9%)
Middlesex	40,412	136,917	233,672
Muncey: Delaware	1,756 (6.2%)	5,007 (17.8%)	6,931 (24.6%)
Muncey: Caradoc	5,065 (6.5%)	11,861 (15.2%)	18,116 (23.2%)
Muncey: Ekfrid	5,655 (10.4%)	9,072 (16.7%)	15,165 (27.9%)

Note: The figures in parentheses represent the amount of cleared land as a percent of total acreage for the townships, based on data from the abstracted census (Canada 1873).

An even more significant impact on Ojibwa livelihood was the rate at which land was being cleared by Euro-Canadian settlers for agricultural fields (table 3.2). Astronomical increases over the 20-year period spanning 1840 to 1861 reflect a radical alteration to the landscape. Despite rapid clearing, however, uncleared, wooded areas remained in existence within a day or two's walk of reserves, affording local Ojibwa the ability to maintain at least some form of traditional hunting.

By 1861, extensive parts of southwestern Ontario were actively cleared and farmed as the Victorian culture of the colonizer imposed "order" on the landscape. Also emerging across the region by then were a few urban centers, smaller service center towns and villages for surrounding rural communities, and transportation networks of wagon roads and rail lines. This pattern of population growth continued into the 1880s, at which point changing demographics reflected a rural depopulation as people started living and earning a livelihood in greater numbers within larger urban centers. While this did not curtail land clearing, since farming operations continued to grow, rural depopulation continued well into the 20th century (e.g., Kenyon 1997; Wood 2000).

Ojibwa Response to Change in the 19th Century

The rise of a colonialist state through the 19th century, complete with both coercive administrative policies that alienated and marginalized Aboriginal nations, and the rise in the population of the colonizer reshaping the land, combined to transform Indigenous groups into enclaves within British southwestern Ontario. These changes required Indigenous communities to define their autonomy and identity within a very different world than had existed even a generation earlier. Change within the three main Ojibwa communities in the region[14] was influenced by the nature and make-up of each group, local Euro-Canadian settlement, and the character of the catastrophic bureaucracy manifest within each community. Nonetheless, at a broader level, each group responded from a similar set of historical knowledge and understanding of their daily life. Thus, while specific differences will be noted, the general patterns documented are of a similar form for all southwestern Ojibwa communities through this period.

Shifting Patterns: Mobility and Settlement

By the end of the 1820s, Ojibwa seasonal round patterns were still largely unchanged from the turn of the century, despite completion of land surrenders for much of the region (Jacobs 1983; Surtees 1985). But the rise of the reserve system during the 1830s began to alter those land-use patterns. Reserves were intended to foster isolation from encroaching Euro-Canadian settlement and to encourage fixed residence and an emphasis on small-plot agriculture. Reserves were mostly established around seasonally aggregated locales and were places where the Indian Department ensured provisions could be obtained. The conceptual construction of these locales as fixed places, even if they were not at first fixed, along with encroaching Euro-Canadian settlement, and the relocation by the Indian Department of other Native people from the United States to these locales (e.g., Clifton 1998), all reinforced the notion through the 1830s that reserves were fixed community enclaves exclusively for Native families and groups.

Ojibwa reserve communities, however, did not develop into villages or nucleated settlements. Descriptions imply a scattered, dispersed pattern of residences across the reserve. Dispersal was also facilitated by the imposition of surveyed lots onto the reserve area (Clench in Britain 1839; Nin.Da.Waab. Jig 1987:33). For example, at the Sarnia reserve, settlement was based on individually owned lots that were concentrated along the St. Clair River, while the interior of the reserve and adjacent unsettled townships were used for hunting (W. Jones in Britain 1839; Canada 1844–45).

At each of the three main Ojibwa settlements in southwestern Ontario, assignment of lots was determined informally, usually by the head of a family. At Muncey and Sarnia this meant choosing a surveyed lot. Selection did not require the consent of community leaders and was rarely challenged (W. Jones in Canada 1844–45, 1847; Clench in Canada 1844–45). At Walpole Island, where Euro-Canadian squatters had already cultivated large areas of open prairie, leaders subdivided farms and arable land for Ojibwa, Odawa or Potawatomi nation use. Separate arable plots were then cultivated by members of a particular nation, with individual priorities determining how much any person cultivated for their family (Keating in Canada 1844–45).

Indian Department records indicate that at each reserve, residences were either apaquois/wigwams or log cabins. At Sarnia, the Indian Department had planned to build log cabins of a uniform size for each family. The Indian agent requested that these cabins be "14 by 16 feet and raised about 2 feet above the upper floor, to give them room to lay by their luggage of different kinds" (PAO 06/1831:1).[15] He also stated that the original plan to build cabins 12 × 14 feet was considered too small by the Ojibwa, who would have chosen to live in "unhealthy camps" if the size was not increased. Since wigwams tended to be about 12 × 16 ft (4 × 5 m) in size (Denke 1993; P. Jones 1861:72), the proposal to increase log cabin size corresponded well with wigwam living space. Any innovative advantage to a log cabin was realized only when it met a key functional characteristic of the traditional, better-known analogue.

At Sarnia, William Jones reported that families who had moved into log cabins appeared to be more "steady" (sedentary) in their habits (PAO 05/1833: 49). At Muncey, the community had built a large number of log cabins, while Walpole Island had few cabins and more camps, a term that was used to refer to wigwams (Canada 1844–45). By the 1850s, most families were said to be living in log cabins, although Talfourd reported that "in the heat of the summer it is usual with some to put up wigwams adjoining their log houses, being cooler, but none from choice reside permanently in them" (Canada 1858). Finally, Wm. Jones also stated that almost all the Ojibwa had either outbuildings or sheds to house their crops, in effect serving as innovative analogues to storage pits.

Census records give a clear indication of the make-up of settlement forms at these Ojibwa reserves mid-century (table 3.3). According to the Muncey data from 1852, a population of 397 people resided in forty-five log cabins, eight shanties (hewn board hybrid-like structures similar to those reported at 1801 from Kitigen) and one frame house.[16] A third of all residences were multi-

TABLE 3.3 Census Data for Land Cleared by Ojibwa Households, 1851–52 (Muncey) and 1861 (Walpole Island and Sarnia)

	Not in the agricultural census	0	1–9	10–19	20–29	30–39	40–59	60+
				Acres				
Muncey Ojibwa								
	34 (63%)	2 (4%)	9 (17%)	5 (9%)	3 (5%)	0	0	1 (2%)
Walpole								
Frame houses	0	0	0	1 (25%)	0	0	1 (25%)	2 (50%)
Log cabins	11 (16%)	6 (8%)	22 (31%)	7 (10%)	13 (18%)	5 (7%)	3 (4%)	4 (6%)
Camps	3 (18%)	4 (23%)	8 (47%)	1 (6%)	1 (6%)	0	0	0
Sarnia								
Frame houses	—	0	2 (50%)	0	1 (25%)	1 (25%)	0	0
Log cabins	—	7 (15%)	15 (32%)	9 (19%)	13 (28%)	2 (4%)	1 (2%)	0
Shanties	—	8 (27%)	16 (53%)	4 (14%)	1 (3%)	1 (3%)	0	0
Camps	—	9 (82%)	2 (18%)	0	0	0	0	0

family. A decade later[17] at Sarnia, census recorders reported ninety-two structures for a population of 399, which included forty-seven log cabins, thirty shanties, eleven camps and four frame houses. There was no indication of multiple family households. At Walpole Island, 504 people resided in ninety-two structures, including seventy-one log cabins, seventeen camps, and four framed buildings. Just over 28 percent of the log cabins were multifamily residences. Only two of seventeen camps were multifamily residences.

Shifting Patterns: Material Possessions

The establishment of fixed reserves, the switch to log cabins—permanent residences to live in and return to—the appearance of merchants in nearby non-Native settlements, and the distribution of annual payments at reserves all contributed to an expansion of Ojibwa material culture. Also, goods distributed from the Indian Department saw a decline in ornamental items such as silver and beads by the 1830s, but the maintenance of utilitarian items such as kettles, guns and shot, along with the addition of items such as shoes, agricultural implements and manufactured clothing (e.g., BHC Ms. R2 Ironside Papers, Record Box 3; PAO MS 296; WIHC Keating Letterbook): "The Majority of Chiefs, in consequence of their late improvement in civilization, have agreed to dispense with . . . silver trinkets, wool hats, scarlet cloth and calico for the present year. And in lieu thereof, wish to get half a dozen box stoves and pipe, fur hats, printed calico, such as worn by whites, women's shoes as well as men's, some finer cloth than they have been in the habit of receiving, and some more farming utensils such as axes, hoes, scythes, wedges, and a good supply of provisions, as they say they will remain and work during the winter, in lieu of roaming in their usual way" (PAO 06/1835:99–100).

Asking for utilitarian goods in lieu of items like silver did not mean a rejection of those items. Silver brooches, pendants, beads and other adornments were commonly used (e.g., Nin.Da.Waab.Jig 1987; Richardson 1848:63). Native dress included a mix of European-style clothes and traditional forms, often combined in personal attire. Indeed, traditional dress for ceremonies and business suits for political interactions with the colonialist state were worn by community leaders through the 19th century (e.g., P. Jones 1861; Karklins 1992).

Ojibwa ownership of goods typical of the time and associated with fashion and innovation were often pointed to as indicating progress toward "civilization." For example, George Henry, an Ojibwa interpreter for William Jones, wrote of the Sarnia Ojibwa in the Christian Guardian in 1837: "Yes Mr. Papermaker, if you had seen these Indians a few years ago, you would think they were the animals you called Orang-Orangs, for they appeared more like them than human beings; but since the Great Spirit has blessed them they have good cloths; plates and dishes; window and bed curtains; knives and forks; chairs and tables; and one of the chiefs has saved plenty of duck and partridge feathers, and has got a good feather bed" (Aum-nid tje wun-nongk, St. Clair, Christian Guardian, March 10, 1837).

While reflecting perceptions of the day with respect to traditional Ojibwa lifeways by the dominant colonialist culture, the description of material items was typical of what one would expect to find in a family's log cabin household, and not in an apaquois/wigwam, where mobility would have precluded possessing such a range of goods.

Historic data indicate that through the mid-century, new classes of goods were used within at least some Native households, and some homes also featured a range of new architectural features (e.g., windows, doors, etc.). These indications are consistent with the last part of the Bellamy site occupation, and with an Ojibwa settlement and mission village from the 1850s in central Michigan (Beld 1990). These sites document a full range of domestic material goods, and an increase in the quantity of farming-related artifacts from earlier periods (Beld 2002). On Beausoleil Island in Georgian Bay, work on a mid-19th-century Ojibwa settlement documented the use of log cabins, cellars, a wide range of contemporary mass-produced material culture, and continued faunal artifact industries, including bird bone beads (Ross 1998, 2004).

Archaeological data were also recovered from a survey of the Enniskillen Ojibwa reserve in the interior of Lambton County, occupied by residents of both Walpole Island and Sarnia (Ferris 1987). While the locale was primarily used for sugaring, one to six families resided there year round after the 1830s (PAO 09/1836:142). Shanties and log cabins were noted, though seasonal visitors used wigwams. Two scatters of domestic debris related to 1840s residences included refined ceramics, bottle glass, smoking pipes and animal remains. A third domestic site yielded a small quantity of material dating to the early 1860s. Presence of mortar chinking with beam impressions suggests that it was the location of a log cabin reported in the 1861 census.

The limited archaeological data available for the mid–19th century suggests that possession and use of new classes of material items, such as ceramics, furniture, and architectural hardware occurred at about the same time that some Ojibwa families began residing in log cabins. Greater accumulation of material goods could occur since they could be kept and stored in a fixed place, without impeding mobility to various resource locales.

Shifting Patterns: Old and New Subsistence Practices

"As the White man has his foot on the Indian hunting-ground, the game, of course, disappears; but more than a substitute is found in swine, horses and cattle, the multiplication of which not only pleasingly occupies their attention but also comfortably supplies their domestic wants with beef, pork, veal, butter, and milk. They have improved in their growing of grain, we judge, fifty per cent" (MSAR 1846–47:11).

A common complaint by missionaries and Indian Department agents was that, despite reserve living, Ojibwa families or individuals still traveled away for long periods of time to harvest seasonally available resources. This mobility, although from a fixed point, was derided as encouraging the continuation of traditional beliefs and lifestyles. Agriculture, as an alternative to the "hunt"

and as a means to keep people on reserves, was seen as critical to facilitating
Christianizing efforts by missionaries, and to achieving assimilation (e.g.,
Wm. Jones and Clench in Britain 1839; Canada 1844–45, 1847; Keating in
Canada 1844–45, 1847; Scott in Canada 1847; MSAR 1846–47:11, 1848–
49:10; Richardson 1848:59–60):

> The friends of the Indian race will also be glad to learn that the Chris-
> tian Indians are making some progress towards Civilization. You will
> form some idea of the temporal condition of the Ojebways under our
> instruction [at Muncey], when you read the following inventory of their
> property . . . 60 log-houses, 20 log-stables, 57 horses, 25 colts, several
> yoke of oxen, 22 milch cows, 40 young cattle, 200 swine, two wagons,
> several ploughs, six harrows . . . one grindstone, one set of carpenter's
> tools, one set of blacksmith's tools, 500 or 600 acres under cultivation,
> etc. Now contrast this with what they had 15 years ago, when all they
> possessed they could carry on their backs: you at once see that the attempt
> to Christianize them has not altogether failed. Facts are stubborn things,
> and speak for themselves. (MSAR, 1842–43:6)

Facts may be stubborn but they are also malleable, and the degree of agriculture practiced by Ojibwa communities was much more variable than implied.
Some increased acceptance of agriculture certainly did occur, and a few families
did raise some livestock by the 1840s (PAO 02/1836:119–120; Clench in Britain 1839:143). Nonetheless, the general trend implied by various observers
from the time was that at some point around the mid-century, the Ojibwa—as
entire communities—developed rural agricultural economies similar to that
seen within contemporary Euro-Canadian settlements in the region. But the
perspective of these sources must be considered. Clearly, in their assessments of
Ojibwa life, any change was read as anticipating a futurist progression toward
an imagined ideal—an ideal that was meaningful to Euro-Canadian observers,
but not necessarily to the Ojibwa themselves. Certainly Indian agents and missionaries, anticipating signs that indicated "improvement" in Ojibwa lifestyle,
would have emphasized certain facts that seemed to substantiate evidence of
improvement. However, there were also plenty of facts in evidence suggesting
a more complex and variable picture, including the retention of traditional
livelihood and the emergence of unique rather than emulative patterns. The
hazard, as always, is with subsequent research accepting historically emphasized "facts" over other, silent "facts" as uncontested historic realities.

The Old: Traditional Subsistence Practices. Traditional subsistence emphases were unchanged into the 1830s. While reserve settlement meant operating from fixed locales, Ojibwa families could still travel to traditional hunting grounds and sugar camps, while reserves, situated near spring fishing grounds, allowed for the continued harvest of that resource (Surtees 1985). What did begin to change was that these reserve/fish camp locales also started to serve as large and permanent summer base camps for an increasing number of families; a place to plant crops while continuing the normal range of subsistence pursuits away from that locale. And with territorial communities coalescing in the face of encroaching Euro-Canadian occupation and State inducements, the operation of small, subterritorial groups of forty to sixty people declined, and mobility away from the reserve became more mobility of families or men.

But as is implied by the Ojibwa seasonal round summary provided by Wm. Jones in 1839, there seems little alteration from the beginning of the 19th century: "Their Pursuits generally are cultivating small fields of Indian Corn, Potatoes, and various kinds of Pulse; and at times in Summer, when their crops do not require their attendance, they follow Hunting and Fishing; in Winter the greater part of them retire to the most favorable situations for Hunting and making Sugar, where they usually remain till the season for preparing to plant and sow their Spring crops. Those Indians may be said to have their locations on which they have fixed themselves, and where they principally make their Home" (Britain 1839:141).

In 1852 most of the Walpole Island community was still characterized as being away from the reserve a good six months of the year (MSAR 1852–53:9). Other missionary accounts reported that the Muncey Ojibwa were away from the reserve for months at a time, hunting and fishing (MSAR 1848–49:10, 1859–60:15). This included a dispersal for the late fall hunt beginning in October, followed by a return to the reserve in January, and then leaving again in the spring (Slight 1844). This is somewhat at odds with the early-19th-century wintering pattern, suggesting a more fragmented series of trips to winter hunting grounds, again from the fixed settlement of the reserve.

Specifically, hunting was being altered in response to changing Euro-Canadian land use and settlement patterns (see also, Cronon 1983). Hunting required families to cover large areas during the course of the summer, fall and winter. And since much of the ceded land in southwestern Ontario incorporated large Ojibwa hunting territories, hunting grounds were afforded little protection from the land clearing and increased settlement across the region. The magnitude of these changes added to pressures on animal stocks, and references to depleted game and the declining reliability of the hunt were noted: "at the same time they [Sarnia Ojibwa Chiefs] express some alarm for their own situation: They observed that, seeing the settlements of whites increasing so fast on every side of them, they find they must soon have to depend on their industry or suffer. They also observed that their crops, though pretty good, will not be sufficient to furnish the whole of the tribe with provisions through the ensuing winter, and that they fear that the game will not supply the deficiency" (Wm. Jones, PAO 09/1833:53–54).

Initially, the Ojibwa response to encroaching Euro-Canadian settlement included avoiding clearances to hunt adjoining wooded areas, or traveling beyond substantial settlements to hunt (Wm. Jones in Britain 1839:141; Clench in Britain 1839:143; PAC RG10 46:576–577, Chase to Clench 04/1846; MSAR 1852–53:9). However, these options would not remain viable for long, as continuing waves of pioneer occupation and clearance increased the distance from reserves to unsettled regions suitable for summer, fall and winter hunts. Of course, individual families could and did choose to move away from reserve settlement into more interior and northerly counties in order to maintain traditional livelihood patterns (e.g., Leitch 1975:38–39), and census records throughout the 19th century record small pockets of Ojibwa residing in rural parts of townships,[18] resisting fixed settlement. But most families did remain on reserves and adapted to a more fixed settlement by modifying hunting practices to accommodate the changed landscape:

> They [Muncey Ojibwa] resort to the unsettled lands in the London and Western Districts [to hunt]; and it is probable, that as soon as those lands are occupied, they will be compelled to abandon the chase. The effect of the gradual settlement of the country has been to assimilate their habits to those of the whites, and to attach them to their homes; they now hunt and fish as near as home as possible. (Clench in Canada 1844–45)

> The greater part of the Ojibwa (at Walpole Island) are away at least 6 months of the year. However, they are now beginning to see the necessity of working their land, as the country around is fast being occupied, and the game is either driven away or killed off. (MSAR 1852–53:9)

Declining game around reserves, the realization that traditional subsistence strategies were not effective if families had to travel too far away, and an increasing focus on agriculture that required maintaining some presence on the reserve over the greater part of the spring and summer, meant that hunting had to change. This is evidenced by the increased fragmentation of hunting trips, occurring as short-term (one-to-two-month-long) trips in the winter and more informal trips of a few days duration otherwise (e.g., P. Jones in MSAR 1848–

49:10). Hunting emphases during peak resource times, such as during the rutting season, were also maintained. In effect, hunting became an intensive activity and winter pursuit, and was augmented by more informal travels and opportunistic, nearby harvests.

Regardless of changes to hunting, other Ojibwa subsistence activities remained largely intact, especially activities carried out on reserves or at specific locales. Sugaring continued to be important throughout the 19th century as both a food source and as a commodity to trade or sell. In fact, the Walpole Island and Sarnia Ojibwa sold off landholdings known as the Lower (Moore) Reserve to purchase individual lots in nearby Enniskillen Township precisely to secure good stands of maple trees suitable for sugaring (PAO 03/1836:120–121, 12/1837:171–72; WIHC Keating Letterbook, 07/1843). The Ojibwa also complained about not receiving enough kettles for sugaring at annual distributions, or the poor quality of the kettles they did receive (e.g., PAO 06/1833:49–50; 07/1833:50–51).

Fishing also remained important, both during spring runs and as a food source through the summer and fall. The Ojibwa received spools of fishing lines during annuity payments, received money to hire a person to make nets out of the lines, and requested the Indian Department provide the materials necessary to build seines for fishing on the St. Clair River. Euro-Canadian poaching was a constant concern (PAO 02/1836:119–120, 06/1836:135).

Archaeological subsistence data are mostly lacking from this period. The Bellamy 1820s–1830s privy data are as diversified as any other deposit at the site, with deer (71 percent) and raccoon (16 percent) making up the majority of mammal bone, augmented by 11 other nondomesticated mammals and three domesticates, including pig (2.2 percent). Fish is dominated by drum (38 percent) and catfish (28 percent), and another four species. Four species of bird are present, including chicken (33 percent). Floral remains are dominated by corn and squash. At the mid-19th-century Beausoleil Island Ojibwa community in Georgian Bay, preliminary faunal data suggest a diverse subsistence base dominated by fish and various aquatic species, and very limited domesticates, comparable to the Bellamy privy (Ross 2004). An even greater diversity of animal remains was documented at mid-19th-century Ojibwa sites in central east Michigan (Beld 1990, 2002; Martin and Richmond 1990, 2002). This included mammal assemblages dominated by deer and, in one case, a massive fish assemblage including over twenty identified species.

The New: Increased Agricultural Subsistence. The degree to which Ojibwa communities opted into broader southwestern Ontario rural agricultural practices of mid-century can be examined through the agricultural censuses from 1851–52 and 1861. While ninety-five adult males in fifty-four residences were listed by occupation in the personal census for the Muncey in 1851–52 as "farmer" (seven were listed as "hunter"), only twenty of fifty-four households were listed in the agricultural census, eleven of which were working less than 10 acres of cleared land (table 3.3). Presumably the "farmer" designation was more honorific than functional, since 67 percent of households at Muncey were not sufficiently farming to warrant the census taker adding them to the agricultural census, while another 17 percent were maintaining very small plots. In other words, just over 15 percent of households in the community were placing a majority of livelihood effort into agricultural activities, while two-thirds of all households were not investing in any agricultural effort (other than, possibly, small garden plots).

A decade later, although cultivated land holdings were more prevalent at Walpole Island and Sarnia, variation remained great. Moreover, looking at Walpole Island and Sarnia households by dwelling type suggests a hierarchy of investment in agriculture by permanence of home, with higher percentages of families in log cabins (45 percent at Walpole Island, 53 percent at Sarnia) working 10 acres or more, higher than families living in shanties at Sarnia (20 percent), or in apaquois/wigwams at either Walpole Island (12 percent) or Sarnia (0 percent). In other words, in 1861, 26 percent of Ojibwa households for both the Sarnia and Walpole Island communities were not engaged in agricultural activities, while another third were only marginally so (i.e., working 10 acres or less).

For all three communities, an agricultural pattern emphasizing traditional crops (corn, potatoes and beans) is reflected in the census data (table 3.4). The predominance of this emphasis by families, regardless of their residence type, likely speaks to the importance of those crops as subsistence staples. Beyond this general pattern, though, there are distinct variations within and across communities. Families in log cabins uniformly invest greater effort in raising livestock, especially pigs as a ready supply of meat. Likewise, log-cabin families generated higher crop yields, likely an indication of a greater investment (or labor pool) in working fields. At Muncey and for Sarnia log-cabin households, raising cash crops such as wheat and oats was more widely practiced than at Walpole Island, where there was almost no interest among log-cabin or apaquois/wigwam families in the raising of these crops.[19] Finally, it is worth pointing out that almost no one in these communities came anywhere near to the Euro-Canadian averages for cash crops, as reflected in the totals compiled for areas adjacent to each reserve (table 3.4). While Sarnia log-cabin households and Walpole Island frame households do exhibit lower yields for corn and a greater emphasis on cash crops than seen

TABLE 3.4 Agricultural Census Data for Ojibwa Households, 1851–52 (Muncey) and 1861 (Walpole Island and Sarnia)

Product	Muncey	Walpole I log cabin	Walpole I camp	Sarnia log cabin	Sarnia shanty	Middlesex County[b]	Lambton County[b]
Wheat in	5 (25%)[a]	1 (5%)	0	14 (34%)	5 (18%)		
bushels	36.0	12	0	23.5	18.9	189.3	125.6
Peas in	8 (40%)	7 (33%)	0	26 (63%)	9 (33%)		
bushels	17.0	6.6	0	12.8	7.4	89.3	67.6
Oats in	11	1 (5%)	1 (6%)	16 (39%)	2 (7%)		
bushels	(55%) 36.0	30.0	5.0	33.0	9.0	158.7	137.0
Corn in	17	21 (100)	16 (89%)	33 (80%)	15 (56%)		
bushels	(85%) 46.0	43.4	33.3	19.5	18.3	11.0	19.1
Potatoes in bushels	13 (65%) 37.0	19 (90%) 26.7	12 (67%) 11.8	38 (93%) 67.5	23 (86%) 37.1	108.0	96.9
Beans in	7 (35%)	14 (67%)	11 (61%)	28 (68%)	8 (30%)		
bushels	3.0	3.8	2.7	3.1	2.8	NA	NA
Cows/ oxen	10 (50%) 1.8	10 (48%) 3.2	1 (6%) 6.0	24 (58%) 3.6	13 (48%) 2.1	NA	NA
Pigs	9 (45%) 4.7	16 (76%) 4.9	7 (39%) 3.6	28 (68%) 4.3	14 (52%) 3.8	7.2	6.3

[a] Number and percent of households raising the crop or livestock listed, followed by the average yields for those households.

[b] County average yields from 1861 are based on total farm yield in the county divided by farmers in the county.

for other reserve households, which suggests a shift toward a more diversified crop base, the pattern overall for the three communities was a general increase in agricultural activities to generate food staples for household subsistence, and perhaps modest surpluses being generated for trade.

Shifting Patterns: Trade and Wage Labor

Increased Euro-Canadian settlement had the effect of making viable both cash-based trading and wage labor opportunities for Native individuals. This included greater opportunities for trade and selling of surplus subsistence yields and goods, with individuals taking items from homestead to homestead for trade or cash. Cottage industries included making brooms, baskets, wooden bowls and ladles, axe handles and scoops, as well as skin bags, war clubs, mats, pipes, etc. (P. Jones 1861:73; Richardson 1848:81–86), and selling or trading fish, meat and firewood (Talfourd in Canada 1858). Money made through these cottage industries provided income for individuals, particularly for those still subsisting through hunting (P. Jones 1861:73). Missionaries objected to these practices, since they were "the undoing of missionary good . . . (by) leaving their houses and sleeping in wigwams" (MSAR 1848–49:10), and so "continue to be exposed to temptation" (MSAR 1851–52:9).

Variable opportunities for wage labor were noted. For example, a laborer could earn a dollar a day working fields, or $2.50 with a team of oxen (Jamieson in Canada 1858). Indeed, in 1858 the Ojibwa of Walpole Island were seen as more successful farmers than at Sarnia, in part because opportunities for wage employment were not as great near Walpole Island as they were for the Sarnia Ojibwa (Nin.Da.Waab.Jig 1987:37).

Shifting Patterns: Summary of Changing Continuities

Ojibwa settlement-subsistence trends through the mid–19th century fail to substantiate claims that there was an abandonment of traditional life and a wholesale shift toward a Euro-Canadian rural cash crop economy. This is not to deny that changes occurred, because they clearly did. But change came from *within* historically understood priorities about livelihood and social organization. Fixed settlement and log cabins were adopted, but on a hot summer's eve the apaquois/wigwam standing next to a family's cabin was the favored place to sleep. Mobility was curtailed due to the changing landscape, but not abandoned. It just changed to individuals or families taking more compartmentalized trips away. Cabins, goods payments from the Indian Department and access to dry goods stores facilitated the expansion of material culture to include mass-produced items, comparable to the goods sitting in the hutches of nearby Euro-Canadian pioneer cabins. But these goods were worn and used in tandem with trade silver, beads, feathers and other style preferences arising from Ojibwa sensibilities, and plates and bowls rarely served up mutton and much more frequently dishes of fish, venison and corn soup than ever would have been found on pioneer tables. Identity, continually challenged by catastrophic bureaucracy and conversion of communities into physically surrounded enclaves within but ideologically marginalized from the colonialist empire, nonetheless persevered.

Change to Ojibwa subsistence can be characterized primarily as one of adjustment to a loss of cyclical mobility and reduction of a home range (fig.

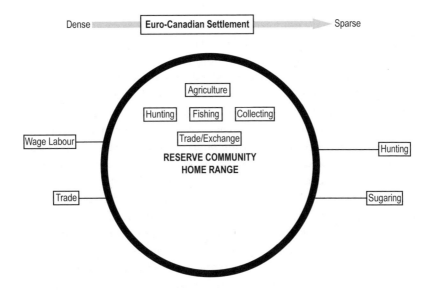

FIGURE 3.9. A representation of the Ojibwa seasonal round ca. 1860. The reserve operated as a kind of reduced home range and fixed base camp. Mobility had been reduced to trips off the reserve, either distant and away from Euro-Canadian settlement for hunting and sugaring, or near and within areas of denser Euro-Canadian settlement for trade and wage labor.

3.9). The home range was reduced to reserve boundaries, and settlement there evolved into an enhanced "summer base camp"—a permanent base from which distant travel continued in order to conduct subsistence activities that could not be carried out locally. As the viability of mobility and distant hunting declined, some Ojibwa took advantage of fixed settlement to increase farming efforts, primarily through the harvesting of corn as a food staple.

Well into the 20th century, this household self-sufficiency for Ojibwa families—manifested through traditional pursuits, subsistence agriculture, trade and wage labor—helped to maintain a viable way of life distinct from surrounding non-Native communities. Agricultural activities intensified further, though variation remained, so that by the end of the 19th century, farming still had not expanded beyond production of food staples for many families.[20] Diversified subsistence also continued and included harvests of sugar, fish, pelts from muskrats, and some hunting (Hedley 1993:194–195; E. Rogers 1994).

Wage labor begins to dominate choices late in the 19th century, especially as the next generation of reserve residents found it difficult to secure sizeable land to work for themselves on reserves (e.g., Canada 1887; Hedley

1993:193; Nin.Da.Waab.Jig 1987:58). But household self-sufficiency declined only after local economic growth occurred (e.g., as Sarnia grew as an industrial center in the early 20th century). At that point, off-reserve labor created on-reserve labor shortages and an undermining of reciprocal social obligations and egalitarian social organization (Hedley 1993:209–211). Since the mid-1940s, a continuing need to balance reliance on wage labor and employment opportunities beyond reserves, and independence through community farming and industrial or commercial projects, has been sought with varying degrees of success. More recently, direct control of internal political matters has allowed for a strengthening of community decision-making processes (e.g., Jacobs 1996).

Absent from southwestern Ontario Anishnabeg Ojibwa archaeological history is any indication of a ruinous loss of identity and culture, or an abandonment of historically informed ways of negotiating self and community in the world, despite significant change occurring to the region and to these communities, especially by the mid–19th century. Rather, a continued autonomy and strategic adaptation to these changes from entirely within an active, Ojibwa-centric agency is evident. This agency enabled innovative incorporation of material culture and colonialist sensibilities to continue a distinct, Ojibwa way of life, while engaged in an ongoing resistance to the emerging colonialist state as manifest in southwestern Ontario.

4

Natives as Newcomers

THE DELAWARE AT FAIRFIELD/MORAVIANTOWN

Our Indians now realize that agriculture and raising livestock are more profit-
able than hunting. They also make them more civilized. Hunting makes them
wild and barbaric. Wild, because they are constantly roaming the bush with
wild animals, and barbaric because the mind is constantly focussed on killing.
At the same time it makes them proud and conceited and full of mean delusions
of freedom and perceived superiority over others. That is why Indians more
than other human beings are ready to kill when they are angry. It is said among
Indian strangers that a converted Indian is no longer a good hunter.
— Gottlieb Sensemann, Moravian Missionary,
November 26, 1798 Fairfield Diaries

Without casting the slightest imputation on the general honesty of the inten-
tion of the missionaries [at Fairfield] and others delegated and well paid by various societies to teach and protect the Indians, still I will say that the enthusiasm
of some, the self-interest of others, and an unconscious mixture of pious enthusiasm and self-interest in many more, render it necessary to take their testimony
with some reservation.
— Anna Jameson, 1838, 2:269

IN CHAPTER 3, THE PATTERN OF CHANGED CONTINUITIES seen for
the 19th-century Ojibwa reflected historically informed adaptation to the rapidly changing social and physical landscape of the region. In this chapter, I
will examine a community that settled among the Ojibwa, arriving around
the time the Bellamy site was first occupied. This was the Delaware (Unami-
Unalachtigo) community that, in 1792, settled at Fairfield on the Thames
River, a day's walk south of the Sydenham River and the Bear Creek Ojibwa.

The surficial contrast of this community to neighboring Ojibwa could
not have been more stark. The Fairfield settlement was a planned Christian
community, directed by European missionaries whose principal doctrine
was the embodiment of religious ideals within day-to-day living, both for

themselves and for their Native "charges." Conventional histories certainly
suggest that Fairfield was a missionary-led home for refugees without a land
or culture, pliant to the word of God and to the message of finding civilization through farming and hard work (e.g., E. Gray 1956; Hamil 1939,
1949). In short, the missionaries' intent for the community was specifically
and consciously a directed effort to create discontinuity from Native-centric
pasts. So the residents of Fairfield, representing an amalgam of dislocated and
dispossessed missionaries, Delaware, and a smattering of others, are seemingly a perfect example of Richard White's (1991) Pays d'en Haut of the
Great Lakes—a community of people creating and holding onto a Middle
Ground in a sea of change. As such, Fairfield should serve as a strong contrast
to the patterns seen for the Ojibwa at 1800, and presumably also will reflect
even starker change in response to the subsequent events of the 19th century.
But a closer look at Fairfield reveals a much more complex series of strategies
and adaptive responses by the Delaware.

Historical Contexts

"Delaware" embodies a number of distinct Aboriginal groups who spoke
a range of Unami, Unalachtigo and Munsee Algonquian dialects, and who
ancestrally occupied the Hudson and Delaware River drainages and Atlantic
coast up to Long Island (Goddard 1978). Into the 18th century, communities
were largely autonomous but shared a common way of life and social organization. Settlements included an unpalisaded area of mostly multifamily
houses, archaeologically characterized as smaller longhouse-like structures
with rounded ends, entrances along a side wall, and the interior partitioned
into separate living compartments and hearth (Kraft 1986).

Fairfield was but one of many Delaware communities scattered north of
the Ohio Valley at the end of the 18th century (Tanner 1987; Weslager 1978).
My use here of the term "scattered" is deliberate, since the postcontact history of the Algonquian-speaking peoples collectively referred to as Delaware is
characterized by over two hundred years of repeated relocations away from the
mid-Atlantic coast. By the 1760s, European settler encroachment and resulting conflicts over land pushed Delaware communities away from their ancestral homeland up the Delaware and Hudson rivers and then into the interior of
Pennsylvania and northern Ohio (Kjellberg 1985; Tanner 1987).

Border disputes, raids and episodes of war between the 1760s and 1790s
had a tremendous impact on Aboriginal nations such as the Shawnee, Miami
and Delaware settled in western Pennsylvania, Ohio and Indiana (Allen 1993;

Stone and Chaput 1978). The following provides a brief historical context of the events that the western Delaware participated in during this period.

18th-Century Conflict in the Old Northwest

European conflicts ended by 1760 with the British as the sole colonial presence in the Northeast. But as the rebellion led by Pontiac in response to British assertions of dominance demonstrated (Allen 1975, 1993), the western frontier was not under the control of any single "power." Rather, it was a place of competing and complementary sovereigns and interests, where intercommunity relations fluctuated depending on temporary alliances and factions between Native people, British and Euro-Americans (White 1991).

Subsequently, the British attempted to establish a cooperative alliance, in response to the widespread perception that they were a real threat to Aboriginal sovereignty and land. The Royal Proclamation of 1763, meant to demonstrate a "benign" colonial power, declared all lands west of the Alleghenies as Native territory, but under British authority, which held exclusive right to negotiate with Aboriginal nations for lands (Allen 1975:16). But the idea that the western frontier was Aboriginal sovereign territory was openly challenged by expansionist American settlement (White 1991:315–316). The Aboriginal "frontier" was then redefined in the Treaty of Stanwix in 1768, which identified the Ohio River as the boundary for "time immemorial" (or less than twenty years, as events would prove). American incursions continued, and harassment of Native villages and retaliatory raids was commonplace. When hostilities broke out between the British and Americans in 1775, the war in the west was a decidedly Native vs. non-Native conflict.

In the west, most Aboriginal nations opposed American interests, though several western Delaware groups did initially ally with the Americans on the promise of a formal homeland (Weslager 1978:40). Some Moravian Delaware remained neutral, but this just meant that they were not trusted by either the British or the Americans (Sabathy-Judd 1999). For example, missionaries were imprisoned by the British, and the British also relocated Delaware villages away from the frontline of the American Revolution to ensure they did not support the Americans. But in 1782 an American force of volunteers killed over ninety Delaware at the Mission town of Gnadenhutten (e.g., Olmstead 1991). This eliminated any Delaware neutrality and directed their support to the British, caused other missions to disperse, and was the impetus for a Delaware diaspora further west (E. Gray 1956; Olmstead 1991; Stonefish 1995a).

Though Native forces were successful during the war, the British surrendered the Ohio Valley to the Americans in the 1783 Treaty of Paris
(Allen 1993:55–56; E. Thomas 1986:107). Aboriginal nations objected that
the British did not sign—or speak—for them, and so refused to recognize the
treaty, asserting that they would respect only the earlier Stanwix boundary
(Allen 1993:56). The British at least proffered an appearance of support to
these views for the region north of the Ohio River, since it would also serve
the British desire to create a "buffer" state of Aboriginal nations between the
advancing American frontier and British occupations north of the Great Lakes
(Allen 1975:31). This pretence was reinforced when the British refused to
abandon their posts on the American side of the Treaty of Paris border and
continued to supply Native forces with arms and rations (Allen 1993; Calloway 1987).

By 1793 skirmishes and raids had escalated into war between American
and Aboriginal peoples. Comments from the British that they expected to
join the war within the year, and the establishment of new British posts in
the disputed territory, convinced Aboriginal leaders that the British were
allied with them. In late August of 1794, however, during a battle in front
of Fort Miamis in northwest Ohio, the direction of the war changed. The
Battle of Fallen Timbers caused many casualties on both sides, but it was the
Native forces that withdrew after British troops in the fort refused to come
out and fight (Allen 1993:83; Calloway 1987). The defeat had great repercus-
sions. The loose military coalition of Aboriginal nations dissolved as groups
returned to homelands and the hunt, and leaders were demoralized. By 1795,
many western Aboriginal nations had signed a treaty with the Americans at
Greenville, relinquishing northern Ohio. While further conflict would again
flare up during the War of 1812, American and British boundaries in this
region were set—though meaningless to Aboriginal nations who retained
their settlements and continued to traverse back and forth across a British-
American border, and continue today to object to the distinction.

Moravians among the Delaware

The Moravian missionary movement was part of the Christian Evangelical
revival of the 18th century, and can be traced to 1722 when Protestant refugees
resettled in Germany from Moravia (Sabathy-Judd 1999:xiv). Incorporating elements of the pre-Reformation evangelical Unitas Fratrum, this "United Brethren" emerged as a mostly missionary institution (E. Gray 1956:21; Sabathy-
Judd 1999:xiv). By the early 1730s, Moravian missionaries were traveling to

the Caribbean, Africa and Russia. By 1741, Moravians in North America had established a base of operations in Bethlehem, eastern Pennsylvania, which ultimately would become their center for all missionary activities. The center in Bethlehem serviced the surrounding, expanding European settlement, and the profits of that work then funded the efforts of other members who went off to undertake mission work (E. Gray 1956:26–27).

Moravian efforts in the Northeast began in the early 1740s with the establishment of missions among the Iroquois (E. Gray 1956:33–35). While these quickly failed, around Bethlehem, missions to various Delaware communities were more successful. But problems between the Delaware and Iroquois, persistent fears by the colonial state of the Moravians acting as spies, and pressures on Native lifeways from encroaching settlement all contributed to various violent episodes, a decline in mission activity and, by 1763, a temporary abandonment of local missions and forced shelter in Philadelphia (E. Gray 1956:37–42). By 1765, the missionaries and the Delaware with them were traveling away from the Moravian base of Bethlehem to the upper Ohio Valley, which at the time was a frontier area including a spectrum of westward-relocated Native communities, resident Ohio Valley Shawnee and more westerly Miami, some trading posts, European settlers and Métis (Mann 2003; H. Tanner 1987:Map 16).

Through the 1770s, the Moravians established five missions in the Ohio Valley comprised of between 350 and 400 Native people (MPHSC 10:540; Sabathy-Judd 1999:xviii). However, the Revolutionary War made the Ohio Valley a battle front. The result of the British order to have the Moravian Delaware settlements relocated to Sandusky in northwest Ohio, followed by the massacre in 1782, was that the next decade was a period of continual relocation, dispersal and missionary attempts to reform scattered Delaware mission communities. Later that year, remnants of one mission were settled on the Huron (now Clinton) River north of Detroit, ten miles upriver from Lake St. Clair (E. Gray 1956:77; MPHSC 10:574). At that time, the population numbered 117 Delaware (16 families; Quaife 1928:238). Four years later, the local Ojibwa had demanded the community leave their land, so the community returned to Sandusky. In 1791, hostilities in the region were again rising, making the entire region south of Lake Erie unsafe (Bliss 1885, 2:158), so the mission temporarily camped on the British side of the Detroit River. In the summer of 1791, Muncey Delaware from the Thames River visited this camp and encouraged the community to settle closer to them on the Thames River (Bliss 1885, 2:250). Ultimately, the Moravian Delaware desire to be near the Muncey community proved to be the impetus to seek permission to settle on the Thames (Kjellberg 1985:41).[1]

In April of 1792, the Delaware and missionaries, about 150 people in all, set out from their settlement on the Detroit River. After spending several days at the end of April scouting out suitable locations up and down the Thames, they chose the spot that was to become the Fairfield village and began clearing fields for planting on May 9th (Hamil 1939; Sabathy-Judd 1999: see 1792: April 29–May 9).[2]

Settlement around the Fairfield Village in 1792

While Fairfield was selected because of its physical setting, the location was also preferred because it seemed so remote, removed from both settlements and the conflicts brewing to the south (Sabathy-Judd 1999:xxvi). Yet that remoteness would soon vanish, as increased non-Aboriginal settlement, existing Aboriginal communities in the area, and the importance of the Thames River as the major transportation route from Niagara and York (Toronto) in the east to Detroit in the west, were all realized.

In addition to the Bear Creek Ojibwa on the Sydenham River to the north and the Ojibwa settlement along the Thames River to the east, there was a Muncey Delaware group settled around the Thames River Ojibwa.[3] According-ing to 1790s accounts, this community consisted of about two hundred indi-viduals, residing in two village clusters (Kjellberg 1985:16). The Munceys traced their history back from the Thames and Grand Rivers to Pennsylvania as an autonomous village group (1798: Sept. 22; Weslager 1972:320). Given the relationship described for Fairfield and Muncey, there was likely a strong tie between these groups that predated the Thames River and extended back to Pennsylvania (D. Stonefish, pers. comm. 1999).

Euro-Canadian settlement in 1792 away from the Detroit River was peripheral: scattered cabins along trails following waterways such as the Thames (Hamil 1951; Johnson 1974:24, 1983:113). By 1805, the entire Western District was marked by only 13,157 acres of cleared land (Johnson 1983:120). In fact, the non-Aboriginal population of the Western District in 1805 was just 3156, of which 59 percent occupied the east side of the Detroit River and south shore of Lake St. Clair (Harris and Wood 1993; Johnson 1974:28). Upstream from the mouth of the Thames was a scattering of clearings and cabins, which had begun to be settled after 1789 (Hamil 1951:16). For example, in 1790, Patrick McNiff reported twenty-eight log houses below the town site of Chatham (20 km west of Fairfield) during a survey of river frontage, and more cabins had appeared within a year (Hamil 1951:12–13; McGeorge 1924:11).

Johnson (1974:24, 28) suggests that by 1800 the Euro-Canadian population away from the Detroit River-Lake St. Clair corridor was just over one
thousand, with less than 10 percent of the land patented. But from the perspective of the Moravian missionaries, the increasing settlement along the
river was rapid and a concern. As early as 1795, Zeisberger (1795: Dec. 7)
wrote: "Since we moved here, the number of settlers on this river has grown
to the extent that they are now on our boundary line three miles from the
town [of Fairfield]. There was no settlement within thirty miles of us when
we arrived. Soon it will be settled like this upstream as well." Later, Sensemann writes: "White people are constantly moving to and fro . . . in droves
from the States . . . and Upper Canada will soon be heavily settled" (1799:
March 8).

Fairfield North of the Thames

Though a prominent place in the local histories and known as the site of the
infamous War of 1812 battle where Proctor ran and Tecumseh died, little has
been written about the Fairfield community. A key challenge to accessing the
community's history had been that while the missionaries kept diaries, this
material was largely inaccessible, as they were written in old-script German
until the 1840s (Dreyer 1997, 1998; Sabathy-Judd 1999). Available data
were limited to the Bliss 1885 translated version of the Zeisberger diaries.
But recently, the first twenty years of the Fairfield diaries, from the founding
of the community until the end of 1813 when it was destroyed by advancing
American forces during the War of 1812, have been translated (Sabathy-Judd
1999). These diaries were formal reports written by resident missionaries
for the wider Moravian community, not published documents (Sabathy-Judd
1999:lxv). They were written by individuals (usually the person in charge
of the mission), but written from a third-person perspective, and very much
document the success and frustration of the community's adherence to the
Moravian concepts of Christianity, daily Christian living, and the spiritual
strength and physical challenges facing the missionaries themselves.

It is critical to recognize the limitations of these records for understanding the Delaware, and the impossibility of avoiding the filter of the recorders
themselves. Certainly, the relative success of the missionaries' Christianizing
efforts, or even if that meant anything to the Delaware, is beyond access.
Also, the practice of the missionaries to constantly admonish residents who
drank to excess, operated on a loose sexual license, or partook in traditional
ceremonies and Native cultural practices gave rise early to a culture of secrecy

in the community. The diaries do note after-the-fact discoveries of such secrecy, or of individuals leaving the community to avoid being admonished for behavior the missionaries frowned on (e.g., 1807: June 17). As well, local oral histories commonly speak of practicing cultural traditions in secret, or going to Muncey or elsewhere to partake in ceremonies and festivals (Stonefish 1995a:32). Given this, the diaries can present only a limited dimension of a much more complex community.

Nonetheless, the diaries are important as they were written from within the community, and so can provide meaningful insight beyond the basic religious agendas of the recorders themselves (Goldring 1984; Whiteman 1986). All the inhabitants of Fairfield, missionary and Delaware alike, had to contend with a limited understanding of the new locale they were in, had to subsist and survive through each year, and had to respond to the changes around them. So the diaries do reflect the seasonal cycle of subsistence and the economic and social relations within and without the community, and provide insights into the community's response to their new settlement, neighbors, and ultimately with the missionaries they lived with.

In addition to the diaries, the site of Fairfield was excavated between 1942 and 1946 by Wilfrid Jury (1945, 1946, 1948; Jury and Jury 2006). The excavations were of a limited utility,[4] as Jury and volunteers used flat-edged shovels to slice through house locations. Only a small sample of the collections remain, and limited observations are available from the published sources. Nonetheless, Jury reports documenting forty individual house sites and other structures in the village area by relocating the road alignment that appeared in a 1793 map of the village and tying that to cellar depressions or house cornerstones. Examination of the field notes at the Museum of Ontario Archaeology, and the remnant collection at the Fairfield Museum located at the site of the original village, confirmed the presence of multiple log cabins, with and without cellars, late-18th and early-19th-century material culture, as well as later 19th-century deposits and extensive Middle Woodland material.

The Fairfield Village Community

Fairfield was laid out as a formal village, with agricultural fields extending outwards and along both sides of the river. Residences were aligned on either side of an east-west lane that ran parallel with the river. Further to the west and east were a number of "huts," likely clapboard cabins, shanties or wigwams, used as sugaring camps each spring (Sabathy-Judd 1999:24). By the end of 1792, thirty buildings existed in the village (Sabathy-Judd 1999: xxxi). Later, in a claim of damages filed following the War of 1812, forty-seven buildings were listed, including a church, school, meeting houses, substantial homes for the missionaries, and Native homes including twenty "dwellings of hewn logs and floored, some with glass windows," and another nineteen "of less value" (E. Gray 1956:337).

Jury reported that most of the excavated residences ranged from 10' × 12' or 10' × 14' (3.5 × 3.7–4.2 m), though some of the structures were as large as 22' × 16' (6.7 × 4.9 m). Jury assumed the smaller cabins to be Native residences, and the larger ones to be missionary residences. He also noted that the Native homes all contained a fireplace in the center of the cabin, as opposed to the more European style of hearths on a side wall away from the doorway; in all, eleven of the house floors excavated included central hearth features. However, since some of the larger structures had central hearths (Jury 1948, field notes; Jury and Jury 2006), it is likely that some of the Delaware-occupied cabins were in fact "more substantial," showing evidence of planked floors, cellars, and glass windowpanes (as opposed to hide or cloth), which had to be transported from Detroit (e.g., 1796: Sept. 17). Smaller cabins (e.g., Jury and Jury 2006:18) were found not to have cellars, planked floors, or doorway sills, few nails, and no door hinges or window glass. Presumably, these are the structures of "less value" noted in the 1812 claim. Jury (1945, 1948, field notes) observed that while these house sites lacked quantities of clay chinking, they did have "compressed" moss likely used as chinking, and some may have had clay-lined floors. All of these houses had cornerstones, or sections of a log used in that capacity. Several cabins also had storage pits along house walls or in corners, rectangular or irregular in profile, 60–80 cm deep, and containing carbonized corn and nutshells (Jury and Jury 2006:18).

Jury noted (1945; Jury and Jury 2006) that some of the central hearths were in fact large circular pits, over a meter in diameter and a meter deep, with either straight-sided walls and rounded bases, or conical profiles and rounded bases. They were lined with clay, the upper 15–20 cm fired by heat. Pit fill consisted of stratified layers of ash, while the bottom portion of the pits contained extensive animal bone and artifact deposits.

It is worth noting that a similar hearth was described in Norah Thompson Dean's oral account of her family attending a Delaware Big House ceremony in Oklahoma in the 1920s. She indicates that the pit was dug to heat a temporary pole and canvas tent her family built and resided in for the duration of the ceremony. She says: "My father then dug a hole about one-and-a-half feet deep inside the tent, almost in the middle. He filled this hole with hot coals from our cook fire which was outside in front of the tent.

The heat from these coals would keep us comfortable and warm, even during the coldest days of fall."[5]

From Jury's description and diary accounts, all buildings were hewn-log cabins. Jury either failed to find or failed to see post moulds, and the presence of cornerstones does suggest conventional log cabin construction, with the outer walls taking most of the structural weight. Gaps between logs were chinked by clay or moss. Logs may have been notched or dovetailed at the corners, consistent with the use of cornerstone supports, and certainly this was an architectural form favored in the German Moravian tradition (e.g., T. Jordan 1985; Rempel 1967). The Jury observations suggest cabins were built almost to a template, presumably reflecting an expediency arising from long experience rather than any mission community rule. Indeed, many of the Delaware families that arrived on the Thames River in 1792 had relocated and rebuilt homes upwards of a half dozen times over the previous decade. Proficiency at construction would have been great, and the preferred house form would have been easy to replicate as the population grew.

But as well, some features of the Delaware houses were distinct from the style adhered to by the missionaries. Earthen or clay-lined floors, side storage features, moss chinking, clay-lined and deep central hearths without chimneys, and presumably smoke holes in the roofs are all reminiscent of traditional Delaware architectural features, particularly of the family compartment within the traditional multifamily Delaware longhouse pattern (e.g., Kraft 1986). The Fairfield form suggests that at the beginning of the 19th century, the Delaware were utilizing a house containing both functional and architectural innovations, as well as traditional elements of spatial and residence organization. The structural features are suggestive of changed continuity: a convergence of earlier traditions, contemporary contingencies and future hopes that reinforced family and social organization in the community (see also, K. Jordon 2002:440). This belies conventional interpretations of Delaware log cabin adoption solely as the result of directed or acquiescent culture change.

References suggest cabins at Fairfield were occupied by single extended families (i.e., parents, children, grandparents, unmarried relations). Widowers and widows without immediate family lived alone, while individuals or families who petitioned to join the community occasionally lived with another family. Collectively, the community worked to clear new fields, tended communal fields, built and maintained common buildings like the school house, and shared tasks such as clearing the road that passed by the village. However, the settlement was not a communal enterprise. Each family was responsible for itself, working their own fields, which were held by the community in common (Sabathy-Judd 1999:xxxii), and keeping income generated by the selling of foodstuffs, crafts, services or labor. Nonetheless, there was a sense of community and communal support beyond simply the shared workload. There are many references in the diaries to collecting food or firewood for poor, hungry, or invalid members of the community; planting someone else's fields or tending to them because they were too old or sick, a single mother, or otherwise unable to keep up with the work; sharing deer from hunting and goods distributed by the Indian Department; and helping with the schooling of children (e.g., 1799: Nov. 18; 1805: June 7; 1812: Nov. 25).

The Moravian Missionaries. The number of missionaries present at Fairfield was limited, usually two to four and their families. Missionaries were not paid salaries but rather were expected to subsist by growing crops, sugaring, selling their surplus, and doing whatever else they could to earn money. They could not rely on the congregation for support except in times of need. That they did not own the houses they lived in or fields they worked was a matter of discord, and the issue was raised with Bethlehem in 1803 (Sabathy-Judd 1999:xxxiii). Daily life for the missionaries was a combination of hard labor, meeting the needs of the congregation and a personal and practical application of their spiritual beliefs. Central was the belief that perfection could not be achieved in life, since this was embodied in the sacrifice of Christ; all they could hope for was to continually move toward that perfection. This meant daily need for them to be aware, in themselves and in the congregation, of the balance between acknowledging that existence of sin in everyone, and avoiding the trap of a self-righteous conviction of having defeated sinfulness, especially when comparing themselves to others, such as Christian and non-Christian Natives and Europeans.

Sabathy-Judd (1999:l) describes the missionary worldview at Fairfield as "circles of grace." The widest circle encompassed the community. A second circle encompassed just those who had been "taken into the congregation": people who attended separate meetings in addition to general sermons and gatherings. Another circle encompassed the communicants: a limited number of people who had reached grace in this life and so could take communion. From this group, the missionaries chose Helpers and Assistants, male and female converts who would set good examples and be responsible for looking after the internal affairs of the village and dealing with outsiders (Graham 1975:57; Sabathy-Judd 1999:l). Ideally, movement was always inward, though there were plenty of instances of slippage (e.g., 1797: Dec. 3).

The daily and seasonal cycle for the missionaries was very much punctuated by meetings, sermons, counseling sessions, baptisms and funerals, as well as responding to crises as they arose, looking after relations with the British government, and even occasionally ministering to surrounding non-Aboriginal communities, all while eking out a subsistence livelihood. In a sense these hardships—the failure and frustration of trying to deliver the message (often through an interpreter) to at least some people who occasionally argued back or committed sin without remorse or acknowledgement—were important burdens to the missionary. They were an affirmation of their own sinful state and allowed missionaries to both contemplate their failings and communicate with Christ. So the missionary impulse served their personal spiritual needs on a daily basis. As such ardent and focused people, they sometimes left others unimpressed, as Anna Jameson noted years later, when meeting Jesse Vogler at the end of his first tenure at Moraviantown on a steamer heading from Chatham to Detroit:

> [He is] very simple and very ignorant on every subject but that of his mission. While speaking with this worthy, simple-minded man, I could not help wishing that he had united more knowledge and judgment with his conscientious piety—more ability with good-will—more discretion with faith and zeal. The ignorance and intolerance of some of these enthusiastic, well-meaning men, have done as much injury to the good cause for which they suffered and preached. I find them civil, but neither prepossessing nor intelligent; in short, I can make nothing of them; I cannot extract an idea beyond eating, drinking and praying. (Jameson 1838:242, 245, 276–277)

For the missionaries to be good at their work, they had to be vigilant at identifying sin and misguided pride. So the diaries tend to focus on admonishing other individuals' sinful behavior, and the need for those people to recognize their sinful ways: to know how "blessed" a sinner they really were, in order to reach salvation after death (Sabathy-Judd 1999:xlviii). Indeed, diarists often expressed frustration when they noted missing an opportunity to admonish, as was the case in 1807 when several people who had "been bad" could not be admonished because the translator, Tobias, had been suspended from his duties because he had gotten drunk and was not remorseful (1807: Nov. 1). For the missionaries, success came as a harsh and sorrowful awakening. After a particularly disturbing series of events and discussion afterwards, Zeisberger reported on how well the congregation took this practice to heart: "It took four days until the brethren were finished talking to one another and many things came to light, especially among those who thought themselves better than others. Everyone found reason enough to be a sinner and one saw many saddened and downcast faces in the town, as if a fast had been called. The work of the Holy Spirit was clearly noticeable" (1797: Dec. 9).

This apparent spiritual contradiction—happy is bad, bad is happy—was a fine line missionaries had to walk. Certainly, the diaries leave the impression that the degree of admonishment varied from missionary to missionary. For example, while it may be just that the issues did not manifest themselves early on, there appears to be less frequent singling out of individuals for admonishment of sinful behavior in the Zeisberger years than in the years following him. Likewise, the perception of certain Delaware practices varied over time. For example, in 1794 (April 5) Zeisberger noted a visitor had come to see his daughter and her husband with the intent of taking them away. However, after a long discussion, the son-in-law persuaded the father that they were happy in Fairfield and wanted to stay. In passing, Zeisberger mentions this took place in a sweat oven (lodge). Yet the missionary Schnall reported sending away a couple in 1806 after they used a sweat oven (Feb. 13). According to oral tradition, Zeisberger was considered less "uptight" about day-to-day Delaware life, including traditional practices, than other missionaries (D. Stonefish, pers. comm. 1999).

The Community: Situating Authority. Any Native person was welcome to join the community. All they had to do was ask permission and demonstrate to the missionaries or helpers that they were joining for the betterment of their soul and spiritual life, and would abide by the community's rules. People would then be admitted for a trial period, to see if they did indeed fit in. The rules or "Congregation Statutes of the Believing Indians in Upper Canada" were drawn up in 1793 by the missionaries *and* helpers together (E. Gray 1956:109). These thirteen rules, in addition to adoring God and not stealing, having sex outside of marriage or being violent, also spoke of not being drunk and not practicing witchcraft or being doctored in "the wild Indian manner." There were rules against owning a Chief's or Captain's medal of silver (usually given by the Indian Department to community leaders); wearing traditional dress, paint, feathers, wampum or silver; or having heads shaved or sheared "as the heathen do" (E. Gray 1956:110).

The community's formal philosophy was that if people did not want to follow the rules, they would be asked peaceably and quietly to leave Fairfield and go elsewhere to live in sin. Beyond breaking the rules, people could also be asked to leave if they failed to demonstrate good contrition and proper behavior (e.g., missing many meetings, failing to confess or acknowledge sins, not seeking guidance, not wanting to be baptized, or not progressing through the circles of grace). Also, pride of religion, confidence of being a good Christian, and claiming to know God were sure signs of a closed heart and an inability to be a good sinner.

Where and how secular authority and leadership were situated within the Delaware community is not clear from the diaries, and indeed secular notions of leadership were inconsistent with the Moravian doctrine of humility (the "no Chief's medals" rule). Nonetheless, it is clear that the inner circle of communicants and elite group of helpers were expected not only to set good examples but also to "police" the congregation and deal with members who caused problems. In many cases, the missionaries would talk to the helpers about the bad conduct of someone in the community, and ask that they speak to the individual. Helpers also dealt with bouts of drinking and problems with visiting Natives, and were expected to tell people to leave and to ensure they did. It was the helpers, as well, who deliberated and discussed with the full community petitions from other Aboriginal nations, such as requests for them to relocate and join Delaware groups in Ohio or Indiana. The missionaries met with all the communicants to review external matters (such as a call to war or a query from the British government) and seek their response. As well, any decisions the missionaries were asked to make that seemed extraordinary or contentious were reviewed with the communicants (Sabathy-Judd 1999:xlix). This was the case, for example, when a freed slave and his Native wife asked to join the congregation (1811: Sept. 5).

Given that the rules of the community, which would be cited as proof of sinful behavior, were both drafted and enforced by the helpers, these people certainly appear to have been vested with community authority and leadership. The helpers certainly are seen by the community today as the original Delaware leaders of Fairfield, who operated within a mix of traditional and church-oriented leadership (Stonefish 1995a:71).[6]

In effect, secular authority within the village arose in the exchange and common agreement reached between the communicants and missionaries. However, there is also no question that the sharing of this authority was not equal. Missionaries ultimately controlled who entered this inner circle of communicants, and could suspend the duties and privileges of communicants whose behavior degraded (e.g., 1797: Dec. 3; 1811: Dec. 31). As well, the missionaries served as the community's contact with the outside world, including the British Crown over the possession of reserve land.

But it is also clear that in those first decades, by preference and in actuality, the authority missionaries asserted was limited. Certainly vesting themselves with a formal authority was counter to basic spiritual tenets. And while the missionaries could recommend and advise helpers to speak to a troubled convert or to admonish the congregation more frequently, they could not force helpers to do these things, and the helpers sometimes did not (e.g., 1804: Nov. 11). Likewise, the missionaries' unwillingness or inability to exercise authority sometimes left them in a no-win situation, as when two of the congregation, Johannes and Samuel, spent an evening getting drunk with a farmer, eventually got into a fight, and injured another man (1804: July 16). Over the next several days, the missionary Schnall tried to resolve the matter informally with the injured person, and told the congregation that it might be possible to avoid a trial. But ultimately he was unable to make that happen (July 25). Feeling that they were nevertheless innocent of the charge, Samuel and Johannes went off hunting so that they would not be present when three constables came to arrest them (Aug. 2). The missionaries were then told by the authorities that a militia would be coming to Fairfield to arrest Samuel and Johannes. When the missionaries next met with the helpers: "They [the helpers] suspect us, as do several other brothers, of calling the militia. We could not convince them that this was not true. Meanwhile the government in Sandwich accuses us of protecting the Indians [since the government assumed the missionaries had the authority to detain the suspects]. This puts us in a critical situation. We have no recourse but to keep silent and hope that the Saviour will help us" (1804: Aug. 19).

The sometimes conflicting relationship between the missionaries and the community shaped the limit of missionary authority. It also demonstrated that the community, and at some level the communicants, had a strong degree of independent will and authority. For example, the diaries note instances when the missionaries' admonishments and recommendations for removal appeared to cross a line considered unacceptable. In 1806, the missionaries asked Caleb to leave, whom they accused of being flippant and proud and of instigating a drinking bout (Sept 8). A few days later, John Schnall reported that Caleb's grandparents, Stephan and Salome, strongly criticized the missionary's action. Because of this, their duties as helpers and attendants were suspended (Sept. 14). Schnall also noted that the complaining harmed the accord in the community, presumably between the missionaries and the residents. Similarly, Christian Denke reported on Aug. 14, 1811 that several communicants were denied taking Holy Communion because they had spoken rudely to the missionaries when the missionaries had admonished their children for being too noisy and making lewd gestures. So, regardless of any authority the missionaries could exercise, they were thwarted when they crossed a line—the line being a separate, commonly understood sense of Delaware community probity.

The Community: The Limits of Authority and the Doctrine of Removal.
The doctrine of sending someone away often proved less than effective, undermining the authority of missionaries and helpers alike. In some cases, this occurred because the people asked to leave were often readmitted, repeatedly. Generally, all a person had to do was plead to return, demonstrate sorrow and contrition, and promise to live properly from then on. No doubt there were many who were genuinely remorseful and needed readmission to settle their troubled spirit. Nonetheless, there are many references in the diaries to individuals being asked to leave, only to return, be readmitted, and then subsequently commit some other infraction and be asked to leave again (e.g., 1799: May 14, 20, July 23). During one instance when the congregation objected to people being readmitted, the diarist complained: "The brethren are no longer sincere in their interest in and prayer for those who have gone astray. No longer do the words of Apostle Paul 'and whether one member suffer, all the members suffer with it' apply here. Each brother and sister, we said, ought to remember his and her own transgressions and to beseech the Saviour to restore what is lost" (1811: June 2).

The diarist's lament over the lack of support for readmitted sinners also reflects a community cynicism toward the sincerity of promises made to adopt a changed life, and their frustration with having to resolve the problems caused by "repeat" offenders, since rarely was a request denied. For example, after threatening to tear down the house of several women who had left their husbands and were operating a brothel in the town, the helpers ordered the women to leave, but some were then readmitted by the end of the year (1804: Nov. 30, Dec. 31). According to diary accounts, for those in the community who wanted to live by the rules and not be disturbed by others living in sin, the constant readmittance of repeat offenders was at times disheartening and frustrating.

But in some cases, the missionaries' efforts to remove someone were thwarted by other residents. This was not uncommon, because often the people told to leave were part of a family (e.g., children or spouses; 1798: April 29). Indeed, while it was simple for missionaries to tell someone that they should send their spouse, children or other family members away from the community, it clearly was not something accepted or willingly done by many, and ensured acrimony. Schnall complained in 1811 (Jan. 27) that people who were told to go away several times were still in the village, mostly because they were receiving shelter and food from their friends.

In one episode, the frustration of dealing with people who did not adhere to the rules, but refused to leave, is clear. Gottfried Oppelt wrote in 1803 (June 20): "Tobias was drunk and spoke very harshly to us, especially to Br. Schnall.

We talked to him in the following days but he was not sorry. Our situation continues to be grave. We cannot get rid of the bad people, the talk about the teachers [missionaries] is terrible and those brethren who still have something in their hearts are discouraged." That Tobias was later re-admitted pleading contrition then sent away after another drinking episode, not once but on several occasions through 1807, was further confirmation of the ineffectiveness of at least some of the community rules.

Alcohol abuse was frequently identified as the root to many of the community's problems. Alcohol was not necessarily banned (though the helpers and missionaries often seized alcohol from residents, or held on to it when brought in by visitors). Rather, drinking to excess was the violation—residents who drank no more than they could tolerate were actually commended (1807: Aug. 25). Sensemann stated in 1799 (May 9) that "To set an example, the missionaries themselves do not take a drop to prove that one can live without it and live a much healthier life." However, at least Denke was fond of the occasional drink and indeed, his increased alcoholism over time contributed to his departure from the mission (E. Gray 1956; Stonefish 1995b:22).

There were plenty of opportunities to obtain liquor. Two distilleries were reported nearby in 1801 (June 29). As well, liquor could be obtained from visiting Natives or traders (especially when they bypassed the village and met residents in their sugaring or hunting camps), or purchased directly when residents visited the settlement. On occasion, drinking bouts would disrupt meetings or other daily activities (e.g., 1802: June 10). On August 25, 1807, two residents, Metemik and Marcus, brought a keg of liquor into town, after having been asked on several occasions not to. The helpers were away at the time, and no one else wanted to help, afraid of threats made by Marcus or because "others who like to drink themselves are sympathetic." Schnall interceded directly, and managed to destroy the keg while Marcus was sleeping. When confronted the next day, Marcus was not apologetic: "Marcus . . . said that he would not stop drinking because he enjoyed it. Getting drunk frequently was his only sin, he exclaimed, unlike others in the congregation whose sins are more numerous" (1807: Aug. 26).

In that instance, Marcus eventually did move away with his family. But there were good reasons to avoid leaving the village. Fairfield was a community, and family and friends were a part of that community. Most families had a home, and cleared fields to cultivate. The community also afforded people a sense of security from the constant conflicts to the south, a valuable commodity especially for the Moravian Delaware. Benjamin Mortimer, the diarist for part of 1798, noted: "In times gone by, it was sometimes necessary to ask our people to stay with us. More recently, especially since we moved to

Canada, it has been the other way around. Nobody wants to leave, no matter how bad their conduct. When it becomes necessary for us to send them away, they usually come back and say they cannot live among the savages" (1798: June 1).

On one occasion (1797: Oct. 12) Bill Henry, a helper, was asked by the missionaries to speak to his son about improper behavior and was told that if it did not stop the boy would need to leave. Henry agreed and was willing to send the boy away himself, but worried about the travails facing a youth sent away from Fairfield: "It is hard to send one's own children into heathenism where their spiritual and physical life is threatened. Our children are naïve and do not know how to adapt to the wild Indians' ways. Many have tried to live among them but have always come back." Clearly there was a lot vested in walking away from the security and safety of the community, far more than simply abandoning one's soul.

But people did leave, including upriver to the Muncey Delaware community. There are many references to extended family connections between the two communities (e.g., E. Gray 1956:110–111), including references to residents visiting friends in Muncey, or Muncey Delaware visiting or overwintering at Fairfield (e.g., 1793: Jan. 10; 1795: May 12; 1807: July 20). More importantly, Muncey provided Fairfield residents with a distinct lifestyle option: "Muncies from upstream have visited regularly these past few days. These heathen neighbors of ours resemble the heathens of antiquity. Just as the latter were tools of Satan, so are these heathen incited by the same hellish spirit to seduce our people to go against Christian teachings" (1798: June 12).

In other words, Muncey offered the choice of a more overt traditional lifestyle, and some Fairfield residents were attracted to that option. Schnall reported on January 6, 1811 that: "Salamo, who seems to have a liking for heathen ways, went back to Muncey Town . . . where he means to stay for the time being" (see also, 1795: May 28). Muncey was also a place where one could partake in more traditional ceremonies, especially if ill and needing a cure. And, of course, this could be done away from the eyes of the rest of the community and the missionaries, unless one later decided to confess, as was the case for one resident who had taken her ill son to Muncey for a conjuring (1811: Dec. 30). Likewise, a repentant Zachaeus confessed that, after being ill and lame and having received no comfort from medicines, he decided to secretly go to Muncey to be treated by a shaman (1798: Oct. 16). Going off reserve for traditional cures, feasts, ceremonies and dances was a practice that continued well into the 20th century (Stonefish 1995a:32).

Another viable option for someone who decided to leave Fairfield was exercised by Abraham and his family. In 1810 he bought some land from the resident Ojibwa six miles upstream from Fairfield and moved there, since he and his family refused not to live in sin (1810: Oct. 30). There are also several references to people who had left and were living with "wild" Natives (e.g., 1799: Feb. 13; 1806: Aug. 13). And when, on occasion, these people returned, the tension between the way the world worked within Fairfield and beyond its edge was underscored, such as when Denke reported in 1812 (July 18) that a large number of former residents had returned to Fairfield to avoid the start of the war further to the west and south:

> Since the outbreak of war, the people who have been sent away have for the most part returned and, along with those not yet whole [i.e., unbaptised residents], have drawn attention to themselves with loose and insolent conduct. Since our recent admonishments were not heeded, we instructed the helpers to have a serious talk with them and impress upon them that, while they are here, they are to heed our regulations. They were to remove all ear and nose ornaments as well as head feathers and cease all heathen conduct including gambling. They said nothing and became a little quieter. Many of them did away with their adornments.

Though refugees in a distant land, the Fairfield Delaware were still connected to the wider Indigenous community of the lower Great Lakes, and the benefits that Fairfield offered were not always desired over and above all other needs. So, as had been done for centuries prior, dissatisfaction could be manifest by leaving and starting up elsewhere. Moreover, living at Fairfield and following the work and spiritual ethic of the community did not mean forsaking Native beliefs, values or a Delaware identity, though maintaining that duality could at times be a guilt-ridden burden or annoyance.

Subsistence and Economic Activities

The Fairfield economy was based on a strategy of exploiting all available resources from a fixed place on the landscape, with a heavy emphasis on agriculture generating surplus yields, and conducting other activities away from the village. This was not a haphazard series of choices selected in response to arriving in southwestern Ontario. Rather, the mixed economy was consistent with Delaware subsistence practices followed during and before the time of Moravian missionaries and in Pennsylvania, and it did not need to change much to adapt to the Thames River environs. The diarists commented on apparent differences and unique problems encountered at Fairfield, but in general the subsistence regime was very similar to that practiced on the Clinton River in Michigan (Stonefish 1995a:14). The climate was similar, and the surrounding market for their produce was the same. This was not a foreign land or experience.

Agriculture. Upon choosing the site of Fairfield for their settlement, the first task the Delaware and missionaries undertook, even prior to building permanent homes, was to clear fields for planting (1792: May 8). By 1798 they were farming over 300 acres of land on both sides of the river (1798: June 16), mostly on river flats that did not require extensive clearing. Over the next two decades, the cultivated land worked by the community increased by another 50 acres (Kjellberg 1985:56). Corn was the staple crop of choice, but wheat was also grown in quantity. Zeisberger noted (1797: Aug. 23) "More and more brethren are following the example of wheat farming. They do not neglect to plant corn, however, since they could not survive without it." While this quote would seem to reflect a community in transition toward a more Euro-Canadian cash crop focus, it is worth noting that, twenty years later in an 1818 submission to the Gourlay survey of Upper Canada (Gourlay 1822, 1:294–298), Denke reported that corn remained the community's principal crop. As well, carbonized corn is reported from all features found from Jury's designated Native house sites (Jury and Jury 2006). Garden plants like potatoes, pumpkins, squash, cabbages and beans were also grown, while potatoes and tobacco, as well as corn and wheat, generated surplus yields for trade. Livestock was also kept, primarily cattle, pig and fowl.

Farming was the primary focus of daily life at the village, from clearing fields, planting, hoeing and hilling, harvesting, drying and storing, to taking crops to the mills. Field work was chiefly women's work (Gourlay 1822, 1:297), though clearing, fence tending and some harvesting was communal (e.g., 1809: July 12), and children and elders would harvest garden crops like potatoes (e.g., 1805: Sept. 18). The Delaware ploughed the fields themselves, purchasing ploughs for the task, or "hired white people to plough their fields for three to five dollars an acre" (1797: Oct. 25). In 1796 (Oct. 3) Zeisberger suggested "We [the missionaries] are their calendar. They observe what we do and plant when we plant. They know from experience that they will not go wrong." While it was the aim of the missionaries to convey principles of surplus yield farming to mission residents, it was also true that the Delaware had plenty of direct experience and their own historical knowledge informing the farming practices they followed. They also imparted knowledge *to* the missionaries: "the brethren were busy picking their so-called sweet corn.

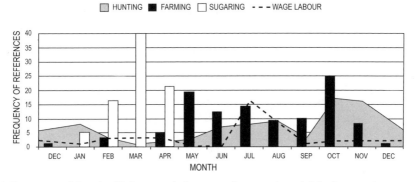

FIGURE 4.1. Moravian Delaware subsistence and economic activities by month, constructed from the Moravian Diaries of 1793–1812.

This corn is picked in its milky stage and roasted or parboiled. It is then cooked and dried" (1809: Sept. 24).

It took most of a month to clear and plant fields in the spring, less time to harvest wheat midsummer, and one to two months for the fall harvest and winter planting (1799: Oct. 17). The diarists worried when the harvest was poor due to bad weather or vermin, and marveled at how productive the harvest was at other times. Beyond providing sustenance, the surplus yields were also a cash currency, heavily sought after by neighbors, traders and British authorities from the settlement and the Detroit River area.

The preoccupation with, and grind of, farming infuses the diaries. At certain times of the year, most residents would stay in the fields to keep pests away, so they were too busy to attend meetings or prayer sessions. Though diarists varied by the degree to which they noted such activity, compiling the number of references to farming by month reflects the seasonal preoccupation of the diarists with this activity and the intensity of farming during those months (fig. 4.1). The annual cycle shows intensity at three points of the year—the spring planting, the summer harvest of wheat and working of the fields, and the fall harvest.

Sugaring. The tapping and boiling of maple sap into sugar was a brief but intensive activity undertaken each spring by Delaware and missionaries alike, "because this work waits for no one" (1796: March 26). Most years a surplus of sugar and syrup was generated, and it was as valuable a commodity as corn or wheat. Once good stands of maple were found in 1793 (Jan. 23), it became the primary economic activity of the community in late winter (fig. 4.1).

In most years, community yields ranged from 200 to 300 lb, while a poor year's yield was noted at 100 to 150 lb (1794: March 29; 1806: April 13). Sugar could fetch upwards of a shilling a pound, depending on quality. Sugaring was carried out away from the village in sugaring camps, situated to the west and east of town and north from the river along small creeks. Both men and women participated (women usually boiling the sap), and during periods when the sap was flowing well or later when boiling had to be completed, entire families would be at the camps. People could be away for weeks from the village, or return only briefly on Sundays for service. Indeed, there are several references to meetings and services having to be cancelled and the town emptied, with perhaps only the missionaries' wives or elders too old to go out staying behind (e.g., 1800: March 9; 1804: March 22; 1806: Feb. 20). Also, being in the sugaring camps was an occasion for visiting and socializing, and, to the missionaries' displeasure, bouts of drinking.

Hunting. The missionaries did not participate in hunting (though they enjoyed the fruits of it), but most Delaware families did. There are references to hunting for every month of the year (fig. 4.1), though never at the same intensity as seen for either sugaring or farming. References to game include deer (referred to 26 times), bear (14), raccoon (6), wild turkeys (4), pigeons (2), and black squirrels (2). There are also references to hunting wolves, though this was more to keep them away from livestock.

Early on, some Delaware still preferred to hunt areas they knew better than around Fairfield, including references in 1793 (Oct. 14) and 1795 (Aug. 22) to members heading to Pettquotting (Sandusky, Ohio) to hunt. In the 1793 example, the head of a household was planning to spend the winter there, "as is his custom." This suggests a retained sense of ownership and expert knowledge of a locale and, just as likely, social interaction with the Native communities in that area.

Despite Zeisberger's claim that "the hunt does not bring much anymore," (1793: Nov. 5), it appears that the community was learning early on exactly what would and would not work locally. For example, in 1795 (July 22) Zeisberger reported: "The Indian brothers who had undertaken to build a deer fence from this river to Lake Erie, a distance of about 20 miles, returned today. They believe a fence to be to their advantage for the hunt. The Chippewa do this as well."

While it is perhaps not surprising that there is no reference to this massive undertaking ever being completed, clearly the community felt that a substantial effort was necessary in the early years to get at local game populations. Also, the community was beginning to learn from the resident Ojibwa, who knew effective hunting strategies and the best seasons for hunting particular game. In a short amount of time, the residents learned where game concentrated, and which hunting strategies, seasonally, were most effective. For example, while hunters were trying to find bear lairs in January of 1793 (Jan. 15), by 1799 (Oct. 7, 29, Nov. 3), hunters had realized that bear were best hunted in the late fall. Building great deer runs in 1795 gave way to hunting deer by jacklighting (use of torches at night; see Lytwyn 2001) or whistles in the summer (1806: Aug. 2; 1799: June 21), and through heavy snow with snowshoes in winter (1812: March 8). Likewise, finding raccoon dens in January or February proved an excellent way to quickly obtain a large quantity of meat (1801: Jan. 21). Indeed, successful hunting in both 1807 (Dec. 5) and 1812 (March 8) led to diarists complaining that the deer hunt was too good, either because meat had been left behind, or because the value of hides was apparently low at that moment.

Hunting was a male pursuit (Gourlay 1822, 1:297), done individually (1793: April 11), in a group (1799: Nov. 3), or in a more formal community activity (1797: May 16). As figure 4.1 shows, the late fall hunt figured prominently in diarists' accounts. This encompassed a communal hunt to bring back food for the community's corn harvest (1806: Nov. 6), and smaller group hunting for hides and meat for the upcoming winter. The late fall hunt was so intensive in 1799 (Nov. 3, 11) that most people were away at "hunting huts" as the women were collecting meat and bringing it back to the village.

Sandwiched between the spring planting and midsummer crop tending was a period for hunting that could be a group activity, but was also informal and described as either a "common" hunt or done by "several" or "some" people (1806: Aug. 26; 1807: July 28). It was also a time to take boys on the hunt to teach them hunting skills (1796: May 16), and to return with dried meat prepared by the hunters in the bush (1805: June 26). The summer hunt was also about choices: one could stay to work the fields, go out to gather meat, or work the fields of nearby European farms to make money. An 1807 diary entry notes that "several brethren went out hunting or harvested crops in the community." If someone wanted to hunt, they could get others in the community to tend their fields in exchange for meat (1798: June 16). Hunting meant leaving the settlement for anywhere from a few days to over a month (1799: Oct. 7; 1801: Nov. 8; 1805: June 10), or just taking a series of day trips. During the summer hunt of 1806 (July 16), Schnall complained that people hunting had been away in the bush for several Sundays. And in 1799 (Nov. 3; Nov. 11), several meetings were cancelled because the translator kept going with the rest of the men to hunt. People went several different places to hunt: into the bush a few days' walk from the village, over to the settlement on the lower Thames and Lake St. Clair, or down to Rondeau Bay and Lake Erie.

At any point in the year, individuals or small groups could be hunting, and references to hunting often appeared indirectly, such as a note that the translator was absent or that someone was drinking at a hunting camp. Also, hunting largely occurred away from the village, and so away from missionaries' "line of sight" and pen. The frequency of references to hunting extracted from the diaries, then, especially those related to individual or informal hunting, are not as abundant in figure 4.1 as might otherwise have been the case.

Incidental hunting in and around Fairfield is infrequently mentioned, even though it seems to have been common practice for women and children to kill squirrels and pigeons or snare rabbits for the cooking pot (1799: June 21; 1807: Sept. 9; Stonefish 1995a:67), which is typical of "garden hunting" practices noted for other sedentary groups (e.g., Kent 1989; Neusius 1996). In 1800 (June 4), the missionaries complained that children's bows and arrows, necessary "since they need to practice their hunting skills," were being used to shoot corn, chickens, and a colt. This underscores both the continued use of this weaponry, and the otherwise invisible agency of children. In this case, children within the village added incidental kills to food supplies and annoyed the missionaries, and thus contributed to community antagonisms and tensions.

Ultimately, Zeisberger's 1793 prediction of the hunt's inevitable failure and an expected shift to a fully farming way of life was not realized prior to the War of 1812. Neither did Sensemann's references to the depravity of hunting (quoted at the start of this chapter), nor the suggestion that Christian lifestyles made the Delaware bad hunters, prove true. In the identified faunal remains from assumed Native house sites, the Jurys (2006) indicated that 80 percent of identified mammal was deer. Over 60 percent of bird bone was duck, and fish, bear, raccoon, squirrel, turkey, crane, partridge and crow were also noted.[7] Jury also observed (1945, 1948; Jury and Jury 2006) that leg and toe deer bones were frequent finds (i.e., shanks brought back from the hunt), and that deer long bone was shattered "peculiar to the Indians . . . and resemble those found in a pre-European site" (W. Jury diary 1943); in other words shattered for marrow extraction and rendering.

Thus, Denke's view in 1812 that "The hunt remains a good part of the Indians' subsistence" (March 8), or later that "men are chiefly occupied with hunting" (Gourlay 1822:297), attests to the maintenance of this traditional practice, in tandem with intensive agricultural practices.

Fishing/Collecting. There are few references to these activities, prob-ably because their apparent casual and individual pursuit left them below the notice of the diarists. In 1793 (May 24), a fish dam was built on the Thames River, and for the next week many fish were speared until rains washed the dam away. There are also references to harvesting spring runs in 1796 and 1797 (April 21; April 29). In 1801, Oppelt (June 1) reported that people were bringing back catfish after spearing them upstream. Stonefish (1995a:67) notes that the community recalls fishing as a much more promi-nent subsistence activity, and fish bones were found archaeologically (Jury and Jury 2006).

The few references to collecting mention blueberries and brambleber-ries taken in July and August (1795: July 13; 1811: July 28), cranberries in March and November (1801: Nov. 16; 1805: Mar 10), and chestnuts in October and November (1795: Oct. 20; 1806: Oct. 12). Blueberries were dried and chestnuts made into a paste or flour. These activities were done by women and children. It is worth noting that the berries ripen at a time when other sources of food may be low. For example, in 1805 (Aug 4) berries were noted as the main food source for the poor. Also, there is a learning curve to collecting strategies, with women early on going over to the former mission site in Michigan to collect berries. The Jurys (2006) also reported bivalve shells in quantity, reflecting another gathering activity.

Crafts and Wage Labor. There are a few references to craft production for selling. Most refer to making canoes (1795: Apr. 20; 1807: May 7), some-thing generally done in early spring. Women were reported going to Detroit and the settlement to trade baskets for apples or to sell baskets, brooms or mats (1798: Aug. 17; 1809: Sept. 7). There are single references to residents making musket stocks and violins (1795: Jan. 21; 1808: July 25), and to people working as carpenters and metal workers, including making mouth harps for children (1798: July 10; 1808: Dec. 17). From the archaeological excavations, there is evidence of tin working, gun repairs, mouth harps, and a range of tools associated with woodworking (Jury 1945, 1948).

Wage labor references generally appear opportunistic—people hiring a resident to guide them (1794: Aug. 1; 1799: Jan. 7) or to take a post to York (1799: Nov. 25), or neighbors asking for someone to help build a house (1793: Oct. 12). There is also a reference to a man who ran a lumber mill, "and thus had frequent contact with our Indians who help him for pay" (1811: March 16). In addition, there is a notable concentration of wage labor references for July and early August (fig. 4.1), when residents went to the European settlement and worked in the fields harvesting hay (e.g., 1795:

Aug. 4; 1810: July 24). This activity is also prominent in the diaries because the missionaries often expressed mixed feelings—pleased that residents were gaining money, and worried that they would fall under the influence of their employers and/or drink.

Trading and Selling. Everything the Delaware harvested or processed, from meat, hides and furs to sugar, corn and even berries, was available for sale or trade. Bear Creek Ojibwa often visited to trade their meat for corn (1794: Aug. 19; 1799: Mar. 8), while corn and sugar were exchanged for dry goods from area merchants or traveling traders (1798: Sept. 14).

This activity occurred throughout the year. However, especially earlier on when traders tended to come directly to Fairfield (e.g., 1794: Mar. 5), trading and selling peaked in November and April. This coincided with the completion of the corn harvest and the sugaring season (e.g., 1798: Nov. 13; 1799: Apr. 29). But the frequency of traders visiting Fairfield declined through time due to the appearance of local dry goods stores at the settlement (Hamil 1951). Mostly the Delaware traded for assorted dry goods that were not available locally.

Discussion—Subsistence and Economic Activities. The economy of the Moravian Delaware was both a product of the intentional design behind the missionary community of which they were a part, and a continuation of traditional subsistence practices that would have been familiar to any other Native group in southwestern Ontario at the end of the 18th century. The two most intensive subsistence activities, agriculture and sugaring, generated surplus yields to be traded or sold. Wage labor was also important. The livestock, supplies, clothing, and other materials traded for or purchased benefited the individual and community, and furthered its economic success. This image of a hardworking, industrious farming community is certainly the single vision of the Fairfield Delaware offered in conventional histories (E. Gray 1956; Hamil 1939, 1951), and in existing anthropological efforts (Graham 1975; Kjellberg 1985). Kjellberg (1985:50) goes so far as to suggest that, by 1801, the Delaware of Fairfield did very little hunting.

But the diaries and archaeological data also reveal that maintenance of traditional lifeways and social organization was a key part of the annual subsistence cycle. Families left for sugaring huts, and men left for weeks at a time to hunt in the bush. Hunting remained a principal means of subsistence throughout the period of the translated diaries (and well after), and most of the community hunted at one point or another during the year. As well, while hunting was a necessity for food, the social dimensions of this activity were also important: hunting was a time away from the settlement and, as such, a chance to reaffirm a connection to the bush, to interact with fellow hunters, and to catch up with, and be part of, the world beyond the edge of the planted fields.

It would be most instructive to compare the Fairfield Delaware with those at Muncey. Unfortunately, very little is recorded for this community from the late 18th and early 19th centuries. The Munceys lived in two loose aggregations of log cabins and apaquois/wigwams on the Thames River, referred to as an upper and lower village by travelers, and noted as being distinct from the surrounding, scattered occupation of the Thames River Ojibwa (P. Jones 1860; Kjellberg 1985). From inferences in the Moravian diaries, the Munceys were seasonally mobile, though less so than the Ojibwa. They likely wintered away from their village—some families stayed at or close to Fairfield. The Muncey were also known to farm intensively and generate surpluses of corn, which the Fairfield community relied on during the early years. In one instance, Zeisberger states "A few brethren went to see their friends in Muncey Town where they received corn. Because of their remote location these people cannot sell their corn and they have a surplus" (1793: Jan. 10).

References in the diaries to the Muncey as "heathen" and "wild" speaks to that community maintaining more overt signifiers of identity as well as more traditional subsistence and mobility. Indeed, dress (buckskin leggings vs. cotton pants) and adornment (trade silver, paint, etc. vs. none)[8] were visible differences between at least some of the Moravian and Muncey Delaware. Importantly, then, the Muncey Delaware provided Fairfield residents with a distinct counterpoint to the missionaries' vision of how life could be led, and provided a connection and continuity to traditional cultural values, beliefs and lifestyle. Nonetheless, the Moravian Delaware did not simply move en masse to the Muncey community whenever they were unhappy with the missionaries or fed up with the admonishments. Rather, their sense of place and self arose from their own community, values, and way of life.

It is also worth comparing Ojibwa and Moravian Delaware patterns. Clearly, the most significant difference is the emphasis on intensive agriculture on the part of the Delaware versus the greater mobility of the Ojibwa. Significantly, the Moravian Delaware pattern of subsistence overall is more reminiscent of the pattern that emerges among Ojibwa communities by the later 19th century (fig. 3.9); i.e., mixed subsistence and some out-mobility operated from a fixed settlement.

While the Moravian Delaware were clearly using a wider array of mass-produced material culture in 1800 than the Ojibwa (from ceramics to agricultural implements), Jury (1945, Jury and Jury 2006) also reported finding

Indigenous items such as small stone triangular projectile points, several schist and stone hoes or adzes, and a clay-ringed bowl pipe from various house sites with central hearths.[9] Diary references to the use of wampum (1809: Nov. 12), bows and arrows, traditional clothing, and reed and grass mats and baskets also speak to maintenance of traditional fashions and technologies alongside mass-manufactured and readily available counterparts.

The Delaware adapted to change by exploiting the opportunities of the southwestern Ontario frontier while also maintaining traditional, Native-skilled ways of living. Change had occurred, but significantly only over the preceding two generations and not at the scale suggested by master narratives for missionized Native communities. As with their architecture, the Delaware incorporated traditional and innovative elements within subsistence and material culture. Evidence of directed culture change, or desires to emulate their missionary coresidents, is absent. Acceptance of innovative strategies and selected use of "useful" things and practices imply changed continuities (Deitler 1998; Moore 1989; J. D. Rogers 1990). There is no indication this was undermining a Delaware sense of identity and continuity with their past, and speaks to a gradual, fluid pattern of response consistent with, and connected to, the general patterns of the previous three centuries.

Fairfield South of the Thames

Information on the Delaware return to the Thames River after the War of 1812 is limited. No archaeological work has been conducted at the resettled site of Moraviantown, and diaries through the mid-1840s remain untranslated (Sabathy-Judd 1999; Veenema 2002). What is known is that upon returning after a two-year abandonment due to the war, most of the Delaware settled south of the river, establishing a nucleated village and communal agricultural fields. Several families lived dispersed beyond the village, including north of the river at the former, now destroyed, site of Fairfield (E. Gray 1956:277). Denke's observations in Gourlay suggest hunting continued to be a principal activity alongside corn agriculture, a pattern that would continue into the mid–19th century (e.g., Canada 1844–5, 1847). Most residences were log cabins, although two frame and two wigwam structures were noted in 1858 (Canada 1847, 1858).[10] The Delaware population grew from around 120 people after the war to over 270 in the 1870s (Canada 1876). There were also periods of out-migrations to Delaware communities in the central United States due to internal conflicts at Moraviantown (e.g., Canada 1858; E. Gray 1956). Opportunities for seasonal or more permanent

wage labor, in the form of new rail lines, the burgeoning lumber industry, and the petroleum industry were increasingly exploited by community
members (E. Gray 1956; Veenema 2002).

Depending on accounts, life at Moraviantown was either a mirror reflection of good Euro-Canadian agricultural settlement (e.g., McCormick 1824;
Pickering 1831), or ruinous, debauched and wasteful for emphasizing a hunt
that was no longer plentiful (e.g., Bond Head 1839; Latrobe 1835). Accounts
indicate that European-style dress was commonplace, though Native features
or modifications were noted for both men and women well into the mid-
century (e.g., E. Gray 1956; Veenema 2002). Hunting continued to play an
important role, but it was increasingly constrained by the 1850s because of
land clearings around the community.[11]

The 1861 manuscript census offers a less subjective picture of the Moraviantown economy. While its value for interpretation is limited due to the
relocation of many families onto individual plots just three years earlier—
some without clearings but all with log cabins or frame houses—it nonetheless reflects the range of practices from the time (table 4.1). Three years
after relocation, 57 percent of families ($n = 35$) were practicing some form of
farming. Of the 57 percent, 28 percent ($n = 10$; 16 percent of all households)
were operating farms with 10 or more acres of cultivated land (crops and
pasture), two of which had 20 acres or more, while 45 percent of farming
households ($n = 17$; 28 percent of all households) had less than 5 acres of
cultivated land. The census data reflect continued reliance on corn-focused
farming and significant potato harvests, while wheat appears to be the only
typical southwestern Ontario cash crop grown in quantity by at least some
of the community. While the number of households with dairy cattle was
relatively high, the low number of cattle per household (1.5) suggests use
more for personal need than generation of dairy products for sale. As with all
Native communities examined, Delaware farmers had no interest in sheep.

Table 4.1 also provides numbers for the Muncey Delaware in 1852.[12]
Thirty-eight (88 percent) of 43 Muncey households were involved in farming. It is also worth noting that while the 1861 Moravian Delaware were all
single family units (nuclear families with some cross-generational occupancy
as well as unmarried siblings), 31 percent of Muncey Delaware homes were
two-family residences. This difference perhaps reflects both the more limited availability of housing stock (which had been provided to all families at
Moraviantown as a result of the Indian Department land sell-off), and continuing traditional residential trends at Muncey. Almost all male adults are
listed as farmers at Muncey, although other professions include shoemaker,
basket maker and hunter, and several households did not list occupation.

TABLE 4.1 Compiled Agricultural Census Data, Moraviantown Delaware, 1861 and Muncey Delaware 1851–52

Product	Moravian farmers	Muncey farmers	Moravian acres	Muncey acres	Moravian bushels	Muncey bushels	Moravian number	Muncey number
Wheat	16 (46%)	16 (42%)	3.4	3.0	51	27		
Peas	4 (11%)	6 (16%)	1.5	1.3	24	18		
Oats	3 (8%)	12 (32%)	2.3	1.8	100	29		
Buck-wheat	8 (23%)	4 (11%)	1.6	1.8	36	23		
Corn	31 (88%)	34 (89%)	2.0	2.4	55	52		
Potatoes	31 (88%)	28 (74%)	1.1	0.6	74	19		
Maple sugar	11 (31%)	29 (76%)					138 lb	181 lb
Steers	18 (51%)	22 (58%)					2.3	1.8
Milch cows	26 (74%)	29 (76%)					1.5	2.8
Horses	14 (40%)	25 (66%)					2.5	3.3
Pigs	21 (60%)	26 (68%)					5.6	5.8

Note: Moravian farming landholders listed: 35; Muncey farming landholders listed: 38.

At Muncey, 29 percent of farming households maintained between 10 and 20 acres of cultivated land, while 39 percent held less than 5 acres of cleared land. Crop and livestock patterns were generally similar between the two communities, although higher yields for all but corn at Moraviantown may speak to regional differences in soil fertility or a more intensive emphasis on surplus yields at Moraviantown. But clearly corn harvesting was the main subsistence staple for both communities.

These data do not suggest marked subsistence contrasts between groups, despite Euro-Canadian observers continuing to situate the Muncey as less industrious, or characterizing Moraviantown as declining toward Muncey. Indeed, the patterns for these two groups are very similar to those documented for the Ojibwa and Six Nations Iroquois (see chap. 3 and 5), and different from broader Euro-Canadian farming practices and emphases.

Despite the relatively successful nature of Delaware small-scale farming efforts, Jesse Vogler, who returned to serve for a second stint as the Moraviantown missionary from 1843 to 1865, became one of the most vociferous critics of the community. He complained of inappropriate behavior, a lack of deference to his position, general laziness, and poor farming practices, like letting weeds grow among crops and not maintaining fences to keep out livestock (Veenema 2002:54). Vogler also had a major impact on the community by undermining Delaware autonomy and shaping the direction catastrophic bureaucracy would take in disrupting community cohesion.

Pressures to give up reserve land emerged in the 1830s and eventually led to a reduction in the size of the community (E. Gray 1956:276–277). That the Moravian missionaries aided the Indian Department in reducing the size of the reserve undermined their credibility in the community, and created resentment and internal community factionalism over the more overt authoritarian role missionaries began to adopt at this time. By mid-century, Vogler had significantly furthered resentment and distrust for the position of missionary, as he actively challenged community interests by aiding and abetting Indian Department policies that sought to constrain the capacity of community members to pursue economic autonomy, especially with respect to control of natural resources such as timber and oil (Graham 1975; E. Gray 1956; Stonefish 1995a; Veenema 2002).

Vogler's diaries characterized the Delaware community as being in decline, dissolute, doomed to extinction and salvageable only through rapid imposition of assimilative policies and the dissolution of the reserve itself (Veenema 2002:63). These views fed into pressures from the surrounding region for even more of the community's lands, and Indian Agent Joseph Clench's desire to sell-off these "wastelands," so they could be put to "productive" use by Euro-Canadian farmers. Between 1853 and 1858, the Indian Department induced the community to surrender the majority of its holdings, in part by exploiting internal factions between those who still supported Vogler and those who did not. In return, all Delaware families received a 40-acre lot of mostly uncleared land. Families that lost improved land were compensated, and then were evicted onto designated lots. Volger's son served as the bailiff (Veenema 2002:67–77; see also, Canada 1858; Graham 1975; Stonefish 1995a).

Not long before these transactions, Clench, who had worked closely with Vogler to facilitate the land sale, was fired for corruption and embezzlement (Graham 1975). It is also clear that Vogler benefited materially from his involvement in these dealings (Veenema 2002:83). Indeed, according to the 1861 agricultural census, he held far more reserve land than any Delaware family, had a far more productive farm (55 acres cultivated) worked by a non-Native hand, and held livestock, including sheep, valued up to eight times more than the most agriculturally focused Delaware family in the community. Missionary subsistence and hard work were no longer good only for the soul; they were also good for the pocket.

Delaware leaders continually decried the role Vogler played in undermining the community and actively refused to acknowledge any assertions he

made to authority (Graham 1975; Veenema 2002). While calculated indifference and the exacerbation of factions undermined the community's ability
to stop the impact of people like Clench and Vogler, the divisiveness they
fomented and the actions Delaware leaders took in response facilitated a secular
maturing of the community. This led to the dispensing of Moravian conventions (e.g., "helpers") and the formal recognition of leaders as chiefs (E. Gray
1956:283). Community members also flaunted rules prohibiting the selling
of lumber or allowing petroleum leases. The disaffection with Vogler also
led to the welcoming of other denominations into the community, including
Methodists by the 1840s and Anglicans by the 1860s (Graham 1975; Stonefish 1995a:18). These other congregations gave members a further option to
go "elsewhere" if they disliked Moravian doctrines or were alienated from
factions in the community "allied" with the Moravian missionary (Stonefish
1995a:33). Eventually, the irrelevance of Moravian doctrines to day-to-day life
led to the abandonment of the mission in 1902 (E. Gray 1956).

Discussion

So who were the Moravian Delaware? A composite community without a
common cultural base assimilated and Christianized by their Moravian missionaries? Or had they retained a distinct cultural identity throughout their
diaspora, and flourished after settlement on the Thames River? There certainly are plenty of allusions offered by the diarists to dependency and loss
of distinct identity. But resituate the emphasis away from the immediate,
personal preoccupations of the recorders and onto the longer rhythms of
daily, seasonally and yearly lived life, and insight into Moravian Delaware
identity and social organization emerges from both the observations and the
omissions in the written record. Indeed, this capacity to read the same written records but interpret them so differently underscores a fatal flaw of the
observer biases found in documentary sources, by allowing researchers to
"cherry-pick" observations in a sea of text to "read" into historical analysis
any particular emphasis which that researcher chooses (Collingwood 1946;
Galloway 1991; Moreland 2001).

    As Anna Jamieson's quote at the start of this chapter implies, the Mora-
vian missionaries could offer only a very narrow and self-interested perspective on the community they were a part of, and judged even more narrowly
the "success" of the mission by the degree of daily adherence to Moravian
Christian doctrines. Actions, persons, things and ideas that fell outside of
those doctrines were a "threat" to Moravian conventions and "civilization"

efforts. So from the missionaries' standpoint, those "wild" Muncey and Ojibwa were a nuisance begging for food, and constantly starving because they "roamed" the land and lived by the hunt. By contrast, the Fairfield Delaware (and local Euro-Canadian settlers) "went hungry" and "borrowed" food (sometimes from the Muncey and Ojibwa) only because of unfortunate circumstances, such as a poor harvest or bad climate. Accounts of starving and begging, in this context, have less to do with real deprivation or collapse of traditional economies (as is erroneously interpreted in many historical analyses), and more to do with judgmental distinctions between self and other (Black-Rogers 1986; Vibert 1997).

Likewise, individual lapses from Moravian doctrine were judged, depending on the diarist, as either disappointing or as clear evidence of mission failure; both also proving the inherent "flaws" of the Native brethren. For example, despite strong social conventions in Aboriginal and Euro-Canadian communities in the late 18th century around the consumption of alcohol as material status and a vehicle for everything from entertaining, to healing rituals and feasts, to respite and release (e.g., Deitler 1990, 1998; Wagner 1998), use of alcohol was characterized by some missionaries as symptomatic of a larger undermining of Moravian doctrines and a vice leading to the ruin of all Aboriginal nations. While alcohol abuse was and is a serious issue for some portion of all communities, the general perception in historic accounts, which has been adopted wholesale in conventional historical analyses, is of alcohol having a universally calamitous impact on "naïve" or "indolent" Aboriginal people, while typically characterized only as a vice for "some" European pioneers.

Being aware of the perceptual differences European observers (and academic researchers) maintain of the world makes it difficult to talk of concepts such as acculturation, assimilation, dependency and civilization, or of resistance and revitalization for that matter, with any degree of utility. For example, are we to assume those helpers and baptized Moravian Delaware praised by the missionaries as members who worked hard in the fields, dressed in the European fashion, faithfully attended church, prayed and wept over their salvation and spiritual beliefs, were "culturally" different from their Moravian Delaware neighbors who preferred the hunt and valued traditional rituals, feasts, healings and beliefs? What if the former liked to hunt, too, which some clearly did? And were these parts of the community then different from Delaware whose spiritual beliefs were more secular and indifferent, regardless of their choice of subsistence, dress or family organization?

Or more inconveniently to pat categorizations, what of individuals who moved between or overlapped differing conventions and values over time and circumstance? How does the historical researcher interpret Zachaeus, for example, who could not get relief from the illness he suffered using conventional medicine, so went to Muncey to have a shaman try to cure him? Is he assimilated one day and not the next? Or is he assimilated because he confessed? And what of Marcus? Was he less acculturated because he talked back to the missionaries and acknowledged that he liked to drink, or was he more acculturated because overindulging in alcohol now and then was his only vice? Indeed, by whose measurement are such things supposed to be evaluated? Should we measure terms like acculturation and assimilation by percentage, in the community and in the individual? Hardly. Individuals, families and communities, both now and in the past, are complex cultural beings whose behavior can be unpredictable and seemingly impossible to measure as parts in a larger, single-minded cultural unit responding to change.

In terms of the relationship between the Delaware and the missionaries, and what being "Christian" meant, there is little indication that the people of Fairfield were pliant supplicants to Moravian missionary masters. There is also plenty of evidence that the Delaware were not reluctant to object, ignore or flaunt the doctrines, values or predilections of the Moravian missionaries resident in the community. While the missionaries offered a particular worldview, it was the Delaware who defined what was important to them individually and as a community, both in terms of spiritual values and day-to-day life, be it Christian or Indigenous. So even though Native religious revivals were going on around them, at Muncey and across the Great Lakes (1807: Feb. 24; see also White 1991), the message did not sway people away from Fairfield. Likewise, while 19th-century religious denominations in Moraviantown reflected social factions within the community, these pre-existed missionary exhortations, and were co-opted into community-centric fault lines and ongoing stresses, existing in and typical of most egalitarian groups. The 18th- and 19th-century Delaware knew who they were, and day-to-day could easily reconcile their Delaware and Indigenous identity with living in a Christian settlement surrounded by an Euro-Canadian occupation, even through dissention and difference in the community. This active engagement in and modification of Euro-Christian doctrine and Indigenous values shows a direct agency in the recursive self-definition of the community throughout the period under study.

Moreover, the diaries reveal that spiritual identity at Fairfield was also very much tied to the community's daily way of life—its pattern of subsistence. Here we saw not a rejection of traditional activities and methodologies, but an active retaining of them. So Christianity, especially the chastising kind found at Fairfield, may have been either welcome or an annoyance, but it did not disrupt core values or force an abandonment of longstanding ways of life and family organization, whatever missionaries may have thought of them. Clearly for some, like Salamo and Abraham, sin-free living at Fairfield was not an attractive option, and so they left. But for those who stayed, the community provided a meaningful home and cultural cohesiveness, consistent with living Delaware traditions and beliefs despite internal tensions.

I would presume members of the Delaware community today would argue that adaptation and changed continuities continue to be negotiated, even though many historians and anthropologists might have previously dismissed the post War of 1812 history of the community as one of dependency and assimilation. It remains that the cultural identity of this community, which emerged as composite and as displaced a Native group as could be conceived of from the turmoil and diaspora of the 18th century, remains strong and fixed today. This, then, is the real testament to the findings in this chapter. Here was a community overseen by Europeans whose sole aim was the intentional acculturation of their Native "charges" at Fairfield—a community founded specifically to facilitate meeting that aim. Yet despite this very intentional focus held by individuals who could, in effect, take a family's home away from them should individuals deviate from a long list of specific social conventions, there is no indication in the data reviewed here that the Delaware lost their historical sense of identity, or failed to be anything other than Delaware and Indigenous. This suggests that the complex social processes of historically based knowledge and lived experience that constantly revised Native understandings of self in and of the world around them, so clearly maintained by the Ojibwa outlined in chapter 3, were equally a critical dimension of Moravian Delaware identity through the emergence of the colonialist state and changed landscape of the 19th century.

5

Iroquoian to Iroquois in Southwestern Ontario

A chain of corroborating events seems to evince them [the Six Nations] that the White people, under whatever pretence, aim at their destruction . . . and the more knowledge [they] acquire, the clearer they will see the impositions which has been practic'd upon them by the White people, and consequently they will be the more averse to adopting the Manners of such people in place of the customs of their Forefathers who liv'd happy, & free from strife before they became acquainted with them.

—Joseph Brant to Rev. Strickland, March 8, 1791; (C. Johnston 1964:269–270)

THE ARCHAEOLOGICAL HISTORY for much of the lower Great Lakes over the last one thousand years is dominated by the emergence of an extensive suite of material culture, settlement-subsistence and mortuary traits found on sites from the 17th century and associated with historically documented Iroquoian-speaking peoples. The written accounts of material life and livelihood, the correlation of historically recorded villages to their archaeological manifestations, and the similarities of those sites to more ancient sites have revealed an antiquity to documented cultural expressions that confirms a deep historical continuity to Iroquoian systems of ideology and thought (Ferris and Spence 1995; Spence 1994). By 1600, this Iroquoian identity was manifest geopolitically by various nations of Huron and Petun north of Lake Ontario to Georgian Bay, the Neutral of southwestern Ontario and the Niagara Peninsula, the Wenro and Erie east and south of Lake Erie, and the Five Nations Iroquois (Seneca, Cayuga, Onondaga, Oneida, Mohawk) south of Lake Ontario.

Continuities to 1650

Conventional histories of the late 16th and early 17th century have characterized that period as one of very rapid and substantial cultural change for Iroquoian-speaking peoples, triggered by the arrival of Europeans, their

values and sensibilities, and the imposition of European material and economic motivations onto the region's Indigenous inhabitants. This supposedly led, by the mid–17th century, to the collapse of Ontario Iroquoian
nations in the face of warfare from the Five Nations Iroquois of New York
state, who attempted to disperse competitors for furs, skins, and ultimately,
European goods (e.g., Delâge 1985; Hunt 1940). Subsequent research has
refined and revised this narrative, attributing a greater complexity to the
processes of interaction and change operating within Indigenous communities, an emphasis on Native-based motivations to historic events, and more
caution toward Eurocentric biases in the written record (e.g., Richter 2001;
Trigger 1985). Nonetheless, most studies of the so-called "early contact" era
continue to emphasize that European-induced rapid and major change took
place by 1650, and to imply that Indigenous history as something that operated beyond European influence ended at that time.

Archaeological research has also echoed these tropes of rapid and major
change, seeing any manifestation of the European presence archaeologically
as evidence confirming this change. Change has been assumed to have arisen
from an insatiable or obsessive desire for things like copper kettles, iron axes
and glass beads causing unprecedented, intense social pressures on Indigenous groups (e.g., Bradley 2001; Fitzgerald 2001; Trigger 1991; Turgeon
2004).[1] This archaeological buttressing of historical narratives is problematic, since these constructions run counter to the complex and robust archaeological histories that antecedent Iroquoian communities lived through during the preceding centuries (e.g., Chapdelaine 1993; Ferris 1999; Warrick
2000). Indeed, by the early 1500s, centuries of internal social and subsistence
development, demographic growth and increasingly complex sociopolitical
organization had facilitated the emergence of broad, interconnected territorial "clusters" of distinct regional village communities. These communities interacted with regional neighbors and further afield across at least
the Eastern Woodlands, exchanging both prosaic and exotic goods, along
with accompanying innovative concepts, ideological frames of reference, and
knowledge of the world beyond the palisade that helped shape worldviews
inside the palisade (Jamieson 1999; Spence 1999).

This deep history speaks of sophisticated and flexible social adaptive strategies at play among Iroquoian communities, as reflected in the material, mortuary and settlement patterns documented in the archaeological record. Such a
history seems incongruous to the naïve-like response Indigenous groups then
supposedly exhibited at European contact, and suggests an overreliance on
the drama of the written record to form interpretations of the archaeological
record—a reading of archaeology through history.

In reconciling the contradictions between these pre- and post-European narratives, a synthetic review of the extensive archaeological record available for at least southwestern Ontario Iroquoian groups, interpreted without concern for finding affirmation of historically described early contact, fails to substantiate claims of significant material or broader social change. Rather, linking that 17th-century record to the deeper archaeological context of the centuries before reveals broad continuities. For instance, settlement-subsistence patterns—including palisaded villages of pole and bark or hide longhouses occupied by multiple, extended, matrilineal families, along with a range of smaller hamlets, single longhouse or cabin sites—remain largely unaltered to 1650, or exhibit changes entirely consistent with long-term trends within communities and between regions. Material culture is mostly unchanged, with the exception of additive functional and ornamental artifact forms largely adopted to augment, or in a few cases replace, existing Indigenous forms. Mortuary patterns remain consistent with earlier practices, though ceremonies and grave good inclusions become more elaborate. This can more easily be read as servicing increasingly complex and entirely Indigenous intra- and intercommunity relations, social ties and reciprocal debt-obligation, than evidence of wealth accumulation or adoption of European values. In other words, the first half of the 17th century archaeologically exhibits only historically informed Native-centric patterns of continuity and surficial patterns of material innovation and incorporation. (For a detailed review, see Ferris 2006, chap. 3).

Discontinuities and Continuities 1650–1750

If the archaeological record for the Iroquoian communities of southern Ontario reflects continuities of lived life through the first half of the 17th century, more significant change is evident after 1650. Epidemics and conflict with the Five Nations Iroquois led to southern Ontario being devoid of large-scale permanent settlement in the 1650s, as the Huron and Petun were dispersed to the western Great Lakes, New York and Quebec, while at least some of the Neutral and Wenro were coerced to relocate and merge with Five Nations communities, especially the Seneca (e.g., Garrad et al. 2003).[2]

While conventionally this period was seen as the culmination of the so-called "Beaver Wars," fought to control the supplies of pelts and access to European trade goods (e.g., Richter 1992; Trigger 1985), revisionist historical interpretations argued that fur trade relations with Europeans, and trade good desires, were not the critical factors, or were subordinate, tertiary considerations to broader Iroquoian social concerns (Brandão 1997; Heidenreich 1987, 1990; Richter 2001). Heidenreich (1990:489, citing Thwaites 1896–1901, 24:297, 43:187[3]) noted instances of the Five Nations Iroquois specifically stating their desire to incorporate other Iroquoian communities into the Iroquois Confederacy—a self-proclaimed policy of "one people one land"—and argued that this policy was critical for replacing significant population losses due to epidemics in the 1630s and 1640s.

Indeed, this one people–one land concept was part of a broader integrative process of individual, group and whole community adoption active within most Iroquoian societies,[4] and certainly Iroquoian matrilineage structures were flexible enough to accommodate community expansion (Engelbrecht 2003:161). This included "associative" forms of adoption (Lynch 1985), which allowed families and groups to retain their former identity alongside their new identity as part of the Five Nations Iroquois.

The success of one people–one land is evident following the events of the 1640s and 1650s. Several historic references note that Five Nation Iroquois villages included, or even were exclusively made up of, both non-Confederacy Iroquois (e.g., Huron, Neutral, Erie, Susquehannocks), and coastal, northern and central Algonquians (Engelbrecht 2003:162). For example, the Jesuits Julien Garnier and Jacques Fremin noted in the late 1660s that New York Seneca villages included large numbers of Neutral Iroquoians, and that one of these villages was almost entirely populated by Neutral, Erie, Huron and others "formerly overthrown by the Iroquois" (Thwaites 54:81). Father Lalemant's comments in 1660 convey the effectiveness of this ancient social practice in maintaining community cohesiveness:

> If anyone should compute the number of pure-blooded Iroquois, he would have difficulty in finding more than twelve hundred of them in all of the five Nations, since these are, for the most part, only aggregations of different tribes whom they have conquered—as the Hurons . . . the Tobacco Nation [Petun]; the Atiwendaronk, called the Neutrals when they were still independent . . . the Cat Nation [Erie]; . . . the Fire Nation . . . and others,—who, utter Foreigners although they are, form without doubt the largest and best part of the Iroquois. (Thwaites 45:207)

The success of this flexible social structure to maintain the vitality of these coalescent communities as well as a broader Iroquois sovereignty can be seen demographically, since population estimates for the Confederacy Iroquois nations were all comparable or slightly larger in the 1660s to those estimated and reported prior to the beginning of the epidemics in the late 1630s (Brandão 1997: Appendix C). Not surprisingly, then, there are no noted abrupt ends to any of the Five Nations village sequences through the 1640–1660 period. Moreover, in less than two decades after dispersal, permanent Iroquoian villages again stood north of Lake Ontario and in southwestern Ontario. These Five Nations Iroquois villages were home to twenty to thirty longhouses and permanent populations of several hundred people, with or without palisades, and with extensive corn fields (Heidenreich and Burgar 1999; Konrad 1981). Research has tended to assume the reason for establishing these villages was to secure military and economic control of the region (e.g., Aquila 1983; Konrad 1981). However, it is also likely that practical knowledge of the region as a place to reside and subsist, knowledge held by newer "adopted" members of Iroquois communities, was influential. For example, the Seneca village of Tinaouatoua was located in the heart of the former Neutral homeland between the head of Lake Ontario and the Grand River, supposedly built at the site of a former Neutral village (Lajeunesse 1960). Given the recombinant nature of coalescent Seneca communities, it does not seem too much of a stretch to see the establishment of Tinaouatoua as a return home for many.

The one people–one land strategy effectively consolidated the Five Nations Iroquois, adding many Iroquois of southern Ontario Iroquoian ancestry to communities, while facilitating Iroquois expansion north of the lower Great Lakes and to the south and west. This widening theater of Iroquois interests entangled the Iroquois with many western Aboriginal nations, leading to both alliances and conflicts, coincident with widening French and British interests in the region. While I do not deny that interest among the Iroquois in the emerging, pan-regional economic frame of the later 17th century might have driven this expansion, I also see something more in the conflicts and interactions between the Iroquois and other Aboriginal nations at this time than simple maneuvers triggered by desires for economic gain and control of trade.

In effect, there were not two nations struggling to advance their interests in the Northeast during this time (i.e., the French and British), there were several: European and Aboriginal. And the struggles, warfare, and Iroquois expansion into regions that were underpopulated due to past group relocations or dispersals were all indicative of efforts to assert or protect sovereignty in an otherwise changing geopolitical landscape. Indeed, French expansionism and assertions of sovereignty for the lands north of the lower Great Lakes clearly aggravated Iroquois anxieties over their own autonomy, given their view that these lands were subject to Iroquois sovereignty (e.g., Brandão and Starna 1996:211–212). This anxiety was likely a key factor behind renewed Iroquois-French hostilities in the 1670s and 1680s.[5]

An Iroquois understanding of their own sovereignty, and a need to protect it from encroaching nations, European or Aboriginal, was poignantly conveyed to the French in 1695: "You thinke your selfes the ancient inhabitants of this countrey & longest in possession yea all the Christian Inhabitant's of New York & Cayenquiragoé [British governor to New York] thinke the same themselves Wee Warriours are the firste & the ancient people & the greatest of You all, these part's and country's were inhabited and trodd upon us the warriour's before any Christian" (quoted in Brandão and Starna 1996: endnote 40). Such statements were fundamentally assertions of a national sovereignty and identity; one that transcended but entwined family and village identities across Iroquoia, including the incorporated Huron, Neutral and others whose descendants had become part of the one-people identity.

Iroquois sovereignty across an expanded geography included war with Aboriginal nations to the north, west and south (e.g., Aquila 1983; R. White 1991). But as these conflicts continued, losses were felt, both in skirmishes inside and beyond the homeland (e.g., Brandão 1997; Snow 1994). By the end of the century Iroquois and other Aboriginal nations sought to resolve these conflicts, culminating in treaties signed between Aboriginal nations (and witnessed by the French), and between the British and Iroquois, in the period 1700–1701 (Brandão and Starna 1996; Havard 1992).

The nation-to-nation nature of these negotiations represents an active agency on the part of the Iroquois, diasporic Huron, and northern, eastern, and western Anishnabeg to assert and clarify pan-regional sovereignty and sovereign territory. The resolution reached was entirely consistent with Indigenous notions of sovereignty and territorial identity. The treaties spoke of sharing lands of disputed sovereignty and contested use—including southern Ontario—between Aboriginal nations as common hunting grounds, citing the metaphor of many spoons taking from one bowl (Brandao and Starna 1996; Lytwyn 1998).[6] This notion of shared use for contested territory is reminiscent of, for example, the co-use of the frontier between Western Basin and Inter-Lakes Late Woodland archaeological traditions ca. AD 1000–1400, reflecting the antiquity and continuing viability into the 18th century of Indigenous concepts of nation, sovereignty and territory (Ferris 2006).

Archaeologically Changing Continuities 1650–1750

Through the 17th century, settlements in the Iroquois homeland mostly consisted of towns and villages (palisaded or not), with larger towns, at least for the Seneca, noted as containing 50 to 120 longhouses, while villages had 25 to 30 longhouses. Longhouses included at least two residential house forms: "ordinary" longhouses, 15–18 m in length with two to four hearths, and longer houses over 40 m in length with six to eight hearths (K. Jordan 2002; Snow 1995; Sohrweide 2001:7).

While nucleated villages continued, a more dispersed form of loosely clustered, smaller residential areas also emerged in the 18th century (K. Jordan 2002:316; Snow 1995:471). Among the Seneca, Jordan documented a broad complex of sites, or "neighborhoods," extending along an 8-km stretch of river. One such neighborhood complex was made up of fifteen to twenty "houselots," scattered up to 80 m apart from each other. Excavation of a houselot revealed a "shorthouse:" a square-ended longhouse just under 8 m long, with a hearth and sleeping compartments on either side of the hearth (K. Jordan 2002:408), reminiscent of small longhouses found on earlier 16th and 17th-century Neutral and New York Iroquois sites (e.g., Lennox and Fitzgerald 1990; Tuck 1971). Historic accounts also suggest there was an increasing use of wood planking, cut logs, and structural hardware such as nails to aid both long- and shorthouse construction (K. Jordan 2002, 2004).

The trend toward dispersed settlement and smaller longhouses have led some (e.g., Richter 1992; Snow 1994) to suggest this reflected a literal example of Iroquois culture and matrilineal social structure breaking down. However, K. Jordan (2002:580) points out that at the time dispersed settlement emerged, Iroquois communities were thriving, due to a relatively secure period of peace, and due to established exchange with western Aboriginal nations and the British. He also notes distinct advantages to a dispersed settlement form in making day-to-day living easier, and argues that the multiple family nature of the shorthouse dwelling (two to four families), along with clustered neighborhoods of like residences (and associated plot cemeteries), should be read as maintenance of lineage and matrilineal structure, not abandonment of it. And significantly, this shift occurred during a settlement relocation that happened at the end of the normal use-life of a previous, nucleated village. In other words, the decision was an active choice to not, at the moment of relocation, construct a settlement as before. This shift was also not permanent, since later settlements still included somewhat nucleated communities (K. Jordan 2002:331–339).

A departure from such settlement trends is noted among the Mohawk after 1711, when the British established Fort Hunter in the Mohawk Valley. This facilitated a large influx of Palantine German settlement, which encroached into the region over the following decades (Guldenzopf 1984, 1986; Snow 1994, 1995). This, in turn, may have encouraged some adoption of European-styled house structures, such as log cabins (Guldenzopf 1986; see next section).

Through the 18th century, subsistence continued to be dominated by swidden agriculture, though fruit orchards and use of domesticates are also mentioned in accounts (K. Jordan 2002; Snow 1994). Kuhn and Funk (2000:41) note over 50 percent domesticates on 18th-century sites, though their data are exclusively for atypical "elite" Mohawk residences. For at least the Seneca, Jordan's data (2002:475) confirm that the traditional emphasis on deer hunting continued, and may have intensified, while European domesticates were limited to less than 3 percent of the site's assemblage.

Change is evident within the material culture on Iroquoian sites, as relatively stable supply networks of European-made goods had been established by the end of the 17th century. Material culture innovations into the 18th century continued to reflect the incorporation of novel goods into Indigenous material culture so as to assist daily life. European materials and goods functioned in augmentative (e.g., glass bead, copper, brass and lead as raw material for Native artisan needs) or labor-saving (e.g., kettles, axes, knives, muskets) capacities, particularly for tasks like craft manufacture, meal preparation and building. Ceramic vessels mostly disappeared from site assemblages by the end of the 17th century, but ceramic pipes continued to be manufactured well into the 18th century. Likewise, while muskets became a more regular part of the toolkit, they did not entirely replace the bow and arrow, as choice preferences continued to shape assemblages, especially related to perceptions of value and functional efficacy. Native-made items such as stone pipes, beads, pendants and effigies of catlinite or pipestone increased through the first half of the 18th century, reflecting ongoing interaction with western Algonquian nations.

The persistence of Native made items such as clay and stone pipes, even as European counterparts become ubiquitous on sites, reflects a preference for traditional forms associated with the attendant social and ritual dimensions of their use. This was especially so for pipes, which were used during meetings of parlay, alliance, and exchange with people from outside the community (Mann 2003; Trubowitz 1992; Wagner 2003). (For a detailed review of archaeological histories from 1650 to 1750, see Ferris 2006, chap. 4.)

Continuing Discontinuities, 1750–1780

Between the 1750s and 1780s, Iroquois settlements included dispersed and somewhat nucleated and palisaded forms. Residences included traditional multifamily longhouse structures, two-family shorthouses, various "hybrid" forms of single or multifamily structures that used hewn boards over pole structures, and even some log cabins—these latter mostly having earthen floors, central hearths, roof smoke holes, bunk alignments and a double hearth for two families (e.g., Blau et al. 1978:495; Faux 1987; Shoemaker 1991). For example, in 1776, Mohawk and Iroquois dwellings along the Mohawk River were described as "very small, consisting only of a little cottage [or hut], in the middle of which is their fire-place . . . with some earthen ware, such as pots and jugs" (Bloomfield in Snow et al. 1996:285, 290). In 1780, François-Jean de Beauvoir (in Snow et al. 1996:293–294) described a village of relocated Montreal-area Mohawk as:

> A miserable assemblage of huts in the woods. . . . These huts are like our barracks in time of war, or like those built in vineyards or orchards, when the fruit is ripe and has to be watched at night. The framework consists of just two uprights and one crosspole; this is covered with a matted roof but is well lined within by a quantity of bark . . . in the middle of the hut is the fireplace, from which smoke ascends by an opening in the roof. On each side of the fire are raised two platforms, which run the length of the hut and serve as beds; these are covered in skins and bark.

While many settlements maintained either traditional forms of residence or hybridized cabins, a few Mohawk families resided in more substantial structures, including larger log cabins or frame houses with barns. Notable was the residence of the Mohawk Brant family for having "all the conveniences . . . [and] more in the English manner" (Bloomfield in Snow et al. 1996; see also Guldenzopf 1986:98). Based on historical and archaeological evidence, Guldenzopf (1986:111) concludes that an "elite Mohawk residence" had emerged by the second half of the 18th century, characterized by the use of frame structures, a cellar, plank floors, limestone foundations, side hearth with a flagstone (or bricked?) base, plaster walls, outbuildings, and a full range of mass-produced goods. This economic elite included the Joseph Brant family and a number of nonhereditary or "pine tree" chiefs and principal warriors. For Guldenzopf (1986) and Snow (1994), this pattern reflected the emergence of socioeconomic stratification among the Mohawk.

Clearly part of the wealth some people held came from their relations with the British and with Indian Agent William Johnson in particular, and from the increase between the 1750s and 1780s of individual landholdings and other practices that Johnson encouraged to both maintain alliances and foster the adoption of European lifestyles among Iroquois communities (e.g., Allen 1993; Tooker 1994). In Joseph Brant's case, the most preeminent of the nonhereditary Mohawk and Iroquois leaders to emerge during this period, his adoption of European lifestyles extended to being educated in East Coast schools and becoming familiar with colonial, urbane sensibilities and values (e.g., Kelsay 1984; Taylor 2006). Those closely linked to British authorities and Johnson in particular received goods, provisions and support in amassing landholdings, which Guldenzopf (1986) saw as causing Mohawk society to split between hereditary sachem chiefs (not so directly interacting with Johnson), and the wealthy principal warriors and their clan wives and mothers who were interacting with Johnson. From a strictly economic measurement, disparity was evident across Mohawk communities in the 1770s. But whether such disparities also undermined traditional authority or merely underscored tensions that continually were in operation between the hereditary council and broader community of nonhereditary leaders (see Engelbrecht 2003; Tooker 1994), remains unresolved.

Certainly material changes had occurred by the third-quarter of the 18th century. Most profound was the partial shift from multifamily dwellings to one- or two-family residences—either earthen-floored cabins or framed stately manors. While not universal until as late as the first two decades of the 19th century (K. Jordan 2002; Shoemaker 1991), this shift had been cited as the decline of the extended family matrilineage within Iroquois society (Wallace 1969; see also, Richter 1992; Snow 1994). But equating log cabins with the loss of matrilineage social structure is a problematic assumption. As Shoemaker (1991:331) points out, extended family lineages do not necessarily end because multifamily residences are no longer in use. The extended family organization of the Seneca, for example, was maintained into the 20th century. Moreover, the continuation of hereditary sachems and inheritance rules for clan council chiefs through matrilineal clan lines (e.g., C. Johnston 1964; Kenyon 1985; Weaver 1972), also confirms maintenance of matrilineage structures, even if lineage segments mostly resided in separately walled (i.e., log cabin) compartments.

Revolutionary Change and Continuity

The Revolutionary War between Britain and its colonial progeny was significant to subsequent Iroquois history. Notably, in the lead-up to the outbreak
of hostilities, the Confederacy could not agree on a united course of action, so
the Council fire was extinguished, and each nation followed a separate path.
This meant some, such as the Mohawk and Cayuga, supported the British,
while others, such as the Oneida, supported the colonialists, while others
were more varied (Graymont 1972; Taylor 2006; Tooker 1994). A united
Council fire would not be lit again for several decades, and animosities over
the events of the Revolutionary War would take a generation to dim, by
which time the Iroquois, wherever they resided, had become enclaves in a
land of and for the colonizer.

The Mohawk settlements along Mohawk Valley, including the upper village or castle of Canajoharie, and the lower village known as Tiononderoge
(Fort Hunter), were mostly abandoned by 1777. Prior to that, Canajoharie had a population of 221 in 1773, and Tiononderoge had 185 (Fenton
and Tooker 1978:475). Most Tiononderoge residents relocated to Lachine
in Quebec, while most of the Canajoharie Mohawk relocated to the western
New York/Niagara River region, joining up with other displaced communities of Iroquois.

By the decline of hostilities and the signing of the Treaty of Paris in
1783, real pressures for resettlement faced Iroquois nations (C. Johnston
1994; Weaver 1994a). The aftermath meant the Iroquois were dispossessed
of land in the United States, either by virtue of support for the British or
through the American formation of reserves followed by a large scale influx
of non-Native settlers (e.g., Hauptman 1999). North of the Great Lakes, the
British negotiated surrenders for land with resident Ojibwa to settle Iroquois
refugees along the Grand River and east of Lake Ontario, and provided provisions and supplies to help their allies resettle.

The consequences of the Revolutionary War changed, at least within the
minds of American and British colonial authorities, the status of Iroquois
sovereignty. British accounts began to refer to the Iroquois as a defeated and
dispossessed people, and of the British providing a kind of charity to aid
them (e.g., C. Johnston 1964:35–53). So in the minds of colonial administrators, the shift from allies to wards of the state was a small leap aided
by transitory Iroquois circumstances as a result of the immediate outcomes
of the Revolutionary War. But it is clear that from the Iroquois' perspective, the British were assisting the Iroquois to secure land in another part of
the Iroquois territory only in order to relocate their sovereignty to this new

place—a reasonable payment for their military alliance to the British during the war.[7]

So while the Iroquois had entered the war as sovereign nations, they exited it under siege from a catastrophic bureaucracy in the form of a British colonial administration that had unilaterally assumed the Iroquois had forfeited their independence (or never had it to begin with). Rebukes by British administrators over the Iroquois' continued attempts to exercise autonomy once they were in southern Ontario were vociferously challenged by both sachems and leaders like Brant, becoming the stuff of a continuous struggle to maintain a sovereignty that was undermined more by colonial oversight and self-serving indifference than by force (D. Johnston 1986; Kelsay 1984; Weaver 1994a).

The Six[8] Nations Iroquois on the Grand River

The return of the Iroquois to southwestern Ontario occurred in earnest in 1784. While close to two thousand people[9] moved onto the lower Grand (C. Johnston 1964:52), others settled at the east end of Lake Ontario, some Iroquois went to northwestern Ohio, and many remained in western New York (Faux 1987; Sturtevant 1978). While those Six Nations communities that settled on the Grand River subsequently created long and varied histories, certain events have tended to stand out as shaping the settlement as a whole, notably the federal imposition of an elected council and banishment of the hereditary Council in 1924, and the Indian Department–imposed "consolidation" of settlement into Tuscarora and Oneida Townships in 1847 (e.g., Weaver 1994a, 1994b). While the former postdates the focus of this study, the latter will serve to bifurcate the narrative history presented here.

Initial "Village" Period 1784–1814

Ian and Thomas Kenyon (1986:4), among others (C. Johnston 1994; Weaver 1994a), have characterized the initial period of Iroquois occupation along the Grand as a series of village settlements. But the term "village" can be applied only loosely here. True, differing Iroquois nations and previously discrete communities maintained that distinctiveness by settling at separate places along the river, extending in all some 70 km upriver from the mouth of the Grand to the area around present-day Brantford (see fig. 5.1). But these were mostly not nucleated villages but rather loose clusters of log cabins, or

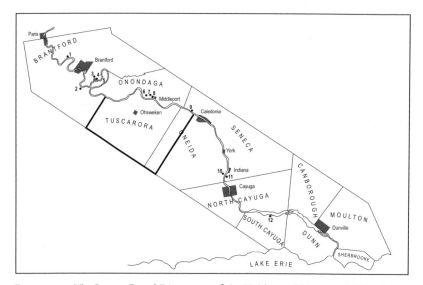

FIGURE 5.1. The Lower Grand River, part of the Haldimand Tract settled by the Six Nations Iroquois in the late 18th century. The map depicts locations of principal river towns and townships (19th century). The solid line around Tuscarora and part of Oneida Townships indicates the location of the Six Nations consolidated reserve. A small portion north of the river, encompassing the area of the sites west of Middleport, also is reserve land. Six Nations sites:

  1 Davisville cluster
  2 Vajko 1 and 2
  3 Mohawk Village cluster
  4 Paulus Powess
  5 Moses Carpenter
  6 Levi Turkey
  7 Thomas Echo Hill
  8 Middleport 2
  9 Dewar
 10 Betsey Syers
 11 May 1 and 2
 12 Susan Cook

sporadic, isolated homes along a definable stretch of the river. For example, surveyor records in the 1790s described settlement along the lower Grand as a scattering of houses on both sides of the river interspersed with river flats planted in maize (Augustus Jones cited in Faux 1984:8).

    A few settlements were more "village-like:" residences in a definable, somewhat more nucleated cluster. This included the Tuscarora Village, which was described as a scattered cluster of thirty houses and a church along the river in the late 1790s (Winnett in Canada 1844–45, 1847; Kenyon 1987b). Another was the upper Mohawk Village, or Brant's Town. This locale was situated atop a ridge overlooking extensive floodplains at an oxbow of the river (Faux 1984; Kenyon and Ferris 1984), with a loose concentration of buildings extending 1.5 km along the oxbow. Prominent was a framed church, school house, and the Joseph Brant residence, which was a two-story frame structure always notable in traveler's accounts as larger and more palatial than anything else, and comparable to upper-class homesteads in the region.

The setting and community landscape at Mohawk Village re-created the layout, architecture, and geographic prominence of the Upper Mohawk Canajoharie settlement left behind in New York, which also had been centered on a frame and steepled church and nearby Brant family home. As at Canajoharie, Mohawk Village was situated along a significant transportation corridor—the main overland route from the head of Lake Ontario to Detroit. As this settlement was located so prominently on the emerging post-frontier landscape of southern Ontario, and known as home to the Brant family, Mohawk Village generated a lot of attention from many travelers and historical figures who passed through, leaving a greater descriptive legacy than for any other Iroquois settlement on the Grand River.

A 1790s painting by Lady Simcoe (fig. 5.2) shows a cluster of buildings overlooking the river, and is described by Littlehales in 1793: "This place is particularly striking when seen from the high land above it, extensive meadows, the Grand River next to it, with a termination of forests. Here is a well built wooden church with a steeple, a school house, and an excellent house of Captain Brant's" (E. Cruickshank 1929, 1:289). In February 1792, Patrick Campbell stayed at Mohawk Village for a few days and found that: "the inhabitants had an abundance of the necessaries of life to supply their wants, and are better and more comfortably lodged than the generality of the poor farmers in my country [Scotland]. Few of the houses I saw but had two apartments, deal floors and glass windows" (C. Johnston 1964:60). And in 1798, Moravian missionaries traveling through the village noted: "The Mohawk Village we passed through is large, irregularly built and scattered. The houses, like all Indian dwellings, are small, having only one room, of a square form. Colonel Brandt has a handsome two story house, built after the manner of white people. Compared with the other houses, it may be called a palace" (L. Gray 1954:120). Often these observations were noted in contrast to the less substantial—i.e., non-Christian, more traditional and so less visibly and materially "normal" to European eyes—lower settlements on the Grand, such as for the Cayuga:

FIGURE 5.2. Lady Elizabeth Simcoe's 1793 watercolor looking up from the Grand River to the southerly core of Mohawk Village. The building on the left is thought to be Brant's home. (Based on a sketch by Robert Pilkington; from the National Archives of Canada, accession number C84448)

The Mohawk village stands on a little plain, looking down upon the Grand River, upon the alluvion of which the inhabitants raise their crops, chiefly of Indian corn. Their houses are built of logs, rudely put together, and exhibiting externally a great appearance of neglect, and want of comfort; some few are in better condition: the house belonging to Brandt's family resembles that of a petty English farmer. The Cayugas seem to have made less progress than the Mohawks . . . : the fire is still in the middle of their dwellings: the earth, or a block of wood, suffices for chair, and table; and planks, arranged round the walls, like cabin births, form their beds. They confine themselves to the cultivation of Indian corn, because it requires little labour, and of that sort which may be performed by women. (Hall 1818:221–224)

In other words, by 1820, some percentage of Iroquois families were still living in cabins whose floorplans continued to echo residential compartments within a longhouse.

The prominence Mohawk Village held, specifically in the first twenty years of the Six Nations settlement on the Grand and prior to Joseph Brant's move to Burlington in 1805, was significant. It was the external "face" of Iroquois diplomatic relations and community, one much to the liking and understanding of European travelers. Duly noted in many accounts was the hospitality afforded non-Native visitors at the homes of Brant and other prominent citizens in the village. Patrick Campbell, again in 1792, wrote:

> Captain Brant who is well acquainted with European manners, received us with much politeness and hospitality. Tea was on the table when we came in, served up in the handsomest China plate and every other furniture in proportion. And after supper was over, we were entertained with the music of an elegant hand organ. Supper was served up in the same genteel stile. Our beverage, rum, brandy, Port and Madeira wines . . . our beds, sheets, and English blankets, equally fine and comfortable. . . . Dinner was just going on the table in the same stile as the preceding night, when I returned to Captain Brant's house, the servants dressed in their best apparel. Two slaves attended the table, the one in scarlet, the other in coloured clothes, with silver buckles in their shoes, and ruffles, and every other part of their apparel in proportion. (C. Johnston 1964:59–61)

But if European travelers were wined and dined to the highest standards of British high society, they were also provided with an exotic flavor of Iroquois culture, in the form of traditional dances and assemblies of people in traditional garb. Lord Fitzgerald noted in 1789 when visiting Mohawk Village that "If you only stop an hour they have a dance for you" (quoted in Kelsay 1984:526). And Patrick Campbell wrote:

> After dinner Captain Brant, that he might not be wanting in doing me the honours of his nation, directed all the young warriors to assemble in a certain large house, to show me the war dance . . . the Indians appeared superbly dressed in their most showy apparel, glittering with silver, in all the variety, shapes, forms, of their fancies, which made a dazzling appearance; the pipe of peace with long white feathers, and that of war with red feathers, equally long, were exhibited in the first war dance, with shouts and war hoops resounding to the skies. The chief himself held the drum, beat time, and often joined in the song . . . the whole exhibition was performed in honour of me, being the only stranger, who they were told by my fellow travellers meant to publish my travels on my return home . . . [then] began their own native and civil [dances]. . . . Here we continued

until near day-light. . . . By my being in a manner under the necessity of often drinking grog with the young Indians and squaws, I got tipsy, though I and one young Indian were the only persons present in the least affected. On the whole, I do not remember I ever passed a night in all my life I enjoyed more. (C. Johnston 1964:61–62)

Significant in the account was the expectation that Campbell would write about the Iroquois in England. In many ways, the Brant hospitality and exhibits of Iroquois ferocity and identity were all part of a marketing campaign of sorts, demonstrating to the emerging, broader colonialities of the region the vibrancy of the Iroquois nations to be autonomous within and without the colonial world. Brant himself embodied this approach,[10] seeing in Six Nations sovereignty the articulation of the "best" from British *and* Iroquois cultures (Kelsay 1984). His emphasis on self-defined important elements of cultural expression from the world of the colonizer (narrowly defined by Brant and his contemporaries as the conventions of British "high" society), and from the historically understood and alive world of the Iroquois, has been noted in other colonial contexts as the maintenance by Indigenous social elites of polyphonic identities in order to negotiate the multiple, sometimes conflicting contexts of being of the Indigenous and being in the colonial (e.g., Alcock 2005). While many of the Six Nations chose not to operate as Brant and his neighbors did, and accepted less of the social meanings in the material innovations they adopted, for at least some families at Mohawk Village, being able to demonstrate an understanding of and the ability to live within both Iroquois and colonial cultures was an important expression of continuing cultural relevance, viability and autonomy.

This outward, public face of the Six Nations at Mohawk Village occurred when the subsequent colonialist state of southern Ontario was not yet fully imagined. The Iroquois' relocation to the Grand River did not end the conflicts between the British, Americans and Aboriginal nations, and the Iroquois continued to play an important role as diplomatic leaders, mediating expectations and influencing actions. For example, dissatisfaction with British views on Six Nations autonomy often led to hints that the Iroquois were going back to New York, or would ally themselves with the Americans against the sparsely populated British settlements of the region (Benn 1998; Kelsay 1984). How the British imagined future consequences of Iroquois autonomy shaped how they accommodated Brant and the Six Nations in the years before the War of 1812.

But while the adoption at Mohawk Village of European "high society" customs and material culture may have reflected economic and class status for a particular social strata, European assumptions that these also reflected the influence of Christian values and assimilation failed to account for the role leadership and politics played in the complex agency of individual, Mohawk and Six Nations interests and identities in the fluid world of the 18th-century Northeast. It was important to demonstrate allegiance and common value to one's partners, whether it was in the formal speech and gift distributions by British authorities, or in the social customs and hospitality exhibited by Mohawk leaders; in the latter case to ensure that British elites interacted with Six Nations elites in the manner to which these British elites were accustomed.

Rural Dispersal

The period after 1815 has been referred to as the "dispersed farm period" (I. Kenyon and T. Kenyon 1986:4), although that term, as with the "village" period earlier, is a misnomer. The sense of dispersal (and implied decline) arises mostly from comments on the deterioration of settlement at and around places such as Mohawk Village and Upper Cayuga (Faux 1984, 1985; Kenyon and Ferris 1984), and more scattered residences appearing along the river.

Certainly the written record for Mohawk Village conveys a sense of decline, including Hall's (1818:224) comments of general neglect. However, it is also the case that after Joseph Brant relocated to Burlington, internal authority among the Six Nations shifted away from Mohawk Village. Gone was authority associated with one individual. Rather, the Confederacy Council formally reasserted authority over Six Nations affairs, and reestablished the general—albeit Grand River based—Council fire at the Onondaga council house, a location more "in conformity to the customs of our ancestors" (C. Johnston 1964:136). In other words, Mohawk Village lost its role as the point of intersection between the world of the Six Nations and the outside, at the same time Joseph Brant's authority within the Six Nations community declined.

Mohawk Village did decline in population. Howison (1821:146) reported the population to be two hundred in 1821. In 1828, John Darling observed that:

> Their principal village, or Mohawk Castle, consists now of half a dozen miserable huts, scattered without any order, and a paltry church. The town was formerly more respectable; but the increasing scarcity of fuel in its neighborhood and the fine quality of the soil induced them by

degrees to separate and settle on the banks of the river, where they cultivate the ground in companies or bands, a certain number of families
dividing amongst them the produce of certain numbers of acres. Their
knowledge of farming is exceedingly limited, being chiefly confined to
the cultivation of Indian corn, beans and potatoes; but those of more
industrious habits follow the example of their white neighbors, and have
separate farms, on which they raise most kinds of English grain. (Darling
in Britain 1834:28) .

By the early 1840s, the area around Mohawk Village was occupied mostly
by non-Native residents: "[Mohawk Village] contains about 24 houses; and
extends in a very irregular form from a quarter to a half mile. All of the
Indian inhabitants of that village, with the exception of four or five families,
have all sold their improvements to white settlers, and have gone to other
parts of the reserve. The houses [of the Six Nations] are all of logs, covered
with inch boards [shingles] for roofs; and in each settlement there are several barns. None of the Six Nations reside in wigwams" (Winnett in Canada
1844–45).

Into the 1840s, the pattern of residence up and down the Grand was
not toward nucleated or even loosely aggregated communities, but rather to
broadly scattered "neighborhoods" along river flats and fields of corn. Patrick
Shirreff wrote in 1835:

A romantic fancy may suppose this tint of the setting sun an affection-
ate evening adieu to nature. The unruffled waters, beneath a cloudless
sky, reflected objects on the surrounding banks; while Indian cots[11], situated on the most prominent points of the terrace, occasionally met the
eye. When contemplating a landscape, where several small islands seem
reposing on the surface of the river, and on which grew luxuriant Indian
corn, overtopped with magnificent sunflowers in full blossom, gentle rip-
ples issuing from beneath a bush on the bank of an island led me to expect
waterfowl, but a squaw standing erect, came gracefully paddling a canoe
filled with children, who had been cultivating the sunflower. (Shirreff
1835:155)

Such a romanticized vista is entirely consistent with the scattered "miserable
huts" quoted elsewhere, or references Indian Department bureaucrats made
of Six Nations–occupied portions of the Grand being wastelands. Moreover,
these dispersed, scattered clusters of residences along specific stretches of the
river are consistent with the pattern of settlement K. Jordan (2002) described

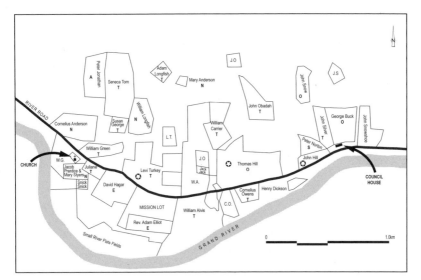

FIGURE 5.3. An Iroquois "dispersed neighborhood," depicting individual improved landholdings near Middleport, 1843, and based on the Thomas Parke "Diagram Showing Indian Improvements on the River Lots at Tuscarora, June 1843," held by the Ontario Ministry of Natural Resources Map Library, Toronto. Circled stars indicate archaeological site locations. Nation affiliations are indicated by letter:

A   Aughquaga (Oneida)

E   Euro-Canadian

N   Nanticoke

O   Onondaga

S   Seneca

T   Tuscarora

for the 18th-century Seneca, with houses spread out along cultivated corn fields and the river, creating a patchwork of neighborhoods. This pattern is evident in Thomas Parke's 1843 map of "Indian improvements" along the Grand, including north of the river near present-day Middleport. This map (fig. 5.3) depicts exactly a patchwork of cleared areas, many of which encompass the landholders' residences (Kenyon 1985, 1987b; I. Kenyon and T. Kenyon 1986). Similar dispersed neighborhoods were also mapped for the lower Cayuga (e.g., Faux 1985:17), and for property holdings around Mohawk Village (Kenyon and Ferris 1984:23). The pattern these maps and written records describe is a documentary manifestation of the archaeological settlement patterns noted by Jordan, and, as he argued, reflects a historically informed adaptive accommodation to the logistics of daily living along the river.

Throughout this period, log cabins make up the bulk of residences in these dispersed neighborhoods, either earthen-floored with central hearths, or more in the style described for Mohawk Village. For example, the home of the Cayuga chief Fish Carrier, located upstream from the Onondaga settlement, is described in the following: "we called on an Indian of reputed wealth, named Fish Carrier. He is a stout middle-aged man, with a wife and family. His log-house had an appearance of comfort, having two large well-glazed windows in front, a door with veranda to the back, and a stone chimney stack. The family seemed to have finished a repast shortly before our arrival,—a good table being covered with plates, knives, and forks, recently used. There were two four-posted beds in the room, five or six chairs, a cat, and several dogs" (Shirreff 1835:152).

Later, Shirreff (1835:158) approached another cabin for a drink of water, and described a woman "sitting under a wooden shade, with a deer-skin, the embers of a fire, and cooking apparatus before her, apart from the house, to avoid heating it." In other words, he was describing an outside activity area entirely consistent with Iroquoian residence patterns noted archaeologically, but now associated with a log cabin.

While communities were broadly dispersed, there were also foci, including churches, schools, and, significantly, council longhouses. These individual nation longhouses served as communal centers and public meeting spaces. Council longhouses, based on descriptions from the 19th century summarized in Kenyon (1985:11–14), were relatively standardized from community to community: log cabins 12–18 meters in length by about 6 meters wide, with deal (plank) floors, open rafters, a peaked roof, a fire (later, an iron stove) at each end of the house, and a standard alignment of benches along each side, with seating arrangements based on Nation and clan affiliations:

> The Council-house of the tribes [is] a long narrow building, with an upper and lower range of benches round both sides, on which the senators recline during counsel. It is kept by two old women, who cook on days of meeting. The roof was hung with ears of Indian corn, considered public property, which are contributed to by individuals in years of abundance, and reserved for times of scarcity. The Council-house is also used for dancing, and contained a number of ornaments worn on such occasions, consisting of strings of bones for fixing on different parts of the body, and prized for the clattering they make when in motion. (Shirreff 1835:152–153)

The care of the longhouse and provisioning of councils by women was commonly noted (e.g., Beavan 1846:46). Proudfoot stated in 1833 that "during
deliberations there was carried into the room and set in the middle of the
floor, a large brass kettle of boiling Indian corn with venison in it, to stand
to cool and then eaten by all" (Priddis 1915:21). Ceremonies conducted at
the council house included the midwinter or white dog sacrifice (Kenyon
1985:14). As well, the area around the Council house served as a cemetery,
so that when the Onondaga longhouse was relocated south of the river in
1858, a Feast of the Dead was conducted (Kenyon 1985:18–19). Clearly the
longhouse was an embodiment of past and present: interior layout echoed
meaningful elements of traditional longhouses, with multiple "fires," corn
hanging from rafters, and defined, segmented and tiered sitting arrangements, while the architecture of peaked log buildings with planked floors
reflected the contemporary world. In effect, the Council house was a very
real physical manifestation of historic Iroquois context and contemporary
innovation, where deliberations on the issues of the present and decisions on
hoped-for futures were made literally "within" historic knowledge of self and
community.

Through the 1840s, the Six Nations generally followed the settlement
trends established when they first arrived on the Grand, which suited the maintenance of personal corn plots and communally farmed river flats and islands.
Given that this pattern was maintained for over sixty years, any increase in
rural dispersal and village "abandonment" can be understood as both the limitations of trying to reside within a single locale for three generations (which
would have been atypical of past Iroquois settlement patterns), and the need to
accommodate second- and third-generation families who could not access lands
around areas of initial settlement since those lands and fields had already been
allocated, or encroached upon by non-Native settlement.

Indeed, the rapid rise of non-Native settlement represented the single most
dramatic change to the lower Grand between 1815 and the 1840s; i.e., the
transformation of the region into a Euro-Canadian rural setting. In large numbers, non-Native farmers were settling among and purchasing, often informally, tracts of land from individual Six Nations families. While this change to
the landscape had been initially encouraged by Brant (to influence agricultural
practices and lifeways), by the 1840s the demand for land was surpassing any
previous experience or capacity to accommodate. Disputes, squatting and other
conflicts were common occurrences: "These Indians suffer a good deal from
the encroachments of the whites, against whom it has been found impossible
entirely to protect them; and they have been rendered very uneasy and unsettled by the uncertainty attending the possession of their farms, in consequence

of the frequent removals rendered necessary by the successive surrenders of portions of their tract" (Winnett in Canada 1844–45).

These anxieties were over the increased sales of reserve land by the Indian Department to non-Natives, which for some Six Nation families meant multiple occasions of relocating households and clearing land. In light of continual Euro-Canadian land pressures, the Indian Department eventually decided to segregate Six Nations and Euro-Canadians by consolidating Native settlement and opening up the rest of the region to even further Euro-Canadian occupation (C. Johnston 1994; Weaver 1994a).

"Consolidation"

By 1847, the Indian Department was actively purchasing individual land-holdings and resettling families onto 100-acre lots within Tuscarora and the west part of Oneida Townships, while actively evicting non-Native squatters from that area (see fig. 5.1 for the location of this reserve). Selection of lots was determined by Iroquois families who chose where they would live within the re-configured reserve: "The land is not subdivided into regular lots. Each Indian selects his own locality, and takes as much land as he can cultivate, or wishes to reserve for himself, without the interference of the Chiefs. They generally are secure from the intrusion of other Indians; and they can transmit their land to their heirs, or convey their interest in it to any other Indian. If disputes arise, they are submitted to the Chiefs in Council, who decide upon the matter" (Winnett in Canada 1847). This meant that specific areas were settled by people belonging to the same nations and communities (e.g., Upper and Lower Mohawk, Kenyon 1986; Weaver 1994a). Issues related to internal factions between Christians and non-Christians, and between reformers and traditionalists, all aggravated by catastrophic bureaucracy and Indian Agent manipulation of authority and decision-making, were played out into the 20th century within this consolidated land mass (e.g., Kenyon 1990; Weaver 1994a, 1994b). By the late 1850s, the majority of the community was assumed to have fully adopted Euro-Canadian agricultural practices (Thoburn in Canada 1858; see also, Weaver 1994a:186), which lasted into the 20th century when wage labor off-reserve led to a decline in farming (Weaver 1994b:241). The degree to which this was the case will be examined next.

Subsistence on the Grand

The initial decades of settlement on the Grand saw preexisting subsistence and seasonal round activities adapted to the local area. While detailed, fixed place accounts were not available for this study to provide a rhythm of daily and seasonal subsistence rounds, accounts do reflect continued emphasis on corn agriculture, augmented by a winter deer hunt, and seasonally intensive harvests of key resources such as fish and sugar (see, for example, John Norton's late-18th-century description in C. Johnston 1964:27–28). The extent of variation within and between nations is not possible to discern from these data.

The winter hunt, extending from November to February, was primarily conducted by younger men and teenage boys; it took them away from the river, settlements, and in the boys' case, from the schoolhouse in Mohawk Village (C. Johnston 1964:60–61, 245; Kelsay 1984:531–533). Howison (1821:147) implied that many residents left Mohawk Village, reducing it to a ghost town when the hunting season began. Hunting territories were up to 100 kilometers away from the settlement (C. Johnston 1964:28), either north and west in what is today east Oxford County, east in the interior of the Niagara peninsula, or south and west of the Grand along Lake Erie (e.g., Winnett in Canada 1844–45).

Late winter sugaring occurred at camps (e.g., Kelsay 1984:531), which were formal sites that could be recognized when not in use (C. Johnston 1964:124). Fishing was also important, so much so that the Council sought specifically to have a fish sluice built as part of a dam proposed near Dunnville to allow fish to swim upstream. When that was not done, the Council complained that they were suffering from the decline in spawning runs upriver (UWORA John Brant letter book, March 13, 1832).

Beyond a strong emphasis on corn, accounts reported that beans, potatoes, sunflowers, and some wheat and oats were farmed, apple orchards were maintained, and livestock holdings consisted primarily of pig, poultry and some cattle (e.g., Britain 1834; Canada 1844–45, 1847, 1858; Shirreff 1835:157).

The impact of non-Native settlement on traditional subsistence became an increasing concern for the Six Nations Council. Beyond objecting to the loss of their river fishery (see also, Nellis in Canada 1847), the Council was concerned by 1811 with non-Native squatters establishing large farms on Six Nations land without rent payment or approval (C. Johnston 1964:282). The Council also sought the Crown, as early as 1806, to purchase lands west of "our narrow slip of land, surrounded by your settlements" (C. Johnston 1964:276), to protect their main winter hunting grounds.

European observers frequently referred to the propensity of the Six Nations to go hunting, and felt it interfered with British "civilization" efforts (e.g., Britain 1834; Canada 1844–45). Indeed, though the British authorities had fought Joseph Brant over his desire to sell reserve lands to create annuities, by 1829 the Crown was touting the sale of lands and rise of Euro-Canadian settlement as an effective assimilative policy to encourage the abandonment of the hunt in favor of farming:

> His Excellency the Lieut. Governor [Sir John Colborne] addressed the Six Nations to the following effect—By representing to them the necessity of their dividing their lands and Cultivating them for their own benefit; That the King had given them one of the finest tracts of land foreseeing that at some period they would be surrounded by a large population of Colonists and their hunting and fishing would be interrupted; That the time had arrived and that for their future Subsistence and Comfort they must become Agriculturalists in recommending that each family should take a certain Number of Acres to cultivate and the lots should descend to their Children and they should not have the power of disposing of them or Selling them, and the remainder of their lands should be leased for the benefit of their Children. (C. Johnston 1964:294)

The response from the Council (C. Johnston 1964:295–297) to this speech hardly acknowledged the suggested benefits of farming. As the Six Nations were "agriculturalists" already, Colborne's emphasis was self-evident, with sachems responding simply that they were indeed attending to their farming. And as the Council noted, the Six Nations already relied on agriculture for subsistence and surplus sale, since the hunt was collapsing. But hunting remained an important, augmentative subsistence activity for the Six Nations well into the 19th century. Accounts note that two-thirds of families were still winter hunting in the 1840s (Canada 1847), and as late as 1857, "some of the young men [still] hunt for deer in their neighbourhood" (Thorburn in Canada 1858).

The Six Nations do appear to have shifted to a more diversified set of subsistence practices, though the degree of this shift within and between nations varied significantly. To Euro-Canadians expecting and imagining "progress," any change in Six Nations practices represented change toward Euro-Canadian patterns (various in Canada 1844–5, 1847, 1858). These anticipatory observations, so similar to the observations offered mid-century for the Ojibwa as noted in chapter 3, can be tested against the patterns documented in census records.

19th-Century Six Nations Agricultural Practices. Available records include an 1843 census (i.e., immediately before consolidation) taken by the Indian Department (table 5.1; Winnett in Canada 1844–5; C. Johnston 1964:305–311). The consolidated numbers for the entire Six Nations settlement on the Grand indicates that 57 percent of landholders held 10 acres of cleared land or less, and that the ratio of cattle holdings (either meat or dairy) to pigs was 1:3, while very few farmers raised sheep. The 1843 manuscript portion of the census (PAC RG10 170336–170340) for the Upper and Lower Mohawk indicate that 61 percent and 45 percent of households, respectively, held 10 acres or less of cleared land. Significantly, while only 5 percent of the Upper Mohawk held more than 50 acres of cleared land, 26 percent of the Lower Mohawk did, with one farm holding 128 acres. In part, this reflects the legacy of smaller parcels held within Mohawk Village, and that the Lower Mohawk farms operated on extensive river flats. This differing emphasis is also reflected by the fact that half of the Lower Mohawk owned ploughs and 24 percent had barns, while only a third of the Upper Mohawk had ploughs and 12 percent had barns. Over 70 percent of all Mohawk households held cattle and pigs, though numbers varied for the Upper and Lower Mohawk, and only six Lower Mohawk households raised sheep. Crop data are not available, though Winnett (Canada 1847) indicated that small farms (which he describes as 5 acres or less) tended to focus exclusively on corn and potatoes cultivated by hoe.

The census data from 1843 suggest that, just prior to consolidation, over half of Six Nations households appeared to be operating garden plot subsistence farming of 10 acres or less, without cash crop harvests and livestock limited to household needs (meat, dairy, labor), while upwards of a quarter of households were engaged in larger scale operations and surplus yield farming tied to the broader rural cash crop economy.

The 1861 manuscript census for Tuscarora Township, taken over a decade after consolidation,[12] offers further insight into the nature of agricultural activities at mid-century (table 5.2). Given the size of the Six Nations community, I chose to concentrate solely on District 1 of the census, which abuts the river. In that district, 196 households were recorded, representing 225 families (i.e., 29 [15 percent] households were made up of two or more families). Of these 196 households, 74 percent (n = 146) lived in single-story log cabins, while 20 percent lived in single-story frame structures.

There were 221 landholdings inventoried in the agricultural portion of the census—in other words 98 percent of families were "agriculturalists." Of these, 36 percent (n = 79) held 10 acres or less cultivated land (crop and pasture), and 27 percent (n = 59) held 11–20 acres. At the other end of the spectrum, 20 percent (n = 44) held 30–100 acres. No one held over 100 acres of cleared land.

TABLE 5.1 Cleared Landholdings for Six Nations (Aggregate Census) and Upper and Lower Mohawk (Manuscript Census) in 1843

Acres	Six Nations (N = 404)	Upper Mohtawk (N = 67)	Lower Mohawk (N = 46)
0–5	146 (36%)	21 (31%)	13 (28%)
6–10	85 (21%)	20 (30%)	8 (17%)
11–20	67 (17%)	6 (9%)	9 (20%)
21–50	68 (17%)	17 (25%)	4 (9%)
51–100	28 (7%)	3 (5%)	8 (17%)
100+	10 (2%)	0	4 (9%)

Note: N = number of landholders

TABLE 5.2 District 1 Agricultural Data for Tuscarora Township (North) from the 1861 Census for 221 Farming Landholders

Product	Farmers Raising crop/ livestock	Average acres per household	Average Bushels per household	Average number	Brant County ac/bu or number	Wentworth County
Wheat	112 (51%)	8.3	110		21/315	14/224
Barley	19 (9%)	3.8	88		na	na
Peas	65 (29%)	3.0	55		4/96	6/107
Oats	66 (30%)	3.8	99		5/136	6/229
Buckwheat	43 (19%)	2.4	30		na	na
Corn	138 (65%)	2.1	53		1/35	na
Potatoes	130 (62%)	1.1	46		1/128	1/146
Beans	90 (41%)		4.0		na	na
Maple sugar	113 (54%)			208 lb	na	na
Steers	91 (41%)			2.7	na	na
Milch cows	111 (50%)			2.2	3.6	4.2
Horses	79 (36%)			2.1	3.7	3.8
Pigs	120 (55%)			7.1	6.9	7.1
Sheep	3 (1%)			10	12.6	12.1

Note: Household averages are based on the number of households with the product. County averages are taken from Canada 1863. County data are from the aggregated compilation (Canada 1863), so average acres and yields are based on all farming households. Unfortunately, this limits comparative value as the Euro-Canadian figures are thus deflated.

The 1861 data indicate a greater diversity of crops than seen for the Ojibwa or Delaware, and a greater number of families raising those crops. However, the predominant crop emphasis remained corn and potatoes (both raised by about two-thirds of all households). Per family corn yield was 53 bushels, a figure notably similar to Heidenreich's (1971) suggestion that a "typical" family of six Huron in the 17th century required 54 bushels of corn a year for subsistence. Beyond traditional crops, wheat was also important (51 percent raised the crop). In addition, a small number of farms raised barley and rye (three farms for the latter), confirming the rather selective emphasis the missionaries at Six Nations (Nelles and Elliot) made in the Canada 1858 report, when they stated that: "formerly few of them [Six Nations families] raised any thing else than Indian Corn and potatoes, but now they raise wheat and other grain." The general implication, that all Six Nations families raised wheat and other grain, is a clear reflection of the observer's own imagined expectations of Indigenous progress toward a European ideal, while at the same time relegated contemporary, predominant practices and diversity to past realities.

Winnett (Canada 1847, 1858) noted that "on the large farms the field labor is performed by the men—the Indian corn cultivation always excepted, as on both large and small farms that culture is always performed by the women." Men focusing on grains illustrates that, with a declining viability of the hunt and increased viability of farming, these new innovations were accepted as male labor contributions to the family. So the plough and scythe represented men's revisions, while the hoe continued to represent reinforcement of tradition within women's labor.

Livestock emphasis in the 1861 data was on pigs, though dairy and steer cattle were also well represented. However, all livestock categories are somewhat lower than that seen for the Ojibwa and Delaware, which could reflect the fact that by 1861 the Six Nations were surrounded by urban centers where barreled meat and dairy products could be obtained. As well, according to Thorburn (in Canada 1858), Six Nations farmers continued to let cattle, pigs and horses graze in the woods during early spring (referred to as a "hard feed"), to the detriment of the livestock.

The 1,871 cultivated landholdings were also briefly examined for District 1 of Tuscarora Township (Canada 1873). Cleared land among the Six Nations reveals greater distribution of larger cultivated landholdings, reflected as a less extreme "J-curve" distribution graph profile (i.e., majority at one end of the spectrum) than seen in either 1843 or 1861 (fig. 5.4). Nonetheless, despite almost a century of settlement on the Grand River, just under half of all residents still maintained only 20 acres or less of cultivated land, a pattern inconsistent with that seen for non-Aboriginal communities.

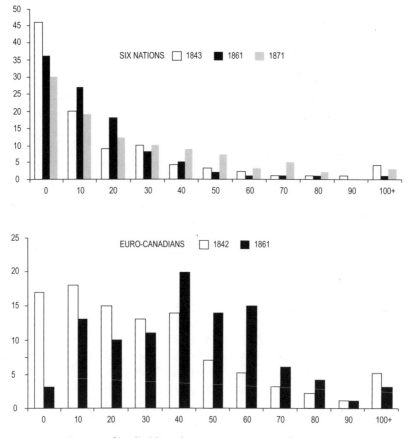

FIGURE 5.4. Percent of landholdings by 10-acre increments for the Six Nations along the Grand River (upper graph), and Euro-Canadians as represented by Mosa Township in Middlesex County (lower graph).

For example, Kenyon and Ferris (1985) noted that clearance rates for Mosa Township (west Middlesex County) in 1842 exhibited a modest "J-curve" (fig. 5.4), at a time when extensive settlement and clearing had been occurring in the township for less than twenty years. This is a fairly typical early settlement pattern for Euro-Canadian communities (McInnis 1992; Russell 1983; Wood 2000), when initial growth of farms was constrained by extensive forest clearing. But in subsequent decades, this pattern changed as communities became more of a rural agricultural landscape. The pattern that emerges then is more a modal or bell-shaped distribution of cleared landholdings. The persistence of the J-curve distribution for the Six Nations into the 1870s, despite the shift in the surrounding region from pioneer to rural landscape, reflects the persistence of subsistence-level farming in these communities, despite the fact that a third of families had adopted a modified form of surplus-yield farming by that time.

Archaeology at Mohawk Village

Archaeological data from Mohawk Village adds insight into the general archaeological history of continuities and discontinuities constructed from the written data just reviewed. Mohawk Village went from a cluster of houses, a church, a schoolhouse, and a short-lived council house in the late 18th century to a small number of houses by 1830, to a rural area by the mid–19th century. By the 1852 census, there were three Mohawk families in the town, including Catherine John (a daughter of Joseph Brant), her son William, and the home of Peter and Elizabeth Powless. In addition, across the street from the Chapel was the Mohawk Institute, a residential school run by missionaries of the New England Company and Church of England (C. Johnston 1964; Weaver 1994a). In 1858, the Institute relocated to the west, and by the 1861 census, only Elizabeth Powless remained in the village.

Archaeological surveys of Mohawk Village were conducted by Thomas and Ian Kenyon and David Faux in the 1970s and 1980s. In all, thirteen locales were identified on either side of the Chapel and the original Mohawk Road (fig. 5.5; Faux 1984; Kenyon and Ferris 1984; I. Kenyon and T. Kenyon 1986:24). While no definitive locale can be associated with the initial Joseph Brant household, several have been associated with other prominent families of the Upper Mohawk community that had originally come from New York.

One large scatter of material northeast of the Chapel and south of Mohawk Road (Area A) corresponds well with an 1845 property holdings map that identifies the area as belonging to the Powless family. The Powlesses came from Mohawk Valley in the 1780s, the adult male at that time being Paulus Sah-on-wad-i, a Mohawk chief, contemporary of Joseph Brant, and schoolmaster. The land his family held included a parcel to the east of the Chapel and near the Brant family's holdings. In the 1843 census, Peter Powless—one of Paulus's sons—held 10 acres of cleared land, and according to the 1852 census, Peter (aged 68 at the time) and his wife Elizabeth resided in a one-story log cabin. Living with Peter and Elizabeth in 1852 were Mary Babcock, Neillen Davids, and Mary Chase, aged 9, 20, and 22, all nonresidents. Peter's brother, Paulus Powless (aged 73), also resided in the village in 1852, living at the home of William John, the son of Catherine John,

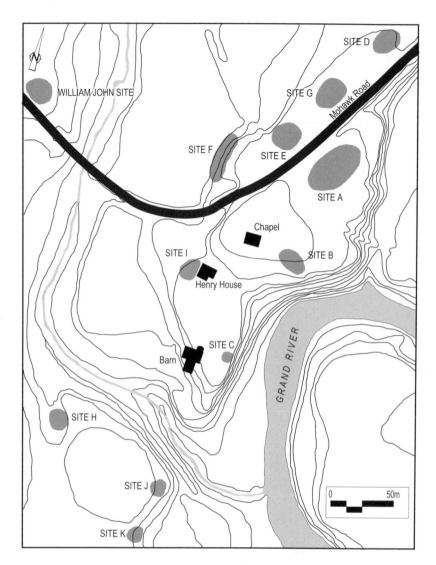

FIGURE 5.5. Archaeological sites at Mohawk Village, based on Thomas and Ian Kenyon surveys. Site A encompasses the Powless residences. Site B was likely the home of Catherine John, while her son's residence is located to the west. Sites E (residence) and F (school midden) are associated with the Mohawk Institute. Other sites are not affiliated. Additional sites are known to the south and east of the map, including Paulus Powless's home situated midway down the eastern side of the oxbow.

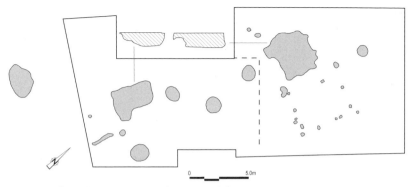

FIGURE 5.6. Settlement patterns documented during excavations at Mohawk Village, Area A. Solid line depicts limits of shovel shining. The early ash pit is to the south of the shined area. Features to the south of the dashed line are associated with the early occupation. Cellar profiles depicted are not to scale.

who at the time was a widow living in a third residence in the village with her granddaughter. Paulus was widowed at the time but had been married to another of Joseph Brant's daughters and had moved in with his wife's extended family. Also residing in the William John house in 1852 was Paulus's grandson, who, in 1857, would inherit through matrilineal descent the Brant Turtle clan Sachem title of Tekarihoken (Brant-Sero 1899; G. Smith 1914).

In 1861, the Powless household was reduced to Elizabeth (aged 81), who still held 6 acres of land and lived with Mary and Jonathan Powless (aged 18 and 9, respectively), and Kitty John. Whether Mary is the same Mary Babcock of 1852 is not known, though, at 81, presumably Elizabeth required support. Elizabeth left the village sometime in the 1860s, living on until 1877 when she died at 96 years of age, according to her headstone in the Mohawk Chapel cemetery.

The location of the Powless family property east of the Mohawk Chapel became a focus of archaeological interest on the eve of the 200th anniversary of the founding of Mohawk Village. In preparation for a celebration of the bicentennial and visit by Queen Elizabeth II honoring the event, landscape alterations and topsoil stripping for a parking lot occurred adjacent to the Chapel. Ministry of Culture archaeologist Ian Kenyon recognized the parking lot as the location of an archaeological site and quickly arranged with all parties involved, including the Six Nations, to conduct a salvage excavation.

The area stripped for the parking lot revealed a tight cluster of features (fig. 5.6), including a series of out-features (ash and spoil pits) and two

keyhole shaped cellars. The southerly of the two cellars and associated features date from about 1800 to the late 1830s, while the more northerly cellar, post moulds, and a limited number of out-features date from the late
1830s to the 1860s. Given landholding and census data, it is believed that
the two cellars were sequentially occupied by members of the Powless family,
and that the later house was the residence of Peter and Elizabeth.

Archaeology of the Powless Homes—Settlement Patterns

The south, or early, occupation consisted of a classic root cellar with a keyhole plan (3 × 2 m by 85 cm deep) and stepped profile. Internal stratigraphy
revealed an occupational deposit sealed by post-use fill; the latter consists
of architectural debris deposited when the structure was taken down and
included a large number of molded red clay bricks that would have framed
a hearth/chimney. An iron hearth hook was found but no iron stove elements. While no foundation or cornerstone was evident, this cellar would
have existed underneath the floor of the cabin, implying the use of floor-
boards. Over one hundred mostly hand-wrought nails were recovered, as well
as door hinges and a door latch, and over three hundred fragments of flat
window glass. No plaster or other interior wall treatments were recovered. A
small number of posts south of the cellar may indicate a veranda or entrance
shelter, suggesting an orientation facing the Chapel and perhaps the Brant
house beyond. A narrow, linear feature southeast of the cellar was devoid of
artifacts and likely was an edge-of-roof drip line. Surrounding the cellar to
the south, east and north were a series of features of limited use duration,
some of which served as refuse pits. Notable was a large pit south of the
cellar (2.8 × 1.8 m), more than a half-meter deep and filled with dense ash,
charcoal, refuse and animal bone. Assuming the cellar was fully under the
cabin floor, and considering feature locations and drip line, an approximate
cabin size of 5 × 5 m (16 × 16 ft) is suggested.

The north feature cluster was dominated by a very large cellar (3.7 × 2.9 m
and 1.1 m deep), that had a similar keyhole plan and stepped profile. To the
east of the cellar were a number of post moulds for a veranda, suggesting the
orientation of the house was toward the river. This is consistent with a number of paintings done in the 1850s and 1860s of Mohawk Village by Robert Whale and his son John Claude Whale, which depict either one or two
single-story log cabins with peaked roofs facing the river north of the chapel
(Kenyon and Ferris 1984). This differing cabin orientation between the early
and late residences also speaks to changes that had occurred to the village at

the time the two Powless cabins were built, with the earlier one facing into the village, and the latter facing out to the river and the rural countryside the area had become.

The living strata in the cellar were overlain by architectural fill, and this material was subsequently overlain by post-occupation infilling. Bricks were mostly recovered from the north end of the feature, consistent with pictorial depictions of a chimney along the north sidewall. Artifacts related to the architecture included several fragments of an iron stove and a clay chimney pot. Close to seven hundred nails were recovered (mostly machine cut), along with a handful of screws, over a thousand fragments of flat glass, door and window latches, door locks and keys, and a small quantity (thirty-five fragments) of plaster, which would have coated the interior walls of the cabin. There were far fewer out-features, although an ash pit similar to that found in the south component was present north of the cellar. A thin sheet midden located to the east of the cellar likely replaced the need for refuse features. Based on veranda/porch width and out-feature placement, a slightly larger 5.5 × 5.5 m size is suggested for this cabin.

The cellars, windows, peaked shingled roofs (and likely interior lofts), and the plastering of interior walls for the later cabin are features consistent with Guldenzopf's (1986) elite house form. This type of residence varies from the earthen-floored central hearth pattern noted more widely in New York, and for at least the Cayuga along the Grand as late as the 1840s, which archaeologically would be more noticeable as an absence of architectural artifacts or features like cellars, porches or foundation cornerstones, and more differential artifact distributions across the site (e.g., Lantz 1980; R. Sutton 2003; Warrick 2004).

Archaeology of the Powless Homes—Subsistence Patterns

Of 6,997 faunal elements recovered, 2,719 were identified (Berg 2005c). Domesticates were an important part of the Powless diet, representing 78 percent of identified elements in the early features, and 54 percent in the later features. Identified domestic bone from the early features includes 82 percent pig, while that number declines to 42 percent in the later features (table 5.3). Notable is the quantity of fowl. While not represented in census records or most descriptions of farming life, poultry would have been an easy food source to maintain near the cabin, requiring relatively little effort to raise. As such it is not surprising to see fowl so strongly represented in the Powless household assemblages, especially the later household which encompassed the latter part

TABLE 5.3 Identified Faunal Remains from Mohawk Village, Area A

	Early features	Late features
Domesticates		
Pig	725 (82%)	324 (42%)
Chicken	120 (13.5%)	302 (39%)
Cow	34 (4%)	82 (11%)
Sheep	5 (0.5%)	64 (8%)
Cat	0	71
Dog	7	0
Total domesticates	**891**	**843**
Other species		
Hare/squirrel	33	47
Chipmunk/vole	19	4
Norway rat	1	204
Racoon	1	0
Muskrat	0	34
Bear	2	0
Deer	8	24
Total mammals	**64**	**313**
Passenger pigeon	16	9
Goose	3	9
Grouse	2	0
Duck	0	11
Total birds	**21**	**29**
Lake sturgeon	2	0
Alewife	0	2
Pike	2	0
Sucker	18	74
Redhorse	67	129
Bullhead	0	33
Rock bass	41	8
Sunfish	0	5
Walleye	4	12
Drum	1	0
Total fish	**135**	**263**
Snapping turtle	1	0
Frog	3	68
Freshwater mussel	34	41
Saltwater bivalve	0	3

of Peter and Elizabeth's lives as a couple, at a time perhaps when they had less ability to raise and care for other livestock.

Consistent with the census data, sheep tends to be rare or nonexistent on most Six Nations Iroquois sites (e.g., Berg 2005a, 2005b, 2005c; I. Kenyon and T. Kenyon 1986; R. Sutton 2003), part of a broader phenomenon that was also noted for the Ojibwa and Delaware. The absence arises in part from the fact that sheep, as pastured herd animals, were more of a European agricultural focus, ill-suited to southern Ontario prior to the opening up of large acreage and establishment of extensive pasture lands (R. Jones 1946:76–77). With second generation Euro-Canadian farmers also favoring pork over mutton (e.g., Ferris and Kenyon 1983; Kenyon et al. 1984), the commodity value of sheep was likely more due to harvesting wool than meat (e.g., McInnis 1987). Of course, this second-stage value to raising sheep was only realized after a further heavy labor investment in shearing, which required specialized training and equipment. So from both archaeological and census data, there is clearly very little investment in sheep as a livestock focus on Native-occupied sites. Only the later Powless household had 8 percent sheep bone, perhaps obtained from Brantford or from nearby Euro-Canadian farmers.

Nondomesticates in the faunal assemblage from the early features are represented by a wide variety of game and fish that would have been obtained around Mohawk Village. Deer is marginally present. Fish includes small quantities of species that either would have been taken in the Great Lakes (e.g., walleye), or perhaps harvested during spawning runs in the Grand (e.g., lake sturgeon, drum). That the latter two species are only present in the early features attests to the impact damming the lower Grand had on upriver subsistence.

While wild game is only an augmentative part of the Powless family diet, greater frequencies are noted for the later period. Significant increases in fish and modest increases in deer, duck and bivalves suggest the active maintenance of all of the activities associated with procuring these species through a period when precisely the opposite would be assumed. On the other hand, this may also be a reflection of the village reverting to a more rural setting through this time. Muskrat certainly speaks to incidental shoreline hunting, or to the use of muskrat pelts in production of cottage industries. Lastly, the identification of a few fragments of Atlantic species of bivalve suggests either exchange or procurement of the item as a food or material exotic.

Only limited floral remains have been identified from the site, including a few fragments of walnut shell, a carbonized plum pit from the later cellar, and seven cupules of traditional northern flint maize (five from the early cellar and ash pit, and two from the later cellar).

The subsistence emphasis for the Powless family was the maintenance of food supplies raised or caught by the household (i.e., pork, chicken and game), augmented by some beef and sheep, which were either raised, purchased or traded. What is distinct about the Powless pattern is that in the latter part of their lives, Peter and Elizabeth were either not raising food crops, or such activities were too marginal for notation (e.g., perhaps a small garden plot by the cabin). While 10 acres of oats were noted in 1852, these were likely raised directly as a commodity, or by someone else renting the land. In this one way, the Powless household appears to be consistent with non-Aboriginal trends, where the typical pattern was never true self-sufficiency (in the sense of subsistence arising solely on the farm), but rather augmented to some degree by commodity or market surplus farming (e.g., McCalla 1985; McInnis 1987:37). But I suspect the Powlesses were less adopting a surplus farming strategy and more a strategy conducive to their needs as an elderly Mohawk couple (see also, Rotman 2005).

Archaeology of the Powless Homes—Material Culture

The material culture recovered displays the obvious temporal changes that occurred through the 19th century for all classes of mass-produced goods. Within the Powless households, this temporal variation is also reflective of provisioning patterns. Specifically, the early features contain classes of artifacts obtained exclusively through annual Indian Department goods distributions. Archaeologically, the early feature assemblage reflects this provisioning in the form of silver ribbon brooches, earbobs and other silver items, guns and gun parts, shot and muskets, firesteels, fishing hooks, awls, needles, and cut fragments of brass or copper, likely from kettles. Also found were smoking pipes, including fragments of a "coat of arms" variety made for the Indian Department and found on the Ojibwa Bellamy site and other Six Nations sites (Ferris 1989; I. Kenyon and T. Kenyon 1986).

The tenor of the rhetoric employed by the State's catastrophic bureaucracy administering the Six Nations during the 1820s to 1850s (e.g., Britain 1834, 1839; Canada 1844–45, 1847, 1858) can be heard in the increasing policy chorus justifying an end to the costly practice of annuity distributions. While cost was a clear motivation behind the shift in practice, various alternate rationalizations dominated the rhetoric, e.g., that these distributions fostered a "dependency" among the Six Nations on the Indian Department and failed to teach communities good economic management, or that trinkets and hunting equipment encouraged "heathen" tendencies and discouraged

"Christian" agrarian lifeways. By the late 1830s, distributions had declined to include only cloth, blankets and gun equipment, and by 1858, goods distributions were discontinued in favor of cash annuities administered by the Indian Agent on behalf of the Six Nations Council (Canada 1858).

While a material "dependency" rhetoric suited the agenda of the colonial state, it hardly reflected the material reality of Iroquois households. Joseph Brant certainly obtained large quantities of finery, enough to impress all visitors who dined with the family. Further, as accounts illustrated, households in the village included an "abundance of the necessities of life" (C. Johnston 1964:60), including tableware, furniture, window panes, etc. These items would not have been obtained through Indian Department distributions, but initially through merchants at Niagara or at the head of the lake (i.e., near present-day Hamilton, see Triggs 2004), transported overland or by bateaux up the river. After the War of 1812, formal transportation corridors were established between Niagara and Hamilton, and people traveled to obtain dry goods, or purchased items from traders traveling up the river. By the 1820s, general stores appeared around Brantford and in smaller communities to the south and west. With the completion of the Welland Canal in 1829, the region significantly opened up, giving rise to a regularized distribution and flow of goods, and facilitating an increase in the number of merchants based locally (e.g., Kenyon 1992).

The later Powless assemblage had several items that would have been obtained locally, including iron stove fragments, a saltglaze beer bottle from the Wm Spencer brewery, a stoneware crock made from Morton & Co. (both companies based in Brantford), and a ceramic chimney pot. Also, ceramic plate sherds were recovered from the later cellar with a black transferware pattern depicting a traditional Iroquois male hunter with bow and arrow shooting at a stag. The plate was manufactured in England for the Kirby Hotel in Brantford, which opened in 1854 (Kenyon and Ferris 1984:fig. 13). Lastly, some glass medicinal or spirit bottles from manufacturers in New York were recovered. Independent provisioning for the necessities and fineries of life were easily met by the Powless households through the period of settlement.

Functional/Artifact Class Considerations. A detailed catalogue of the material culture recovered from the Powless homesteads was grouped into broad functional categories (table 5.4) modified from historic site analyses such as South (1977), Resnick (1988), Groover (2003), and MacDonald (2002). I recognize that this kind of "lumping" of artifact classes is of limited interpretive use, since these groupings impose assumptions of function potentially alien

TABLE 5.4 Artifact Counts from Mohawk Village, Powless Household Excavations

Category	Early features	Late features
Meal systems	1061 (21.7%)	1572 (17.5%)
Ceramics (refined and coarse)	950	1314
Glassware and containers	96	221
Cutlery	15	37
Armaments/hunting	59 (1.2%)	17
Gun gear	55	17
Fish hook/harpoon	3	0
War club spear point	1	0
Architecture	647 (13.2%)	2097 (23.3%)
Flat glass	351	1005
Metal (nails, hinges, locks, etc.)	275	1008
Bricks	21	16
Plaster	0	35
Chimney pot	0	33
Domestic furniture	7	19
Furniture elements	5	10
Clockworks	1	0
Hearth/stove	1	9
Personal	376 (7.7%)	931 (10.3%)
Smoking pipes	199	404
Trade silver	25	1
Costume jewelry	1	16
Beads	43	220
Clothing (buttons, buckles, etc.)	71	208
Coins/discs	16	8
Combs/razors	4	14
Writing implements	14	40
Eyeglass lens	0	6
Toys	1	12
Mouth harps	2	2
Tools and equipment: Domestic activities	19 (0.4%)	61 (0.7%)
Thimbles/pins	6	37
Scissors	3	2
Bi-pointed needles	2	7

TABLE 5.4 Artifact Counts from Mohawk Village, Powless Household
Excavations *(cont.)*

Category	Early features	Late features
Bone-handled awls/punches	4	2
Firesteels	2	0
Tin scoop/bucket	0	8
Whetstone fragments	2	4
Files	0	1
Transportation	3	12
Wagon furniture/sleigh bell	3	12
Miscellaneous Iron rings/washers	6	5
Faunal remains	2713 (55.6%)	4280 (47.6%)
Total	**4881**	**8999**

to the site inhabitants themselves, and so mask context-specific variation in object use. Nonetheless, at a general level it can be noted that the Powless data deviate from South Carolina or Frontier patterns, and from patterns seen at other 19th-century, southern Ontario, Euro-Canadian domestic sites (e.g., Ferris and Kenyon 1983; I. Kenyon and T. Kenyon 1982; MacDonald 1997, 2002). As such they are worth exploring here.

There was limited variation between the cellar and out-features for the early period, and the later features lacked any sizeable content with the exception of the cellar, so artifact patterns for all early and for all late features are grouped in order to provide a basic early–late comparison. Early features are dominated by faunal remains (55.6 percent), which is significantly higher than faunal percentages from non-Native domestic sites, where they range between 20 and 30 percent. Meal system or kitchen artifacts in the early features make up just over 21 percent of the assemblage, well below the 45–60 percent range seen for Euro-Canadian sites, or for the South Carolina pattern. Architectural items, at 12.9 percent, are within the range noted for Euro-Canadian sites.

The later features had more from most artifact categories, presumably due to improved material-good provisioning by this time. Variation from the early features included a much higher quantity of architectural items, especially flat glass fragments and nails. This contributed to lower percentages for meal system artifacts and faunal remains. At a gross scale, this reflects similar trends noted by South (1977), but means little other than the later Powless home was either more substantial, or, more likely, that there was less harvesting or dismantling of the structure after abandonment, and thus greater contribution of architectural artifacts to the cellar fill.

A decline in armaments/hunting items from later features is notable. But given that faunal data suggest an increase in wild game procurement in the later features, the distinction may be less a decline in hunting and perhaps either a decline in Peter Powless's own ability, or greater conservation of muskets after the distribution of guns by the Indian Department had stopped.

Another counterintuitive trend is the significant increase in glass beads in the later features: five times as many as in the earlier features. This is substantiated in flotation samples, where early feature fill averaged 0.3 beads per liter and later features averaged two beads per liter. The early assemblage was made up almost entirely of seed beads (plus three tubes and one facetted), while there were thirty-seven nonseed beads in the later assemblage, including tubes, facetted and large round forms. Most striking was the difference in color between the two assemblages, with less than 10 percent of the beads in the early features being a color other than white, while 97 percent of the late beads were not white. Speck (1955:54) noted that the early-19th-century Iroquois beadwork he examined was characterized by simple beaded borders using minor frequencies of white beads. However, by the mid–19th century that beadwork became more elaborate and incorporated multi-colored floral designs (Speck 1955:64).[13] This pattern is reflected in the Powless households.

The higher frequency of beads, along with a notable increase in pins and thimbles, may reflect a cottage industry practiced by Elizabeth and/or the resident women, making beaded craftwork such as moccasins and bags (Karklins 1992).[14] Early and late assemblage differences are also noted for clothing items (e.g., buttons—early: 51; late: 188), and may suggest that seamstress or tailor work was carried out by some of the residents.

The buttons, as well as shoe fragments, buckles, blacking bottles, and other clothing items, also reflect changing clothing fashions through this time. From the late 18th century to the mid–19th century, Iroquois dress incorporated European fashions such as long coats, shirts, boots, breeches and undergarments (Ferris 1984; Karklins 1992), alongside more traditional headdresses, sashes, robes, moccasins, face paint, beaded clothing and silver jewelry (C. Johnston 1964; Karklins 1992). Indeed, maintenance of traditional dress elements was identified as late as the 1830s by Confederacy Council members as "a sign of our independence of the rules and customs of the whites" (Echo Hill, Indian Council, Feb 4, 1834; in Faux 1985:22). But by the mid–19th century, increased access to mass-produced clothing led to colonial fashions being incorporated into family wardrobes, and by the 1870s, suits were the formal dress of sachems (Karklins 1992; Weaver 1994a, 1994b). Despite this, beaded objects, the use of silver ornaments, wampum, headdresses and war clubs continued through the 19th century to be key signifiers of identity and historically based distinctiveness.

Rather than view these clothing trends as acculturative or evidence of cultural abandonment, the long-term pattern suggests additive incorporation and innovative revision. For example, the two Powless household assemblages reflect an expected temporal decline in the kinds of artifacts associated with Indian Department distributions, particularly for trade silver items (down from twenty-five items in the early features to one). But there is a notable increase (from one to sixteen items) of costume jewelry in the later features, especially rhinestone-studded pins and pendants, finger rings and bangles for earrings. This suggests a replacement strategy for items of personal adornment (Beauchamp 1903; Karklins 1992). Given that silver items were still manufactured by the Iroquois themselves, costume jewelry seems to have filled a personal aesthetics void, without inheriting the identity signifiers that silver ornaments continued to have through the 19th century.

Also noteworthy is that someone in the later household collected objects of Native antiquity. Found in the cellar were three ancient artifacts, including a Meadowood point, a Vanport point, and the bowl portion of a 16th-17th century ring pipe. Though Archaic and Transitional Woodland components are known in the area of the Powless cellars, Early, Middle and Terminal Woodland components are not. Clearly these objects were found elsewhere, brought home and kept, presumably conveying very different meaning to the possessor than they would have had to a non-Native discoverer.

The examination of the Powless household assemblages through the classification of artifacts into broad functional categories has illustrated some general variation between those two households, and with 19th-century, southern Ontario, Euro-Canadian domestic site patterns. However, differences noted at this gross level encapsulate many factors of broadly temporal, depositional or methodological nature, so comparisons can be subject to arbitrary interpretation. To access deeper insights into the material manifestation of the Powlesses' daily rituals of lived life, and the ways they negotiated tradition and innovation through the rise of the colonialist state, I next will examine some specific artifact contextual patterns.

Powless Households' Ceramic Trends. In both early and late features, a wide range of refined ceramics were recovered, dominated by flatware (plates), "teas" (referring only to cups and saucers) and bowls, along with a few serving dishes, condiment bowls, teapots, pitchers, and coarse earthenware pots

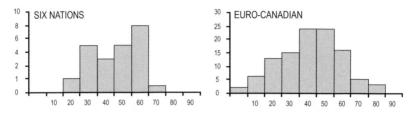

FIGURE 5.7. Number of Six Nations (*n* = 23) and Euro-Canadian (*n* = 107) ceramic sherd assemblages by percent of printed sherds (in increments of 10 percent). Six Nations data come from the Mohawk Village collections, I. Kenyon and T. Kenyon 1986; Kenyon 1987b; Warrick 1998, 2004. Euro-Canadian data are from I. Kenyon and T. Kenyon 1986: fig. 13.

and bowls—collectively the tools of formal and family dining and preparation of meals.

Counts of decorated, nonvessel attributable ceramic sherds included 56 percent transfer-printed wares from the early features, the most abundant "expensive" category of ceramic commonly available for purchase from merchants (e.g., Kenyon 1991, 1992; Miller 1980, 1991), while the later occupation had 62 percent transfer wares. In comparing sherd counts from mostly surface-collected Six Nations Iroquois sites along the Grand River, Ian and Thomas Kenyon (1986:21) noted variation between Iroquois sites, and between the general Iroquois pattern and a broader Euro-Canadian Ontario Rural Domestic Pattern they had previously documented for over one hundred 19th-century sites (1982, 1986; fig. 5.7). Six Nations sites with 51–80 percent printed sherds—all above the Euro-Canadian mean of 46 percent printed wares—all mostly date after the early 1820s and came from Mohawk Village and upriver homesteads of larger farm operations. The sherds from sites with lower percentages mostly came from downriver communities, including residences from the more traditional Cayuga and Onondaga nations. These variations suggested to the Kenyons (1986:22) variable exposure to and incorporation of British-imported trends in dining rather than spatial differences in wealth.

Sherd analyses are helpful for ordering limited, surface-collected samples of material, and in the case of the Six Nations, do reveal broad-scale differences from general colonial patterns. However, the limitations of sherd analyses, especially for interpreting social dimensions of artifact use, have been noted (e.g., Beaudry et al. 1991; Majewski and O'Brien 1987). In addition, several factors would have influenced and constrained choice during the purchase of ceramics (Klein 1991). Indeed, Ian Kenyon (1992) has shown that, prior to the establishment of a fixed transportation network regularizing distribution from wholesalers to retailers, retail supplies were constrained by seasonal availability and the common occurrence of what merchants referred to as "stockouts," meaning very limited choice of stock in the weeks or months before the shop was restocked. This meant that, during the first few decades of the 19th century, choice was limited for consumers to what was locally available in stock, regardless of preference or economic capacity. This constraint on the Grand River would have eased by the early 1830s, when supply and distribution needs were met with the creation of multiple road networks and the Welland Canal.

Given the higher-than-average printed percentages on post-1830s Six Nations sites, use of expensive wares *could* reflect some greater capacity to actively choose ceramics in keeping with "fashion" trends for those wares, unimpeded by limited choice. It is certainly the case in the later Powless household assemblage that there is more evidence of brown transferware ceramic "setts" (multiple settings of plate and teaware), likely reflecting a greater capacity to exercise consumer choice. There was also a tea set of the flow blue "Versailles" pattern, multiple plates of blue and black willow pattern, a tea and bowl service of blue-sponged and Ironstone cups and saucers, all of which were only available late in the occupation during the time Elizabeth lived there as a widow, underscoring the age and gendered agency of dining customs and choice in the household (Rotman 2005).

Ceramic Vessel Analyses. Ceramic fragments that could be assigned to a vessel form were separated from general sherd analyses. Vessel form was based primarily on rim sherd shape, angle, body form, foot ring, and location of decoration. Multiple sherds from the same vessel were not counted separately. Both the early and late features show a roughly similar variation in the three dining wares of plates, saucers, and bowls (table 5.5). There are also a similar number of teapots from each period, including black basalt and Chinese export porcelain examples from the early cellar and an ironstone one from the later cellar. Other vessel forms included platters, tureens, condiment or slop bowls and salt cellars.

Though the samples are small, a consistent variation seen across the two components is the difference between larger and smaller sized plates. A variety of plate sizes were available in the 19th century, including tea and dessert plates (muffins and twifflers), 5–8 inches in diameter; and larger dinner, table or soup plates, 9–10 inches in diameter (Coysh 1982; Kenyon 1991; Miller 1991). Though not exclusively, smaller plates were typically used during the serving

TABLE 5.5 Vessel Forms Recovered from Early and Late Powless Households

	Early features	P/T/B¹	Number	Late features	P/T/B	Number expensive
Large plates (> 8 in.)	28 (76%)		10 (36%)	17 (57%)		11 (65%)
Small Plates (≤ 8 in.)	9 (24%)		6 (67%)	13 (43%)		13 (100%)
Plates of indeterminate size	2		2	10		8
Total plates	39	45%	18 (46%)	40	44%	32 (80%)
Saucers	35	40%	16	35	39%	27
Plate:saucer ratio	1.1			1.1		
Cups	21		13	35		22
Total teas	56		29 (52%)	70		49 (70%)
Total plate/ tea	95		47 (49%)	110		81 (74%)
Bowls	13	15%		15	17%	
Teapots	4			3		
Other	5			8		

¹ Refers to percent of plates/teas (saucers only)/and bowls in the assemblage

of an afternoon tea, for desserts, or during single-serving meals like breakfast, while the larger plates were more commonly used for main courses during the principal dinner meal of the day, associated with casseroles or roasted meats, or as serving platters for a mix of foods (MacDonald 2002:87). MacDonald (2002, 2004) notes that the use of small plates varied by regional diet; for example, a northern English dietary pattern required the use of more small plates for the single portion breakfasts that were common to the region. Alternatively, she notes (MacDonald 2002:87–88) a high frequency of large plates among German immigrants, reflecting a diet more focused on simmered foods for dinner. Similarly, a high representation of bowls in assemblages has been interpreted as reflecting the maintenance of traditional diets based on single-pot stews, soups or gruel among conservative Six Nations families (I. Kenyon and T. Kenyon 1986), and among crofters of the Western Scottish Isles (Barker 2005).

In the Powless assemblages, identifiably larger diameter plates (i.e., more than 8 in) in the early features represent 76 percent of all plates whose diameter could be ascertained. This is similar to the numbers for German immigrants and far higher than seen for British-Canadian assemblages of the same time, suggesting a meaningful difference in culinary needs at the dinner table, likely based on a diet heavy on meat casseroles and stews. Moreover, given that smaller plates were used for single-item servings and to provide finger foods served at tea time, it is possible that this element of Western dining culture had not been incorporated extensively within the early household.

However, data from the later features indicate that western dining conventions were being incorporated into Powless daily meals, as the frequency of larger plates dropped to 57 percent and smaller plates increased to 43 percent. The larger plate percentage, although higher than Euro-Canadian patterns and dining conventions noted elsewhere (Kenyon 1991; I. Kenyon and S. Kenyon 1992, 1993; MacDonald 2002, 2004), suggests that the consumption of foodstuffs served as single-portion meals increased in the later household or complemented larger plate use; in other words, meal presentation at the table had shifted.

Of course, the household residents who made decisions about meals, dining etiquette and provisioning were not unaware of European and Euro-Canadian dining conventions. Certainly, descriptions of dining with Joseph or John Brant and other prominent individuals all reflect being favorably impressed by a fully stocked table with all wares in order and proportion for the style and conventions of upper-class British dining and entertainment. So any variation from these formal conventions arose from the private "domus" or domestic space where social meanings and structures operate within and between household residents (Hodder 1990, 1998), and embedded in the daily rituals of dietary choice and dining culture, where personal household identity operated beyond the conventions of formal group dining (e.g., Blanton 1994).

Indeed, the differences in percentages of smaller and larger plates may be reflecting the boundary between personal and external presentations of self—that intersection of the polyphonic planes of identity where the historically known self negotiates its understanding of the way the conventions of the colonizer are to be implemented (e.g., Bhabha 1994). Specifically, in the early assemblage, 36 percent of large plates were expensive (printed), while 67 percent of the smaller plates were expensive. In the later features, 65 percent of large plates were expensive, while 100 percent of smaller plates were (printed and ironstone). The consistently higher percentage of expensive smaller plates, and their association with the social act of offering tea to visitors and other formal dining conventions inspired by the British upper class, suggests a conscious effort by the Powless families to utilize a form of plate not critical for personal consumption as a signifier of "colonial" sensibilities and awareness in the theater of more formal meal settings.

This is reinforced by looking at the percentages of ceramic teas in the assemblages. A combined 52 percent of cups and saucers from the early features were expensive, compared to 70 percent for the later features. So despite the variation of expensive large and small plates through time, an effort to maintain more expensive, matching setts of several cups and saucers was practiced. Indeed, this occurred in the early household despite limits on supply at that time, and despite the apparent lack of a similar effort made when procuring the large plates used most frequently at the family dining table. It should also be mentioned that inexpensive ceramic teas in the later features included a set of bluesponged ware (minimally seven cups and five saucers). Presumably these were purchased for personal use rather than for formal occasions. If so, in Peter and Elizabeth's household, it seems that the convention of tea drinking had been adopted *both* for formal presentation, serviced by expensive wares, and as a dining innovation accepted within their own personal domus, but serviced by less expensive wares.

Peter and Elizabeth's household is remarkable for the maintenance of consistently high percentages of expensive wares, with only larger plates being notably below the general average of 74 percent (based on identified vessels). Clearly, there was an active interest in displaying the latest fashion trends for these objects, and an acceptance of at least some of the colonialist sensibilities behind owning and using these wares (see also, Lawrence 2003). In some ways, the images depicted on those printed ceramics included a pictorial narrative of the world around the Powless household, such as transfer-printed pastoral scenes on plates and teas (e.g., Ivanhoe pattern, British North American scenes) that would have been visible reminders of the landscape outside their door during this later occupation. Significantly, the use of the Kirby Hotel Iroquois hunting scene plates, at a time when bow and arrow hunting in traditional dress was in decline or gone locally, would have had personal significance to household members and served as visual reminders of the familiar, historic landscape the Powlesses had been a part of—personal meaning from mass-produced material.

But do the Powless ceramic data emulate broader Euro-Canadian or Six Nations trends? One means of comparing data previously outlined by Ian and Thomas Kenyon (1986:21–23) consists of plotting both the percentages of expensive wares and the plate/saucer ratios from different sites.[15] The Kenyons focused on the ratio of all plates within an assemblage to all saucers because of the variable social dimension they believed this ratio could convey within European dining conventions, ranging from a laborer's daily eating practices to the multiple courses of the economic upper classes, where plates in particular were switched from course to course (Goodwin 1999; I. Kenyon and S. Kenyon 1992; Wall 1991). Among the upper classes, this translated into a higher plate-to-saucer ratio[16] that correlated neatly with increased percentages of expensive wares[17] in the vessel assemblages compiled by the Kenyons. In other words, the higher the plate-saucer ratio, the higher the percentage of expensive wares present in a vessel assemblage. A somewhat meaningful correlation (r^2 = 0.482) between these two variables is reflected in fig. 5.8 and the resulting trend line mapped for the Euro-Canadian data.

However, plotted Six Nations site assemblages with sizeable samples of ceramic vessels on the graph reflect a very different scatter. At best, a very slight trend (r^2 = 0.290) may suggest that the higher the plate-saucer ratio, the lower the percentage of expensive wares in Six Nations assemblages. For Ian and Thomas Kenyon (1986:22–23), that the low percentage of expensive wares and high plate-saucer ratios appeared on downriver sites indicated that these households had not incorporated tea drinking into their dining practices. However, eliminating the Styers site (Site 1) as an outlier effectively undermines the Kenyons' trend for this admittedly limited dataset, as statistically there remains no correlation between the two variables (r^2 = 0.096).

But what is noteworthy here is that this lack of a correlation between wealth and tea drinking among the Six Nations is so counter to Euro-Canadian patterns, underscoring that ceramics were incorporated into Six Nations households differently. British and European customs of tea drinking and mealtime display either were not adopted or were variably incorporated within households, with families like the Styers seemingly operating outside any kind of broader colonialist convention toward mealtime behaviors.

For the Powless households, the ceramic assemblage can be read as reflecting a more active engagement with some of the colonialist ideas of mealtime behaviors, in that when tea drinking was adopted, so too were some of the social conventions around public display and formal dining. In the early household, with its predominance of large, inexpensive plates, few but expensive smaller plates, and overall fair use of expensive wares (56 percent by sherds or 49 percent by identified vessels), the incorporation of tea into dining practices appears to be part of the adoption of understood conventions of formal table presentation and meal etiquette practiced by British upper classes. These understandings were then the gestures translated back in the public displays of meals and performance Brant and his neighbors follo~ at Mohawk Village. Thus, teas and smaller plates, as primary "to~' in public presentations of food sharing, were disproportionate'

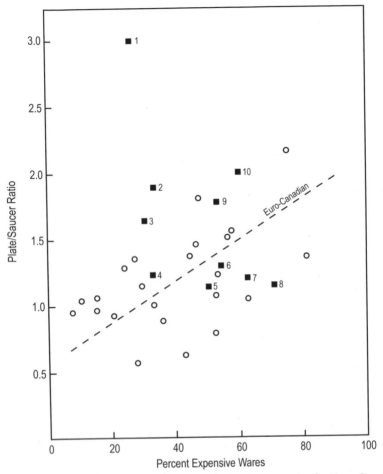

FIGURE 5.8. Percent of expensive wares and plate/saucer ratios for Euro-Canadian and Six Nations sites. Circles are Euro-Canadian sites, and squares are Six Nations sites. Euro-Canadian data are from I. Kenyon and T. Kenyon 1986; Dodd 1990; B. Morrison 1991; MacDonald 2002 (Robinson data). Six Nations sites:

1 Styers
2 Cook
3 Hill
4 Dewar
5 Powless early features
6 MV Area C
7 Carpenter
8 Powless late features
9 Middleport 2
10 MV Area B

from expensive categories, though smaller plates were underrepresented and perhaps used solely for formal dining contexts.

Within the later household, there is a greater awareness of fashions and economic variation in ceramic use, and more incorporation of those distinctions into daily customs, thus blurring the line between personal and public meal presentation, as seen in strategies such as maintaining expensive and inexpensive services. But the trend is also consistent with the previous generation and the earlier understanding of public/private identities played out among this "elite" class at Mohawk Village, since there continued to be more frequent use of expensive wares for vessel forms used in formal dining presentations and less concern for that privately. As well, overall vessel form ratios still reflected a continuing dietary set of practices based more on an "Iroquois meal system" than a mirror of broader trends and fashions in mid-Victorian southern Ontario.

Being of the Indigenous and Being in the Colonial

Descendent from what Guldenzopf referred to as "elite patterns," archaeological and historical data reflect a distinct socioeconomic locus for some families in Mohawk Village. Moreover, given the limited agricultural activities of the Powless households, this distinct status appears to be discrete from the trend in the 20–30 percent of Six Nations households that had invested in larger scale farming by the mid–19th century. Indeed, though not explored in detail here, the emergence of these surplus yield farm operations appears to be a phenomenon of the 19th-century agricultural landscape in the region. The sense of place and status that these people had may reflect more innovative notions of success and identity through cash crop farming as these emerged through later Victorian times.[18]

Despite Joseph Brant's extensive landholdings, the distinct socioeconomic status of families like the Powlesses in Mohawk Village seems to have been associated more with earlier notions of situated class conventions, arising out of the distinct intersection and interactions Mohawk Village (and Canajoharie previously) served between "elites" within and without the Six Nations. This sense of social status and place seems to have been maintained transgenerationally, a memory marker that was passed on to the next generation of Powlesses within notions of decorum and etiquette—not a "nouveaux riche" emerging from rural farming, but more political and social privilege (and duty), tied to a self-defined family legacy and place in the community.

This is not to say that the Powless families (or Brants, Johns and others) found identity and defined their place in their community solely from colonial values and conventions, any more than Six Nations families operating large farms should be assumed to have fully incorporated a rural Euro-Canadian set of social values, or that families of garden plot homesteads defined themselves in opposition to such values.[19] What the archaeological record demonstrates is continued adaptation and innovation informing notions of value and self, but not undermining or replacing historically based notions of identity arising from specific cultural contexts (Given 2004; Jordan and Schrire 2002; J. D. Rogers 2005). For example, given that innovative ceramic fashions continued to be purchased for the later Powless household after Peter died and up until the house was abandoned, it is reasonable to assume Elizabeth was the active agent stocking the china cabinet and entertaining visitors and residents alike, perhaps also displaying a penchant for mid-Victorian paste jewelry. But it is also reasonable to assume that Elizabeth was involved in the manufacture of Native beaded crafts as a possible income-generating household practice, or for personal use—or most likely both. Likewise, it was probably Peter who maintained his musket and perhaps continued to hunt and contribute wild game to the dinner table, alongside poultry, pork and beef from limited livestock holdings or barrels purchased from local merchants—a hybridized blending of past practice and present opportunities in daily life.

Though using much of the same material culture as surrounding Euro-Canadians, the internal meanings and signifiers for these items in specifically the Powless households, and likely more generally among the Six Nations, differed, suggesting to me that there was less of an internalized acceptance of a differential or coveted value placed on these items, and more a recognition of the social meanings tied to the use of these material items. Therefore, while the preponderance of mass-produced materials on these sites could be read as normative patterns reflecting an assimilated people no longer distinct from the broader society around them, a consideration of historical context and recognition of the interplay of tradition and innovation revises the meaning and agency reflected in these households. As such, the patterns documented can best be understood by thinking of the Powless household as a material "collage" of fluid and contested meanings (see Manina Jones 1993), with mass-produced ceramics, brace buttons used for undergarments, and blacking bottles used for coloring European-styled boots recovered alongside silver earbobs and brooches, beads, and iron spikes from ceremonial war clubs—all invoking and being instilled with distinct contemporary *and* historically derived meanings, while also being blended by the Powlesses innovatively to signify additional meanings and definitions of self.

We need to think about what this represents: signifiers of tradition and identity operating alongside more exaggerated signifiers of European conventions, fashion, and decorum. For the Powless family, whose Grand River patriarch was a chief and social contemporary[20] of Brant, and whose son married into the Brant family eventually leading to a grandson inheriting the maternal clan sachem from the Brant line, the Powlesses lived in a time tied to the past and present and hoped-for future of continued importance. In this way, the silver brooches, war club, beads and other material expressions of tradition are tied up in the formal status of a former chief and important family in the community, a status that continued into succeeding generations. Thus, the expensive ceramics used for teas and formal dining demonstrated, to the Powlesses and others, a sophisticated, urbane set of sensibilities and appreciation of the family's social position within Mohawk Village, the enclaved lower Grand of the Six Nations, and the emerging colonial world.

Indeed, the continued use of traditional cuisine and wild game creates a compelling image of that food on and in those ceramics, and serves as metaphor of the Powlesses in a colonial world: a venison roast placed on a flow blue platter with an image of the Versailles palace, for example, being a poignant and visible reminder of difference for dinner guests and family alike; an affirmation of identity and tradition physically "overlaid" onto innovative change. This is the significant ritual of memory, history and identity that gets played out in everyday gestures like meal times (e.g., Hodder and Cessford 2004; Martin Jones 2002; Scholliers 2001; D. Sutton 2001), continually reaffirming self-referential notions of past and present to both the outside world and to the family itself. For the Powlesses, that venison shank, at a time of pork and mutton and decline in venison as a regular part of meals, could have become an important, luxury foodstuff itself (e.g., van der Veen 2003), something desirable because of its rarity and intimate connection to Powless and Iroquois history, and different from the common cuisine of the surrounding Euro-Canadian world.

Such everyday metaphors are the kinds of daily lived experience[21] that both underscored and empowered the traditional authority and importance held by or at least perceived to be held by the Powless family through their time at Mohawk Village. For me, this complex identity maintenance within the Powless households, as well as the diverse and variable maintenance strategies reflected more broadly across Mohawk Village and the Six Nations, are far more compelling and active narratives than those offered in conventional histories. The families and individuals making up the Six Nations communities exhibited patterns of revision in response to both the constraints and opportunities the changing world offered, as had their ancestors during the centuries before the 19th-century colonial world first emerged. As with their ancestors of the previous centuries, the Six Nations communities and individuals that settled on the Grand River also exhibited the reinforcement of continuity one can expect from active agents, knowledgeable of who they are, where they came from and how they articulate with the broader world around them—in other words living the 19th century within their own time, worldview and knowledge of past, present, and future, and not one imposed by the colonial bureaucracy of the day, or by historians and archaeologists reading the past through the present.

6

Archaeological Histories of Native-Lived Colonialisms

I HAVE ATTEMPTED TO TEST AND CHALLENGE conventional notions and assumptions of Indigenous histories within emergent European colonialisms by looking beyond the observations and tropes found in historical records to seek more direct archaeological histories of peoples under study. By "archaeological histories," I do not mean solely understanding history through material remains. Rather, I mean examining data from material *and* documentary sources through an archaeologically oriented lens that provides fuller and more robust interpretations of past human life, as evidenced through those unique, archaeologically accessible contexts and rituals of daily living seen in settlement-subsistence and material procurement, use and disposal. These are some of the datasets archaeologists use to generate interpretations for the vast expanse of the global past lacking written records, and should be the way archaeologists approach the period of written records, rather than differentially weighing the significance and meaning of the written over the material (Andrén 1998; Reis 2005).

This approach shifts the weight of evidence away from assumptions of acculturation, dependency and cultural obscurity, so caught up with the baggage that arises from misunderstandings and biases in both original accounts and subsequent research, contributing to narrative constructions of the Indigenous as a passive backdrop for the socioeconomic motivations and histories of Europeans (Murray 2004; Rubertone 2000; Williamson 2004). The consequence of adopting revisionist archaeological histories, I believe, is that every theme and trope, and the timing and import they are given within conventional historical narratives of the last five hundred years in at least the Great Lakes region can be called into question, contradicted, and even repudiated, by degree if not in totality. The resulting archaeological history situates the past as that experienced by Indigenous agents living that past, revealing an understanding of those events from within the time and place of the Indigenous.

Constant Contacts

For example, I have attempted to contextualize the colonialisms and lived life experienced by the Ojibwa and Six Nation Iroquois of southwestern Ontario from the later 18th through 19th centuries within a deeper archaeological history that reaches back through the early contact era and into the more ancient past. This is critical in its own right to understanding the events of the 19th century and the agency evidenced by these Native communities. But it has also proved critical in undermining the conventional assumptions of the impacts tied to that initial period of "contact" with Europeans, by situating the AD 1550–1650 period within the rhythm of changed continuities Native peoples experienced in the centuries both *before* and *after* this initial "contact" (see Ferris 2006).

The implied opposition inherent in the concept of "contact" (as between European and Aboriginal) is entirely an artifice that masks the complex social and political relations occurring between Aboriginal nations, between each Aboriginal nation and each individual European nation, and between individuals from each of those constituencies interacting within and without their particular communities. This artifice, in turn, has contributed to shaping much of the marginalized history of the Other within European experiences and the histories of their emergent colonialist states.

Rather than advocating greater caution in distinguishing between archaeologies of "contact" and "colonialism" as Silliman has argued (2005), I would prefer to jettison the distinction and the concept of "contact" altogether. Colonialism, in whatever asymmetrical form or enclaved constraint that hatched from the initial interactions of European and Indigenous, only emerged in the Great Lakes well into the 18th century. Prior to that, historical contexts of the 16th to 18th centuries can be read more as changing continuities of broad Woodland material innovations, social structures, geographic relocations and broad contacts with external peoples—a continuation of the Terminal Woodland period, the end of which was variable by community and nation and arguably continued for at least the Ojibwa well into the first half of the 19th century.

This is not to say that the events of the 17th and early 18th centuries were simply shrugged off by Indigenous communities. They were devastating to live through, and those events became the memory markers for people who subsequently framed both their own sense of self and an understanding of the world in which they lived by those experiences. But, as seen from the wider historical context of the generations before and after, those moments were no instant triggers to dependency, loss of identity or rapid unprecedented change. To adopt Bourdieu's language, events of the 17th and 18th century laid bare dispositions, challenged doxa, and shook individuals and groups into *both* orthodox and heterodox assessments of self, group and the way the world works. Given that all humans experience the world through a histori-cal understanding of the way things are, it is clear to me that Indigenous responses (from nations, communities or individuals) served to reinforce core identities and social structures, while allowing more tertiary or "surface" ways of negotiating the world (material, settlement, tools of prestige and ritual) to be revised.

Ironically, an important implication of these stable, changed continuities into the 18th century is that the archaeological record, and archaeologically oriented data from historical records, can feed back into a better understand-ing of the more ancient past. In other words, dismissing the comparative value of ethnohistory and historical archaeology to provide insight on the precontact era, as Lightfoot (1995) and others have suggested, is premature, since clear continuities of Native-lived life can be mapped at least from the Indigenous record for the Great Lakes well into the rise of colonial contexts in the region (see also, Ferris 2006). As such, the archaeological patterns documented from this late Terminal Woodland period, informed as they are by written records that can access less tangible aspects of a Native world-view, in turn offer approximate understandings of more ancient archaeo-logical patterns. This can be seen, for example, by comparing Anishnabeg Ojibwa seasonal round scheduling in 1800 with preagriculturally focused Western Basin Late Woodland patterns. This is how the written record, or the archaeologically derived interpretations of that record, in turn contrib-utes to archaeological interpretations of the more distant past.

Creeping Colonialisms

But what of the archaeological history of the colonial period examined here, where there is no question that the imposed influence of the colonial State impacted Native communities in southern Ontario? It is critical to think of this period as a series of context-specific processes, both external and internal to Indigenous peoples, shaping those always changing continuities and his-torical trajectories (Lightfoot 2005a).

To begin, it is certainly the case that in southern Ontario, the nature of impacting colonialities was distinct from experiences elsewhere. Here, any European dimension to influencing, constraining or altering the world of the Indigenous occurred not through overt military force, slavery, genocide or deprivation, but rather from the more insidious and unacknowledged impact of massive population increases that created a previously unimaginable scale of non-Native settlement, encroachment and land clearance. The impact of this indirect process was also aided and abetted more directly by the self-interested and constantly revisionist catastrophic bureaucracy that callously and casually undermined Indigenous autonomy and continually reconfigured Native dispositions of the way the world worked. These two external impacts, one physical and material, the other ideological and illogical, changed Native communities into manufactured enclaves of the colonial experience, a legacy still visible today.

All three of the groups examined here experienced and responded to these "creeping colonialisms," which were first manifest for the Delaware on the Eastern Seaboard, and the Six Nations in New York State, around the early to mid–18th century. In a sense, the Delaware fled from creeping colonialism into the Ohio Valley and western Lake Erie, "aided" by their association with Moravian missionaries who negotiated with other colonial manifestations to keep communities coherent. For Iroquois communities, early encroachment and British administrative bureaucracy were not only problems, but also opportunities to shape the emerging colonial landscape to serve Iroquois nations and individual ends. Yet after the Revolutionary War, the Iroquois, too, were moving away from encroachment. Eventually, both the Delaware and the Iroquois were enveloped by continual expansion of non-Native settlement and land clearing, in effect fixing their communities through the happenstance of time and events onto the Lower Grand and Thames Rivers. The Ojibwa, located further to the west in smaller, more mobile communities, logistically maintained traditional land use and settlement patterns, modifying practices by shifting settlement slightly to avoid pockets of encroachment. Eventually though, the landscape became so altered that the viability of their settlement-subsistence was also undermined. Then these communities, too, became fixed in place.

This fixedness converted these autonomous groups, formerly traveling free across the landscape pursuing their own political, economic and social motivations, into marginalized, "ethnic enclaves" (Spence 1996, 2005) in a world of and for the colonizer. All three of the groups continued to interact with the world beyond their enclave, but the heightened distinctions between the world inside and outside led to increased heterodox and ortho-

tenets of identity and social organization built around that mobility and territorial sense of place.

It seems to me this transgenerational dimension of change—a gestation period prior to florescence—is significant beyond this study. For archaeologists, it is this combination—introduced innovation and its subsequent normalizing through the enculturation and acceptance by the next generations, who have been exposed to the innovation from birth—that is potentially so revealing of a social process underlying the long-term rhythms in the archaeological record. And this is so whether the innovation happens to be trade goods, corn cultivation introduced a millennium earlier, or fired clay ceramics introduced even earlier.

Over this longer term, then, changing continuities operate within the existing *habitus* as a constant, dynamic revision to historically understood lived experience. For example, understandings of who Europeans were and what they represented to Indigenous people certainly shifted through time, from recognition of Europeans as people from away, to people here to stay, to Europeans as an infestation causing the very landscape to be changed, and finally to Europeans as a dominant constraint on all dimensions of life. More directly, the internalization of innovation—the revising of *habitus*—created novel ways of constructing identities *within* the community, as the Powless family explored at Mohawk Village, or in the authority the helpers at Fairfield held between community and missionary. This is the nature of change operating over the long-term and as part of historical trajectories, leading to external expressions of a changed "culture" distinct from earlier periods yet arising entirely from the ongoing continuity of understanding the world internally, to define self and community in that world. Understanding this multiscalar process, then, fundamentally denies the logic of discontinuous change as imagined in past conventional tellings of Indigenous histories over the last five hundred years.

Epilogue

An important dimension to this study has been the demonstration that archaeological history can more directly access the past as experienced by Indigenous peoples than more conventional interpretations based on European accounts that have been constructed into dominant colonialist histories, or imagined through normative descriptions of material remains. While my aim has been to recontextualize understandings of the last half millennium for the Aboriginal communities of southwestern Ontario, I believe a wider

use of this perspective will be critical to revising similar conventional understandings of European-Indigenous interactions across at least North America. Moreover, this resituating of the last five hundred years through tellings
of archaeological histories can place the southern Ontario experience within
a broader, global context of research, moving beyond the marginalized fields
of regional cultural historical archaeology or particularistic ethnohistory of
Iroquois/Algonquian contact with the French and British.

Beyond this, I also feel there is a further, contemporary importance to
the narratives archaeological histories offer of the past. Increasingly, the real
challenge facing those who examine the past (no matter whose past is being
examined) is to recognize how the present infuses their constructions of the
past. Archaeological histories cannot ignore the fact that the descendants
of the ancestors under study also live in the world of the researcher: being
together and together beings. As individuals who choose to construct the
pasts of neighbors living alongside us today and sharing some common elements of contemporary community and society, we must reconcile an obvious fact: that those neighbors, relying on historical remembering and contemporary living, are constantly maintaining an identity still ongoing and
directly connected to that past we are exploring. Archaeological histories,
then, are living histories of a living people that really cannot contain fixed
endings since they are always connected by time to present and future contexts. In other words, we as researchers are also a part of—and directly connected to—the same temporal processes, rhythms and contexts we talk about
and explore in our work.

In accepting the open-ended nature of the temporal rhythms flowing
through past, present and future, the narratives of archaeological histories
have the capacity to connect the present with the past, providing a broader
relevancy beyond just a historical narrative. This is the means of weaving
together all our presents with all our pasts and so eschewing the marginalization, racism and irrelevancy of the Other (e.g., Kelly 1998). Instead, we draw
out the connection to the present by understanding, ultimately, the deep
temporal continuities to the archaeological histories of the Americas, Europe,
Africa and Asia as intertwined and belonging to the contemporary global
communities we are all a part of, without denying the multiple, contradictory, conflictual pasts inherent in those multiple histories.

To me, weaving together this deeper archaeological history to the changing continuities of the last half millennium should more directly shape the
interpretation of concepts like Orser's (1996, 2005) construction of a global
historical archaeology. Rather than an emphasis on European colonialism
giving rise to a global capitalism that then defines the modern world, we can

provide a historical depth to those networks of human interaction and agency that Orser (2005:83–88) sees as so critical to understanding the processes of a global modern history. This engages the pasts of a place with the pasts of the contemporary peoples in that place.

Critically, this is not a co-opting of the histories of the Other for the consumption, ownership and creation of a deeper historical relevancy for the descendants of the colonizers living within the contemporary, pseudo postcolonialism of places like North America. Rather this is an acknowledgement of the past as being made up of many multiple histories connected to always deeper temporal contexts, all welcome as essential to an understanding of difference and commonality in the present and critical to imagining future pasts. If the contextual archaeological histories to be told of the last half millennium can access that balanced footing and alternative perspective, and in so doing abandon the privileged histories of the colonizer that have so dominated lay and research understandings of the past, archaeologists can provide a contemporary relevancy to archaeological knowledge that will be far more significant than simple revisionist tellings of the past.

Notes

Chapter 3. Changing Continuities

1. Indeed the irony is that, by my reckoning of past research on Indigenous peoples interacting with Europeans in the Northeast, over a dozen specific dates *prior* to the 19th century have been cited as the moment when decline and irrelevancy occurred for Aboriginal peoples. Suffice to say that within these narratives, 19th-century patterns of Native life were assumed to be meaningless, or experienced even further ruin in that Native people were so changed as to no longer reflect "Native culture," or at least were submerged beneath the tide of the inevitable.

2. For example, Nangi, the St. Clair River community chief who gave the Moravian missionary Christian Denke permission to establish a mission among the St. Clair Ojibwa on Harsen's Island, was referred to as one of the three "head" chiefs of the St. Clair Ojibwa (Curnoe 1996:76–77; Denke 1991).

3. Nangi had no authority to grant Denke consent to settle on the Sydenham River, but Denke assumed his earlier consent to establish a mission on Harsen's Island made it alright, much to the consternation of the Bear Creek Ojibwa (Dreyer 1997; Ferris 1989).

4. Several species present speak to nonsubsistence activities. Head, wing and leg bones of a raven, golden eagle and hawk, and perhaps lynx and mink bones, may have been the remains of skin bags used frequently by the Ojibwa to hold medicines and other objects of importance (e.g., Nelson 1984). Dog bones (NISP = 7) may have been associated with a dog feast, as described by Denke (1996:7): "we butcher a dog because that is our favorite animal, burn his pelt and eat all the rest. After the meal we must dance for a long time . . . and at the same time sing in a loud voice."

5. When speaking to Denke in 1801, the residents of Kitigen told him they could not keep domestic animals, in part because their children would kill them for sport (Denke 1996:6).

6. River flats adjacent to summer base camps for raising corn were sometimes communally planted, and the use of those flats could include people who did not reside at the base camp itself (Denke 1996:4).

7. "Apaquois" is a French modification of an Algonquian word meaning mat covering. It typically referred to Central Algonquian Anishnabeg dwellings—wigwams or tepees covered with sections of bark, hide or mats.

8. For example, the Odawa chief Onagan from St. Anne's Island mentioned to the
Moravian missionary Denke in the early 19th century that he was feeling old
and did not want to travel south with his community to Sandusky Bay on Lake
Erie for the winter. Instead, he was hoping to winter with his son-in-law's family, Nabbawe, upriver on the Sydenham (Denke 1993; Dreyer 1998).

9. Dreyer (1997) has suggested the Bellamy site *is* Kitigen, due to the setting of
the site in comparison to Denke's account, and the general distance from what
would be Denke's mission site on the Sydenham, some three or four miles further upstream. I am sympathetic to the assertion, but reluctant to endorse it,
since excavations have been too limited, and several settings within a mile of
Bellamy also fit Denke's description.

10. Eighty-seven post moulds of 350 sectioned contained material, confirming
casual waste disposal practices as well as continual reuse of the site.

11. Ten from storage features, 50 from the privy, and one from a post mould.

12. This includes a preponderance among nonseed beads of tubulars and a
small assemblage of wire-round barleycorns, and the absence of facetted beads
or polychrome seed beads.

13. Perhaps the most extreme example was Lieutenant-Governor Francis Bond
Head's (1839) idea that Native people were destined to become extinct. He felt
that civilizing policies were doomed to failure due to the Aboriginal maintenance of traditional lifeways, which condemned them to destitution and victim-
ization by unscrupulous Euro-Canadians. As such, he wanted to remove Natives
from the influences of Europeans by creating one reserve on Manitoulin Island
in northern Lake Huron, where Native people could live out the "sun setting"
on their way of life. Native groups refused to go and the plan failed (Leslie and
McGuire 1978:15–16).

14. The communities to be discussed include the Upper St. Clair—or Sarnia—
reserve (Aamjiwnaang) at the north end of the St. Clair River, Walpole Island
(Bkejwanong) at the north end of Lake St. Clair, and Muncey (Chippewas of the
Thames) on the Thames River west of London (see fig. 3.8).

15. Letterbook of William Jones, Indian Agent at Baldoon and Port Sarnia,
Upper Canada, 1831–1839. Public Archives of Ontario, Private Manuscript
section, Letterbook collection (MS 296).

16. The absence of wigwams may be accurate, as the Indian Department
undertook to build log cabins for many of the families, in part to accommodate
the earlier 1830s relocation of the Bear Creek Ojibwa to Muncey (Gulewitsch
1998).

17. It should be noted that the 1851–52 census for Lambton County, which
would have included Walpole Island and Sarnia, has been lost. Likewise, while
the 1861 census for Walpole Island distinguishes Ojibwa from Odawa and

Potawatomi, the 1861 Muncey census makes no distinction between Ojibwa and Delaware, which was provided in the 1851–52 census.

18. In the 1871 Camden Township, Kent County personal census (Schedule 2, page 96, family 383), an Ojibwa family is recorded along the Sydenham, in the area of the former Bear Creek community. All adult males were listed as hunters. Two to three married couples, two with a child, a widowed woman listed as 40 years old (mother?) and a widowed 80-year-old (grandmother?), along with two unmarried young men (total = 11) all resided in a single shanty.

19. Three of four frame-dwelling families at Walpole Island did invest in these crops, with bushel yields of wheat at 72 bu, peas at 40 bu, and oats at 73 bu. These families had far lower yields for corn (27 bu) than for either log or apa-quois/wigwam families, suggesting these three families were indeed adopting more of a diversified agricultural practice. A similar pattern is seen for John Riley, the single Ojibwa farmer in a frame house at Muncey, who was working over 100 acres of land with a wheat harvest of 250 bu of wheat in 1852.

20. For example, over 50 percent of households on Walpole Island in 1891 were working holdings of 10 acres or less (Hedley 1993:192; Nin.Da.Waab.Jig 1987).

Chapter 4. Natives as Newcomers

1. The British thought they had the authority to allow this settlement, since it was assumed the mission would settle within land recently surrendered by resident Ojibwa in 1790 (Canada 1891, vol. 1; Jacobs 1983). That assumption proved false, since the missionaries selected a site further upriver from the surrender boundary, so the Delaware never held title to the original village location.

2. When citing excerpts from the Moravian diaries, the Sabathy-Judd publication will simply be cited as year of entry, followed by the date of the entry.

3. Kjellberg (1985:14) notes that between 1783 and 1785 the number of Delaware on the Grand River had decreased by some 164 persons, and attributes the drop to the formation of the Thames Muncey Delaware settlement.

4. The nature of the excavation technique used—a kind of systematic chunking through of house floors and features from one corner to the other—is reflected in Jury's field diary from 1943. In discovering a particularly productive cellar feature, he notes "I will leave it [to be excavated] till Saturday when the girls, Miss M and Miss B of the University of Western Ontario, can look over the soil as I throw it out."

5. I am indebted to Jim Rementer, who transcribed and compiled Norah Thompson Dean's oral history in 2005 and shared with me the section describing her childhood experiences traveling to and staying at that Big House ceremony.

6. William Henry Killbuck, or Gelelemend, the grandson of the Delaware chief Netawatwees who had joined the Moravian settlement with his family in the 1770s, was made an attendant in 1798, and is considered the community's first secular leader (Curnoe 1996:36; E. Gray 1956:53; Stonefish 1995a:71).

NOTES

7. The Jurys (2006) did not report any domestic species from Native cabin sites, though there was a circular logic at play, in that Native-occupied cabins were recognized as those lacking domestic animal remains. They did note butchered cattle bones and hen bones from "European" house sites.

8. Nonetheless, traditional dress continued well into the 19th century for the Moravian Delaware. For example, Hamil (1949:100) quotes from Latrobe (1835), who described the Moravian Delaware he met as wearing a mixture of "Indian and European costumes." Denke reported that people valued the vermillion they received from the British to paint their bodies (Gourlay 1822, 1:298).

9. True, the site does have Middle Woodland material on it, and Jury's excavations are suspect. But the pipe and points are artifact classes associated with later technologies (i.e., Terminal Woodland)—a part of the archaeological record not otherwise documented from Fairfield and not common in this stretch of the Thames River.

10. They may be dwellings for Moraviantown residents, or associated with a Potawatomi settlement of about thirty to forty individuals living in tents and apaquois/wigwams, and reported in the 1861 manuscript census as living adjacent to the Delaware.

11. Fur trapping is still noted in the community as late as the 1870s (Canada 1876).

12. Comparable data from the same census period is not available, so the 1851–52 census for Muncey is compared with the 1861 Moraviantown data.

Chapter 5. Iroquoian to Iroquois in Southwestern Ontario

1. For example, Bradley (2001) has pointed to the appearance of small scraps of cut and rolled European-derived copper on 16th-century sites in the lower Great Lakes as evidence of the rapid emergence of a kind of "scrap metal cult" among Aboriginal groups precipitating major culture change. But a longer term perspective underscores the fact that these items, made by Native artisans from cut pieces of copper kettles, are entirely consistent with Indigenous copper artifact forms that had begun appearing on sites in the Great Lakes as early as the 14th century (Ehrhardt 2005; Fox et al. 1995). Trigger (1991; Trigger and Swagerty 1996) and Turgeon (2004) have argued that the emergence of Indigenous long-distance trade networks only began *after* Europeans introduced the concept of long-distance goods exchange. Turgeon argued specifically that northeastern Indigenous groups lived in a period of "profound localism" during the Late Woodland, during which there was little contact with distant communities, and so is a period of time that stands in stark contrast to what happened after Europeans arrived. But the archaeological record fails to support this idea, since long-distance exchange of Indigenous exotics such as shell and copper extended across the Northeast, Great Lakes and beyond, well before European exchange began (e.g., Ferris 2006; Fox 2002, 2004; Jamieson 1999).

2. Iroquois oral tradition states that the Erie and Neutral were offered the choice to either join the Confederacy or face death (Morgan 1851:76).

3. These citations are taken from the *Jesuit Relations,* which were originally written in the 17th century.

4. This included ceremonial resurrection of a community leader by the person replacing the deceased (e.g., Wrong 1939:209–210), and adoptive incorporation of groups of people at the community level; for example, when the Wenro moved north and joined the Huron in 1638 (Branstner 1991:296). The antiquity of this social community formation process—the coalescent nation—is evident archaeologically during the Late Woodland, with many examples of village expansions incorporating external populations, or the merging of two separate villages into a single community (e.g., Ferris 1999; Williamson and Robertson 1994).

5. Similar to French incursions down the Richelieu River to Lake Champlain and into Iroquois territory in the early 17th century, which was also seen as a threat to Iroquois sovereignty and a major catalyst for the subsequent conflicts between the Iroquois and French at that time (Heidenreich 1990).

6. The disputed sovereignty arose from Iroquois claims to the area based on their view that they had been successful in dispersing other Aboriginal nations from those lands, and various of those dispersed nations that had not been incorporated into the Five Nations, such as the Odawa and Huron-Wendat, still claiming some of the region, compounded by newer Aboriginal (e.g., Ojibwa) and French encroachment into the region.

7. It is also clear that British colonial officials felt they were placating a potential threat to British sovereignty, in the form of angry Iroquois nations whose support for the British had been ignored in the provisions of the Paris treaty. In that treaty, Britain surrendered claim to Iroquois ancestral homelands, which, from the Iroquois perspective, the British had no claim to nor the authority to surrender.

8. The Five Nations became the Six Nations in the early 1720s, when the Tuscarora nation was adopted into the Confederacy. The Tuscarora had been dispersed by warfare a decade earlier, and had settled near the Onondaga and Oneida as refugees from that conflict (Landy 1978).

9. A 1785 census included 448 Mohawk, 381 Cayuga, 225 Onondaga, 162 Oghguagas (Oneida), 129 Tuscaroras, 47 Seneca, 51 western Iroquois, 31 eastern Iroquois, 231 Delaware, 74 Tutelos, 53 Creek and Cherokees, and 11 Nanticokes (C. Johnston 1964:52).

10. For example, upon returning from a trip to the United States, Brant is reported to have stopped just before entering "Indian Country" (western New York), and changed from western attire into Native attire and gear, "to appear among his own people like one of them" (Kelsay 1984:536).

11. The meaning of cot used here is of a small cottage or cabin (OED).

12. By 1857 only 12 to 15 families were living outside of the consolidated reserve (Thorburn, in Canada 1858).

13. Triggs (2004:164) misinterpreted these observations, assuming Speck (and Kenyon and Ferris 1984:40) was identifying a distinct "Iroquois cultural pattern." He then notes that his findings at an early 19th century Ojibwa encampment were also dominated by white beads, undermining any "Iroquois" exclusivity to the trend. But then no "ethnic" exclusivity had ever been implied, and certainly the predominance of white beads was also seen at the Ojibwa Bellamy site (see chap. 3; Ferris 1989; Ferris et al. 1985). Use of mass-produced white beads, commonly obtained from British distribution, was a pan-Native pattern in the Great Lakes in the early 19th century, since choice would have been shaped by this common source.

14. Ian Kenyon points out (Kenyon and Ferris 1984:40) that another Upper Mohawk, Moses Carpenter, paid off his debt to a shopkeeper in Brantford in 1833 with several pairs of beaded moccasins.

15. Notwithstanding limitations argued elsewhere in ascribing meaning to ceramic patterns (Monks 1999:209), meaningful differences were demonstrated by the Kenyons and so they are worth exploring here.

16. A figure obtained by dividing the number of plates in an assemblage by the number of saucers.

17. A figure obtained by adding the number of expensive (porcelain, ironstone, printed) and inexpensive (painted, sponged, stamped, edged and C.C. or plain) plates, saucers and cups, then dividing by the total number of specimens.

18. Kenyon's 1986 unpublished paper attempted to explore this dimension of Six Nations society and did find some correlation with multiple criteria of elevated status in the community (i.e., landholdings, religious affiliation, Council membership). He found, within the 1871 census data, a greater emphasis on larger scale agriculture among Christian families compared with non-Christian families, and a greater emphasis among Council members compared with non-Council members, regardless of religious affiliation. This suggested some correlation between social status (i.e., Council leaders), landholdings, and surplus yield farming.

19. It is important to keep in mind that Mohawk Village families like the Powlesses, and Six Nations cash crop farming households along the Grand, lived alongside 50 percent or more Six Nations families who, whether as a form of resistance, maintenance of historic practices or alternative livelihood, pursued various forms of a traditional, self-reliant garden-plot subsistence.

20. Masonic pipe fragments from the early Powless cellar are significant in this regard, given that Brant was also a Mason (Kelsay 1984).

21. Manifest materially, but also through other behaviors, such as the maintenance of gendered labor distinctions in tending to corn fields.

References

Albers, Patricia

2002   Marxism and Historical Materialism in American Indian History. In
        Clearing a Path: Theorizing the Past in Native American Studies, edited by
        Nancy Shoemaker, pp. 107–136. Routledge, New York.

Albers, Patricia, and Jeanne Kay

1987   Sharing the Land: A Study in American Indian Territoriality. In *A
        Cultural Geography of North American Indians*, edited by Thomas Ross and
        Tyrel Moore, pp. 47–92. Westview Press, Boulder, CO.

Alcock, Susan

2005   Roman Colonies in the Eastern Empire: A Tale of Four Cities. In *The
        Archaeology of Colonial Encounters: Comparative Perspectives*, edited by Gil
        Stein, pp. 297–330. School of American Research Press, Santa Fe.

Alexander, Rani

1998   Afterword: Toward an Archaeological Theory of Culture Contact. In
        Studies in Culture Contact Interaction, Culture Change and Archaeology, edited
        by James Cusick, pp. 476–495. Center for Archaeological Investigations
        Occasional Papers 25. Southern Illinois University Press, Carbondale.

Allen, Robert

1975   The British Indian Department and the Frontier in North America
        1755–1830. *Canadian Historic Sites: Occasional Papers in Archaeology and
        History* 14:5–125.

1993   *His Majesty's Indian Allies: British Indian Policy in the Defence of Canada,
        1774–1815*. Dundurn Press, Toronto.

Andrén, Anders

1998   *Between Artifacts and Texts: Historical Archaeology in Global Perspective*.
        Plenum Press, New York.

Aquila, Richard

1983   *The Iroquois Restoration: Iroquois Diplomacy on the Colonial Frontier, 1701–
        1754*. Wayne State University Press, Detroit.

Axtell, James

1984   *After Columbus: Essays in the Ethnohistory of Colonial North America*. Oxford
        University Press, Oxford.

Axtell, James *(cont.)*

1992   Columbian Encounters Beyond 1492. *William and Mary Quarterly* 49 (3): 335–360.

1997   The Ethnohistory of Native America. In *Rethinking American Indian History*, edited by Donald Fixico, pp. 11–27. University of New Mexico Press, Albuquerque.

2001   *Natives and Newcomers: The Cultural Origins of North America.* Oxford University Press, New York.

Bamforth, Douglas

1993   Stone Tools, Steel Tools: Contact Period Household Technology at Helo'. In *Ethnohistory and Archaeology Approaches to Postcontact Change in the Americas*, edited by Daniel Rogers and Samuel Wilson, pp. 49–72. Plenum Press, New York.

Barker, D.

2005   Pottery Usage in a Crofting Community: An Overview. In *From Clan to Clearance—History and Archaeology on the Isle of Barra c. 850 to 1850*, edited by Keith Branigan, pp. 111–122. Oxbow Books, Oxford.

Barrett, John

2001   Agency, the Duality of Structure, and the Problem of the Archaeological Record. In *Archaeological Theory Today*, edited by I. Hodder, pp. 141–164. Blackwell Publishers, Oxford.

Beauchamp, William

1903   *Metallic Ornaments of New York Indians.* New York State Museum and Science Service Bulletin 73, Archaeology 8. Albany.

Beaudry, Mary, Lauren Cook, and Stephen Mrozowski

1991   Artifacts and Active Voices: Material Culture as Social Discourse. In *The Archaeology of Inequality*, edited by Randall McGuire and Robert Paynter, pp. 150–191. Blackwell Publishers, Oxford.

Beaven, James

1846   *Recreations of a Long Vacation; or, a Visit to Indian Missions in Upper Canada.* H&W Rowsell, Toronto.

Behm, Jeffery

1998   The Bell Site: Community Plan of the Grand Village of the Meskwaki. *Wisconsin Archeologist* 79 (1): 131–174.

Beld, Scott

1990   Gratiot County Archaeology, Phase V, S89–273: Shin-gwah-koos-king/ Bethany Mission (20–GR-186/187/199). Report Submitted to the Bureau of History, Michigan Department of State by Alma College, Alma.

2002   A Preliminary Report on the Cater Site, 20MD36, Midland County, Michigan: Early and Mid-Nineteenth Century Occupations in Central Michigan. *Michigan Archaeologist* 48 (1–2): 1–86.

Benn, Carl

1998   *The Iroquois in the War of 1812.* University of Toronto Press, Toronto.

Theorizing the Past in Native American Studies, edited by Nancy Shoemaker, pp. 3–28. Routledge, New York.

Culin, Stewart

1975   *Games of the North American Indians.* Dover Press, New York. Reprint of the 1907 Twenty-Fourth Annual Report of the Bureau of American Ethnology.

Curnoe, Greg

1996   *Deeds Nations*, edited by Frank Davey and Neal Ferris. Occasional Publications of the London Chapter, Ontario Archaeological Society 4. London, Ontario.

Cusick, James

1998   Historiography of Acculturation: An Evaluation of Concepts and Their Application in Archaeology. In *Studies in Culture Contact Interaction, Culture Change and Archaeology*, edited by James Cusick, pp. 126–145. Center for Archaeological Investigations Occasional Papers 25. Southern Illinois University Press, Carbondale.

Deitler, Michael

1990   Driven to Drink: The Role of Drinking in the Political Economy and the Case of Early Iron Age France. *Journal of Anthropological Archaeology* 9:352–406.

1998   Consumption, Agency, and Cultural Entanglement: Theoretical Implications of a Mediterranean Colonial Encounter. In *Studies in Culture Contact Interaction, Culture Change and Archaeology*, edited by James Cusick, pp. 288–315. Center for Archaeological Investigations Occasional Papers 25. Southern Illinois University Press, Carbondale.

2005   The Archaeology of Colonization and the Colonization of Archaeology: Theoretical Challenges from an Ancient Mediterranean Colonial Encounter. In *The Archaeology of Colonial Encounters: Comparative Perspectives*, edited by Gil Stein, pp. 33–68. School of American Research Press, Santa Fe, NM.

Deitler, Michael, and Ingrid Herbich

1998   Habitus, Techniques, Style: An Integrated Approach to the Social Understanding of Material Culture and Boundaries. In *The Archaeology of Social Boundaries*, edited by Miriam Stark, pp. 232–263. Smithsonian Institution Press, Washington, DC.

Delâge, Denys

1985   *Bitter Feast: Amerindians and Europeans in Northeastern North America, 1600–64.* 1993 English translation. UBC Press, Vancouver.

Deloria, Philip

2002   Historiography. In *A Companion to American Indian History*, edited by Philip Deloria and Neal Salisbury, pp. 6–23. Blackwell Publishers, Oxford.

Denke, Christian

1990   The Diaries of Christian Denke on the Sydenham River, 1804–1805. (Translated by Irmgard Jamnik) *KEWA* 90 (5): 2–21.

Denke, Christian *(cont.)*

1991   The Diaries of Christian Frederick Denke on the Sydenham River, 1802–
        1803. (Translated by Irmgard Jamnik) *KEWA* 91 (7): 3–18.

1993   Diaries of Christian Frederick Denke on the Sydenham River, 1806.
        (Translated By Fred Dreyer) *KEWA* 93 (7): 2–13.

1994   Chippewa Mission Diary of Christian Frederick Denke. (Translated by
        Irmgard Jamnik) *KEWA* 94 (6): 2–17.

1996   Ojibwa Mission Report: Christian Frederick Denke's First Visit among
        the Ojibwa 1801 (Translated by Irmgard Jamnik) *KEWA* 96 (8): 2–10.

Dening, Greg

1994   The Theatricality of Observing and Being Observed: Eighteenth-Century
        Europe "Discovers" the ?-Century "Pacific." In *Implicit Understandings:
        Observing, Reporting, and Reflecting on the Encounters between Europeans and
        Other Peoples in the Early Modern Era*, edited by Stuart Schwartz, pp. 451–
        483. Cambridge University Press, Cambridge.

Densmore, Francis

1979   *Chippewa Customs*. Minnesota Historical Society Press, St. Paul's.
        Originally Published in 1929 as Bureau of American Ethnology Bulletin
        86, Washington, DC.

Dirlik, Arif

2000   Whither History? Encounters with Historicism, Postmodernism,
        Postcolonialism. In *History After Three Worlds: Post-Eurocentric
        Historiographies*, edited by Arif Dirlik, Vinay Bahl, and Peter Gran, pp.
        241–257. Rowman & Littlefield Publishers, London.

Dobres, Marcia-Anne

2000   *Technology and Social Agency: Outlining a Practice Framework for Archaeology*.
        Blackwell, Oxford.

Dobres, Marcia-Anne, and C. Hoffman

1994   Social Agency and the Dynamics of Prehistoric Technology. *Journal of
        Archaeological Method and Theory* 1 (3): 211–258.

Dobres, Marcia-Anne, and John Robb

2000   Agency in Archaeology: Paradigm or Platitude? In *Agency in Archaeology*,
        edited by M. Dobres and J. Robb, pp. 3–17. Routledge, New York.

Dodd, Christine

1990   Excavation of the Drake Site, a Nineteenth Century Cabin Site on the
        403 Right-of-Way, Ancaster to Brantford. Report for and on file with the
        Ontario Ministry of Transportation, Toronto.

Dreyer, Fred

1997   The Moravian Mission to the Chippewas. *Ontario History* 89 (3): 181–198.

1998   *Chippewas, Delawares, and Germans: Records of the Moravian Mission to the
        Indians in Upper Canada*, vol. 10. Kent Historical Society Papers and
        Addresses, Chatham, Ontario.

Drooker, Penelope

1997   *The View from Madisonville: Protohistoric Western Fort Ancient Interaction Patterns*. Museum of Anthropology Memoir 31. University of Michigan, Ann Arbor.

Duke, Philip

1992   Braudel and North American Archaeology: An Example from the Northern Plains. In *Archaeology, Annales, and Ethnohistory*, edited by B. Knapp, pp. 99–110. Cambridge University Press, Cambridge.

1995   Working through Theoretical Tensions in Contemporary Archaeology: A Practical Attempt from Southwestern Colorado. *Journal of Archaeological Method and Theory* 2 (3): 201–229.

Dunham, Sean

2000   Cache Pits: Ethnohistory, Archaeology, and the Continuity of Tradition. In *Interpretations of Native North American Life: Material Contributions to Ethnohistory*, edited by Michael Nassaney and Eric Johnson, pp. 225–260. Society for Historical Archaeology/University Press of Florida, Gainesville.

Ehrhardt, Kathleen

2005   *European Metals in Native Hands: Rethinking Technological Change 1640–1683*. University of Alabama Press, Tuscaloosa.

Ellis, Christopher, and Neal Ferris (editors)

1990   *The Archaeology of Southern Ontario to A.D. 1650*. Occasional Publications of the London Chapter, Ontario Archaeological Society 5. London, Ontario.

Engelbrecht, William

2003   *Iroquoia*. Syracuse University Press, Syracuse, NY.

Evans, John

2003   *Environmental Archaeology and the Social Order*. Routledge, London.

Farnsworth, Paul

1992   Missions, Indians, and Cultural Continuity. *Historical Archaeology* 26 (1): 22–36.

Faubion, James

1993   History in Anthropology. *Annual Review of Anthropology* 22:35–54.

Faux, David

1984   The Mohawk Village: An Interpretive Approach to Historical, Archaeological, and Genealogical Investigations. Presented at the Iroquoian Historical Conference, Woodland Indian Cultural Educational Centre, Brantford, Ontario.

1985   Lower Cayuga Settlements Prior to 1850: Documentary Evidence. *KEWA* 85 (6): 6–24.

1987   Iroquoian Occupation of the Mohawk Valley during and after the Revolution. *Man in the Northeast* 34:27–39.

Fenton, William, and Elisabeth Tooker
1978   Mohawk. In *Handbook of North American Indians, Volume 15 Northeast*, edited by Bruce Trigger, pp. 466–480. Smithsonian Institution Press, Washington, DC.

Ferris, Neal
1984   Buttons I Have Known. *KEWA* 84 (5): 2–16.
1987   Preliminary Findings from Enniskillen: A Mid-Nineteenth Century Ojibwa Reserve. *KEWA* 87 (1): 4–11.
1989   *Continuity Within Change: Settlement-Subsistence Strategies and Artifact Patterns of the Southwestern Ontario Ojibwa, A.D. 1780–1861.* Master's thesis, Department of Geography, York University, Toronto.
1990   Rescue Excavations of the Younge Phase Cherry Lane (AaHp-21) Site, Leamington, Essex County. License report submitted to and on file with the Ministry of Culture & Communications, Toronto.
1999   Telling Tales: Interpretive Trends in Southern Ontario Late Woodland Archaeology. *Ontario Archaeology* 68:1–62.
2003   Between Colonial and Indigenous Archaeologies: Legal and Extra-Legal Ownership of the Archaeological Past in North America. *Canadian Journal of Archaeology* 27:154–190.
2006   *In Their Time: Archaeological Histories of Native-Lived Contacts and Colonialisms, Southwestern Ontario A.D. 1400–1900.* PhD dissertation, Department of Anthropology, McMaster University, Hamilton.

Ferris, Neal, and Ian Kenyon
1983   There was an Englishman, a Scotsman, and an Irishman. *KEWA* 83 (4): 2–12.

Ferris, Neal, Ian Kenyon, Rosemary Prevec, and Carl Murphy
1985   Bellamy: A Late Historic Ojibwa Habitation. *Ontario Archaeology* 44:3–22.

Ferris, Neal, and Michael Spence
1995   Woodland Traditions in Southern Ontario. *Revista de Arqueología Americana* 9:83–138.

Fitzgerald, William
2001   Contact, Neutral Iroquoian Transformation, and the Little Ice Age. In *Societies in Eclipse: Archaeology of the Eastern Woodlands Indians, A.D. 1400–1700*, edited by David Brose, C. Wesley Cowan, and Robert Mainfort Jr., pp. 37–47. Smithsonian Institution Press, Washington, DC.

Fixico, Donald
1997   Methodologies in Reconstructing Native American History. In *Rethinking American Indian History*, edited by Donald Fixico, pp. 117–130. University of New Mexico Press, Albuquerque.

Fogelson, Raymond
1989   The Ethnohistory of Events and Nonevents. *Ethnohistory* 36 (1): 133–147.

Foster, George
1960   *Culture and Conquest: America's Spanish Heritage.* Quadrangle Books, Chicago.

Fowler, Loretta
1987   *Shared Symbols, Contested Meanings: Gros Venture Culture and History, 1778–1984.* Cornell University Press, Ithaca, NY.
Fox, William
2002   Thaniba Wakondagi among the Ontario Iroquois. *Canadian Journal of Archaeology* 26 (2): 130–151.
2004   The North-South Copper Axis. *Southeastern Archaeology* 23 (1): 85–97.
Fox, William, Ron Hancock, and Larry Pavlish
1995   Where East Meets West: The New Copper Culture. *Wisconsin Archeologist* 76 (3–4): 269–293.
Fredrickson, N. Jaye
1980   *The Covenant Chain: Indian Ceremonial and Trade Silver.* National Museums of Canada, Ottawa.
Funari, Pedro Paulo, Siân Jones, and Martin Hall
1999   Introduction: Archaeology in History. In *Historical Archaeology: Back from the Edge*, edited by P. Funari, M. Hall, and S. Jones, pp. 1–20. Routledge, New York.
Galloway, Patricia
1991   The Archaeology of Ethnohistorical Narrative. In *Columbian Consequences Volume 3: The Spanish Borderlands in Pan-American Perspective*, edited by David Hurst Thomas, pp. 453–470. Smithsonian Institution Press, Washington, DC.
1992   The Unexamined Habitus: Direct Historic Analogy and the Archaeology of the Text. In *Representations in Archaeology*, edited by Jean-Claude Gardin and Christopher Peebles, pp. 178–195. Indiana University Press, Bloomington.
Garrad, Charles, Tim Abler, and L. Hancks
2003   On the Survival of the Neutrals. *Arch Notes* 8 (2): 9–21.
Giddens, Anthony
1982   *Profiles and Critiques in Social Theory.* MacMillan Press, London.
1984   *The Constitution of Society: Outline of the Theory of Structuration.* Polity Press, Cambridge.
Given, Michael
2004   *The Archaeology of the Colonized.* Routledge, London.
Goddard, Ives
1978   Delaware. In *Handbook of North American Indians, Volume 15 Northeast*, edited by Bruce Trigger, pp. 213–239. Smithsonian Institution Press, Washington, DC:
Goldring, Philip
1984   Religion, Missions and Native Culture. *Journal of the Canadian Church Historical Society* 26 (2): 43–49.
Goodspeed, William (publisher)
1889   *History of the County of Middlesex.* Wm. Goodspeed, Toronto.

Goodwin, Lorinda

1999   *Archaeology of Manners: The Polite World of the Merchant Elite of Colonial Massachusetts*. Plenum Publishers, New York.

Gosden, Chris

2004   *Archaeology and Colonialism: Culture Contact From 5000 BC to the Present*. Cambridge University Press, Cambridge.

Gourlay, Robert

1822   *Statistical Account of Upper Canada, Compiled with a View to a Grand System of Emigration*. 3 vols. Simpkin and Marshall, London.

Graham, Elizabeth

1975   *Medicine Man to Missionary: Missionaries as Agents of Change among the Indians of Southern Ontario, 1784–1867*. Peter Martin Associates, Toronto.

Gray, Elma

1956   *Wilderness Christians: The Moravian Mission to the Delaware Indians*. Russell & Russell, New York.

Gray, Leslie (editor)

1954   From Bethlehem to Fairfield, 1798, Diary of the Brethren John Heckewelder and Benjamin Mortimer. *Ontario History* 46:107–131.

Graymont, Barbara

1972   *The Iroquois in the American Revolution*. Syracuse University Press, Syracuse, NY.

Groover, Mark

2003   *An Archaeological Study of Rural Capitalism and Material Life*. Kluwer Academic/Plenum Publishers, New York.

Guilday, John

1963   The Cup-and-Pin Game. *Pennsylvania Archaeologist* 33 (4): 159–163.

Guldenzopf, David

1984   Frontier Demography and Settlement Patterns of the Mohawk Indians. *Man in the Northeast* 27:79–94.

1986   *The Colonial Transformation of Mohawk Iroquois Society*. PhD dissertation, Department of Anthropology, SUNY Albany, Albany.

Gulewitsch, Victor

1995   *The Chippewas of Kettle and Stony Point: A Brief History*. The Chippewas of Kettle and Stony Point Historical Claims Research Office. Forest, Ontario.

1998   Big Bear Creek Narrative. Report prepared for the Chippewa of the Thames First Nation, Muncey, Ontario.

Hagan, William

1997   The New Indian History. In *Rethinking American Indian History*, edited by Donald Fixico, pp. 29–42. University of New Mexico Press, Albuquerque.

Hall, Francis

1818   *Travels in Canada, and the United States, in 1816 and 1817*. Longman, Hurst, Rees, Orme & Brown, London.

Hamell, George

1987   Mythical Realities and European Contact in the Northeast during the
        Sixteenth and Seventeenth Centuries. *Man in the Northeast* 33:63–87.

Hamil, Fred

1939   Fairfield on the River Thames. *Ohio State Archaeological and Historical
        Quarterly* 48:1–19.

1949   The Moravians of the River Thames. *Michigan History* 33 (2): 97–116.

1951   *The Valley of the Lower Thames, 1640 to 1850.* University of Toronto Press,
        Toronto.

Hamilton, Tom

1980   *Colonial Frontier Guns.* Fur Press, Chadron, NE.

Harris, Cole, and David Wood

1993   Plate 4: Eastern Canada ca. 1800. In *Historical Atlas of Canada, Volume
        II: The Land Transformed 1800–1891*, edited by R. Louis Gentilcore.
        University of Toronto Press, Toronto.

Hauptman, Lawrence

1995   *Tribes and Tribulations: Misconceptions about American Indians, 1790 to the
        Present.* Macmillian Press, New York.

1999   *Conspiracy of Interests: Iroquois Dispossession and the Rise of New York State.*
        Syracuse University Press, Syracuse, NY.

Havard, Gilles

1992   La Grande Paix de Montréal de 1701: Les Voies de la Diplomatie Franco-
        Amérindienne. *Signes des Amériques* 8. Recherches Amérindiennes au
        Québec, Montréal.

Hedley, Max

1993   Autonomy and Constraint: The Household Economy on a Southern
        Ontario Reserve. In *The Political Economy of North American Indians*,
        edited by John Moore, pp. 184–213. University of Oklahoma Press,
        Norman.

Heidenreich, Conrad

1971   *Huronia, A History and Geography of the Huron Indian, 1600–1650.*
        McClelland and Stewart Limited, Toronto.

1987   Inland Expansion. In *Historical Atlas of Canada I: From the Beginning to
        1800*, edited by R. Cole Harris, Plates 34–35, 37–38. University of
        Toronto Press, Toronto.

1988   An Analysis of the 17th Century Map 'Nouvelle France.' *Cartographica* 25
        (3): 67–111.

1990   History of the St. Lawrence-Great Lakes Area to A.D. 1650. In *The
        Archaeology of Southern Ontario to A.D. 1650*, edited by Chris J. Ellis
        and Neal Ferris, pp. 475–492. Occasional Publications of the London
        Chapter, Ontario Archaeological Society 5. London, Ontario.

Heidenreich, Conrad, and Robert Burgar

1999   Native Settlement to 1847. In *Special Places: The Changing Ecosystems of*

Heidenreich, Conrad, and Robert Burgar *(cont.)*
    the Toronto Region, edited by Betty Roots, Donald Chant, and Conrad
    Heidenreich, pp. 63–75. University of British Columbia Press,
    Vancouver.

Herrick, Ruth
1958   A Report on the Ada Site, Kent County, Michigan. *Michigan Archaeologist*
    4 (1): 27–58.

Herskovits, Melville
1938   The Significance of the Study of Acculturation for Anthropology.
    American Anthropologist 39:259–264.

Hickerson, Harold
1970   *The Chippewa and Their Neighbors: A Study in Ethnohistory*. Holt, Rinehart
    and Winston, New York.

Hodder, Ian
1986   *Reading the Past: Current Approaches to Interpretation in Archaeology*.
    Cambridge University Press, Cambridge.
1987   The Contribution to the Long Term. In *Archaeology as Long-Term History*,
    edited by Ian Hodder, pp. 1–8. Cambridge University Press, Cambridge.
1990   *The Domestication of Europe*. Blackwell Publishers, Oxford.
1991   Interpretive Archaeology and Its Role. *American Antiquity* 56 (1): 7–18.
1998   The Domus: Some Problems Re-considered. In *Understanding the Neolithic
    of North-western Europe*, edited by Mark Edmonds and C. Richards, pp.
    84–101. Cruithne Press, Glasgow.
1999   *The Archaeological Process: An Introduction*. Blackwell Publishers, Oxford.
2001   Introduction: A Review of Contemporary Theoretical Debates in
    Archaeology. In *Archaeological Theory Today*, edited by Ian Hodder, pp.
    1–13. Blackwell Publishers, Oxford.
2004   The "Social" in Archaeological Theory: An Historical and Contemporary
    Perspective. In *A Companion to Social Archaeology*, edited by Lynn Meskell
    and Robert Preucel, pp. 23–42. Blackwell Publishers, Oxford.

Hodder, Ian, and Craig Cessford
2004   Daily Practice and Social Memory at Çatalhöyük. *American Antiquity* 69
    (1): 17–40.

Hoover, Robert
1992   Some Models for Spanish Colonial Archaeology in California. *Historical
    Archaeology* 26 (1): 37–44.

Howison, John
1821   *Sketches of Upper Canada*. G. & W. B. Whittaker, Ave-Maria Lane, London.
    Reprinted in 1970 by Coles Publishing Company, Toronto.

Hunt, George
1940   *The Wars of the Iroquois: A Study in Intertribal Trade Relations*. University of
    Wisconsin Press, Madison.

Jacobs, Dean

1983   Indian Land Surrenders. In *The Western District: Papers from the Western District Conference*, edited by Kenneth Pryke and Larry Kulisek, pp. 61–68. Essex County Historical Society Paper 2, Windsor.

1996   'We Have but Our Hearts and the Traditions of Our Old Men:' Understanding the Traditions and History of Bkejwanong. In *Gin Das Winan Documenting Aboriginal History in Ontario*, edited by Dale Standen and David McNab, pp. 1–13. Champlain Society Occasional Paper Number 2, Toronto.

Jacobson, H.

1895   Narrative of an Attempt to Establish a Mission among the Chippewa Indians of Canada. *Moravian Historical Society* 5 (1): 1–24.

Jameson, Anna

1838   *Winter Studies and Summer Rambles in Canada*, 3 vols. Saunders and Otley, London.

Jamieson, Susan

1999   A Brief History of Aboriginal Social Interactions in Southern Ontario and Their Taxonomic Implications. In *Taming the Taxonomy Toward a New Understanding of Great Lakes Archaeology*, edited by R. Williamson and C. Watts, pp. 175–192. eastendbooks, Toronto.

Jochim, Michael

1991   Archaeology as Long Term Ethnography. *American Anthropologist* 93 (2): 308–321.

Johnson, Leo

1974   The Settlement of the Western District, 1749–1850. In *Aspects of Nineteenth Century Ontario*, edited by Fred Armstrong, H. Stevenson, and J. Wilson, pp. 19–35. University of Toronto Press, Toronto.

1983   The State of Agricultural Development in the Western District to 1851. In *The Western District: Papers from the Western District Conference*, edited by Kenneth Pryke and Larry Kulisek, pp. 112–145. Essex County Historical Society Paper 2, Windsor.

Johnston, Charles

1964   *The Valley of the Six Nations: A Collection of Documents on the Indian Lands of the Grand River*. Champlain Society, Toronto.

1994   The Six Nations in the Grand River Valley, 1784–1847. In *Aboriginal Ontario*, edited by Edward Rogers and Donald Smith, pp. 167–181. Dundurn Press, Toronto.

Johnston, Darlene

1986   The Quest of the Six Nations Confederacy for Self-Determination. *University of Toronto Faculty of Law Review* 44 (1): 1–32.

Jones, Manina
1993   *That Art of Difference: 'Documentary Collage' and English-Canadian Writing.*
        University of Toronto Press, Toronto.

Jones, Martin
2002   Eating for Calories or for Company? Concluding Remarks on Consuming
        Passions. In *Consuming Passions and Patterns of Consumption*, edited by
        Preston Miracle and Nicky Milner, pp. 131–136. McDonald Institute for
        Archaeological Research, University of Cambridge, Cambridge.

Jones, Peter
1860   *Life and Journals of Kah-ke-wa-quo-na-by (Rev. Peter Jones), Wesleyan
        Missionary.* Anson Green, Toronto.
1861   *History of the Ojebway Indians.* A. W. Bennett, London.

Jones, Robert
1946   *History of Agriculture in Ontario, 1613–1880.* University of Toronto Press,
        Toronto.

Jones, Siân
1997   *The Archaeology of Ethnicity: Constructing Identities in the Past and Present.*
        Routledge, New York.

Jordan, Kurt
2002   *The Archaeology of the Iroquois Restoration: Settlement, Housing, and Economy
        at a Dispersed Seneca Community, ca. 1715–1754.* PhD dissertation,
        Department of Anthropology, Columbia University, New York.
2004   Seneca Iroquois Settlement Pattern, Community Structure, and Housing,
        1677–1779. *Northeast Anthropology* 67:23–60.

Jordan, Stacey, and Carmel Schrire
2002   Material Culture and the Roots of Colonial Society at the South African
        Cape of Good Hope. In *The Archaeology of Colonialism*, edited by Claire
        Lyons and John Papadopoulos, pp. 241–271. The Gerry Research
        Institute, Los Angeles.

Jordan, Terry
1985   *American Log Buildings: An Old World Heritage.* University of North
        Carolina Press, Chapel Hill.

Jury, Wilfred
1945   *Fairfield on the Thames Report of Excavations Made on the Site of the Early
        Mission Village 1942–43.* Bulletin 3. Museum of Indian Archaeology,
        London, Ontario.
1946   *Fairfield on the Thames Report of Excavations Made on the Site of the Early
        Mission Village 1945.* Bulletin 4. Museum of Indian Archaeology, London,
        Ontario.
1948   *Fairfield on the Thames Report of Excavations Made on the Site of the Early
        Mission Village 1946.* Bulletin 5. Museum of Indian Archaeology, London,
        Ontario.

Jury, Wilfred, and Elsie Jury

2006   Excavations at the Fairfield Moravian Mission on the Thames, Kent
County, Province of Ontario, Canada. *KEWA* 6 (1–2): 12–22. Reprint of a
1976 paper presented at the Society for American Archaeology Meetings,
St. Louis.

Karklins, Karlis

1992   *Trade Ornament Usage among the Native Peoples of Canada: A Source Book.*
Studies in Archaeology Architecture and History, Parks Canada,
Ottawa.

Kelly, Robert

1992   Mobility/Sedentism: Concepts, Archaeological Measures, and Effects.
Annual Review of Anthropology 21:43–66.

1998   Native American and Archaeologists: A Vital Partnership. *SAA Bulletin*
16 (4): 24–26.

Kelsay, Isabel

1984   *Joseph Brant, 1743–1807: Man of Two Worlds.* Syracuse University Press,
Syracuse, NY.

Kent, Susan

1989   Cross-Cultural Perceptions of Farmers as Hunters and the Value of Meat.
In *Farmers as Hunters: The Implications of Sedentism,* edited by Susan Kent,
pp. 1–17. Cambridge University Press, Cambridge.

Kent, Susan, and Helga Vierich

1989   The Myth of Ecological Determinism—Anticipated Mobility and Site
Spatial Organization. In *Farmers as Hunters: The Implications of Sedentism,*
edited by Susan Kent, pp. 96–130. Cambridge University Press, Cambridge.

Kenyon, Ian

1985   The Onondaga Settlement at Middleport. *KEWA* 85 (3): 4–23.

1986   Wealth, Status and Power among the 19th Century Six Nations Iroquois.
Paper presented at the Canadian Archaeological Association meetings,
Toronto.

1987a   An Archaeological Study of 19th Century European Settlement in the
Gore of Camden, Kent County. *KEWA* 87 (4): 8–16.

1987b   Levi Turkey and the Tuscarora Settlement on the Grand River. *KEWA* 87
(1): 20–25.

1988   Late Woodland Occupations at the Liahn I Site, Kent Co. *KEWA* 88 (2):
2–22.

1990   Union Jack over the Longhouse. Paper presented at the 1990 annual
meeting for the Society for American Ethnohistory, Toronto.

1991   *A History of Ceramic Tableware in Ontario: 1780–1890.* For the Association
of Professional Archaeologists workshop on ceramics, Toronto.

1992   Spilled Ink and Broken Cups: The Distribution and Consumption of
Ceramic Tableware in Upper Canada, 1800–1840. *KEWA* 92 (4): 2–20.

Kenyon, Ian *(cont.)*

1997   'Weeds Upspring where the Hearth Should Be:' Rural House
        Abandonment in Southern Ontario. *Ontario Archaeology* 64:39–55.

Kenyon, Ian, and Neal Ferris

1984   Investigations at Mohawk Village, 1983. *Arch Notes* 84 (1):19–50.

1985   *Hard Times in Cashmere: The Archaeology of a Southern Ontario Ghost Town.*
        Ontario Ministry of Culture and Recreation, Conservation Archaeology
        Report, Southwestern Region, Report 12. London, Ontario.

Kenyon, Ian, Neal Ferris, Christine Dodd, and Paul Lennox

1984   Terry Lynch: An Irish Catholic in a Protestant Township. *KEWA* 84 (9):
        2–23.

Kenyon, Ian, Neal Ferris, and Wayne Hagerty

1988   Western Basin Occupations of the Robson Road (AaHp-20) Site. *KEWA*
        88 (5): 3–24.

Kenyon, Ian, and Susan Kenyon

1992   'Pork and Potatoe, Flour and Tea': Descriptions of Food and Meals in
        Upper Canada, 1814–1867. *KEWA* 92 (5): 2–15.

1993   Household Ceramic Stocks in Mid-19th Century Ontario. *KEWA* 93 (1):
        2–26.

Kenyon, Ian, and Thomas Kenyon

1982   Social Dimensions of Ceramic Use in Southwestern Ontario, 1814–1867.
        Paper presented at the 1982 meeting of the Society for Historical
        Archaeology, Philadelphia.

1986   Echo the Firekeeper: A Nineteenth Century Iroquois Site. *KEWA* 86 (2):
        4–27.

Kinietz, Vernon

1940   *The Indians of the Western Great Lakes.* Occasional Contributions from
        the Museum of Anthropology, University of Michigan 10. Reprinted in
        1965. University of Michigan Press, Ann Arbor.

Kjellberg, Erik

1985   *Seeking Shelter: Canadian Delaware Ethnohistory and Migration.* Master's
        thesis, Department of Anthropology, McMaster University, Hamilton.

Klein, Terry

1991   Nineteenth-Century Ceramics and Models of Consumer Behaviour.
        Historical Archaeology 25 (2): 77–91.

Knapp, Bernard

1992   Archaeology and Annales: Time, Space, and Change. In *Archaeology,*
        Annales, and Ethnohistory, edited by B. Knapp, pp. 1–21. Cambridge
        University Press, Cambridge.

Konrad, Victor

1981   An Iroquois Frontier: The North Shore of Lake Ontario during the Late
        Seventeenth Century. *Journal of Historical Geography* 7 (2): 129–144.

Kraft, Herbert

1986   *The Lenape Archaeology, History, and Ethnography.* Collections of the New
        Jersey Historical Society, vol. 21. Newark.

Krech III, Sheppard

1988   The Hudson's Bay Company and Dependence among Subarctic Tribes
        Before 1900. In *Overcoming Economic Dependency*, D'Arcy McNickle Center
        for the History of the American Indian, Occasional Papers in Curriculum
        Series Number 9:62–70. Newberry Library, Chicago.

1991   The State of Ethnohistory. *Annual Review of Anthropology* 20:345–375.

Kuhn, Robert, and Robert Funk

2000   Boning Up on the Mohawk: An Overview of Mohawk Faunal Assemblages
        and Subsistence Patterns. *Archaeology of Eastern North America* 28:29–62.

Lajeunesse, Ernest

1960   *The Windsor Border Region. Canada's Southernmost Frontier.* Champlain
        Society, Toronto.

Landy, David

1978   Tuscarora among the Iroquois. In *Handbook of North American Indians.
        Volume 15: The Northeast*, edited by Bruce Trigger, pp. 518–524.
        Smithsonian Institution Press, Washington, DC.

Lantz, Stanley

1980   Seneca Cabin Site: Historic Component of the Vanatta Site (30CA46).
        Pennsylvania Archaeologist 50 (1–2): 9–41.

Last, Jonathan

1995   The Nature of History. In *Interpreting Archaeology: Finding Meaning in the
        Past*, edited by Ian Hodder, Michael Shanks, Alexandra Alexandri, Victor
        Buchli, John Carman, Jonathan Last, and Gavin Lucas, pp. 141–156.
        Routledge, New York.

Latrobe, Charles

1835   *The Rambler in North America, MDCCCXXXII-MDCCCXXXIII.* 2 vols.
        R. B. Seeley and W. Burnside, London.

Lawrence, Susan

2003   Exporting Culture: Archaeology and the Nineteenth-Century British
        Empire. *Historical Archaeology* 37 (1): 20–33.

Leclair, Laurie

1988   *The Caldwells of Point Pelee and Pelee Island: A Brief History and Survey of
        Documents.* Research Branch, Indian and Northern Affairs Canada, Ottawa.

Leighton, Douglas

1981   The Compact Tory as Bureaucrat: Samuel Peters Jarvis and the Indian
        Department, 1837–1845. *Ontario History* 73 (1): 40–54.

Leitch, Adelaide

1975   *Into the High Country: The Story of Dufferin the Last 12,000 Years to 1974.*
        Corporation of Dufferin County, Orangeville.

Lennox, Paul

1982   *The Bruner-Colasanti Site: An Early Late Woodland Component, Essex County, Ontario.* Mercury Series, Archaeological Survey of Canada Paper 110. National Museum of Man, Ottawa.

Lennox, Paul, and William Fitzgerald

1990   The Culture History and Archaeology of the Neutral Iroquoians. In *The Archaeology of Southern Ontario to A.D. 1650*, edited by Christopher Ellis and Neal Ferris, pp. 405–456. Occasional Publications of the London Chapter, Ontario Archaeological Society 5. London, Ontario.

Leslie, John, and Robert McGuire

1978   *The Historical Development of the Indian Act.* Treaties and Historical Research Centre. Indian Affairs and Northern Development Canada, Ottawa.

Lightfoot, Kent

1995   Culture Contact Studies: Redefining the Relationship between Prehistoric and Historical Archaeology. *American Antiquity* 60 (2): 199–217.

2005a   The Archaeology of Colonization: California in Cross-Cultural Perspective. In *The Archaeology of Colonial Encounters: Comparative Perspectives*, edited by Gil Stein, pp. 207–236. School of American Research Press, Santa Fe, NM.

2005b   *Indians, Missionaries, and Merchants: The Legacy of Colonial Encounters on the California Frontier.* University of California Press, Berkeley.

2006   Mission, Gold, Furs, and Manifest Destiny: Rethinking an Archaeology of Colonialism for Western North America. In *Historical Archaeology*, edited by Martin Hall and Stephen Silliman, pp. 272–292. Blackwell Publishing, Malden, MA.

Linton, Ralph (editor)

1940   *Acculturation in Seven American Indian Tribes.* D. Appleton Century, New York.

Little, Barbara

1994   People with History: An Update on Historical Archaeology in the United States. *Journal of Archaeological Method and Theory* 1 (1): 5–40.

Lynch, Peter

1985   The Iroquois Confederacy, and the Adoption and Administration of Non-Iroquoian Individuals and Groups Prior to 1756. *Man in the Northeast* 30:83–99.

Lyons, Claire, and John Papadopoulos

2002   Archaeology and Colonialism. In *The Archaeology of Colonialism*, edited by Claire Lyons and John Papadopoulos, pp. 1–23. Gerry Research Institute, Los Angeles.

Lytwyn, Victor

1998   A Dish with One Spoon: The Shared Hunting Grounds Agreement in the Great Lakes and St. Lawrence Valley Region. In *Papers of the Twenty-Eighth Algonquian Conference*, edited by David Pentland, pp. 210–227. University of Manitoba, Winnipeg.

2001   Torchlight Prey: Night Hunting and Fishing by Aboriginal People in the Great Lakes Region. In *Papers of the Algonquian Conference 32*, edited by John Nichols, pp. 304–317. University of Manitoba, Winnipeg.

Macaulay, Jane

1988   Floral Analysis of Six Features from the Bellamy Site. Report in the Possession of the Author.

MacDonald, Eva

1997   The Root of the Scatter: Nineteenth Century Artifact and Settlement Patterns in Rural Ontario. *Ontario Archaeology* 64:56–80.

2002   *'In a Country Where There is not as yet a Village': Towards a Historical Archaeology of Markham's Berczy Settlement*. Master's thesis, Department of Anthropology, University of Toronto, Toronto.

2004   Towards a Historical Archaeology of the German-Canadians of Markham's Berczy Settlement. *Northeast Historical Archaeology* 33:13–38.

Mainfort, Robert Jr.

1979   *Indian Social Dynamics in the Period of European Contact: Fletcher Site Cemetery, Bay County, Michigan*. Anthropological Series 1(4), Publications of the Museum. Michigan State University, East Lansing.

1985   Wealth, Space, and Status in a Historic Indian Cemetery. *American Antiquity* 50 (3): 555–579.

1996   Time and the Fletcher Site. In *Investigating the Archaeological Record of the Great Lakes: State Essays in Honor of Elizabeth Baldwin Garland*, edited by Margaret Holman, Janet Brashler, and Kathryn Parker, pp. 415–454. New Issues Press, Kalamazoo, Michigan.

Majewski, Teresita, and Michael O'Brien

1987   The Use and Abuse of Nineteenth-Century English and American Ceramics in Archaeological Analysis. In *Advances in Archaeological Method and Theory* 11:97–209.

Mann, Robert

1999   The Silenced Miami: Archaeological and Ethnohistorical Evidence For Miami-British Relations, 1795–1812. *Ethnohistory* 46 (3): 399–427.

2003   *Colonizing the Colonizers: Canadien Fur Traders and Fur Trade Society in the Great Lakes Region, 1763–1850*. PhD dissertation, Department of Anthropology, SUNY Binghamton, Binghamton.

Martin, Patrick, and Robert Mainfort, Jr.

1985   The Battle Point Site: A Late Historic Cemetery in Ottawa County, Michigan. *Arctic Anthropology* 22 (2): 115–130.

Martin, Terrance

1996   Wais-ke-shaw at Windrose: Animal Exploitation in the "Country of Muskrats." In *Investigating the Archaeological Record of the Great Lakes State Essays in Honor of Elizabeth Baldwin Garland*, edited by Margaret Holman, Janet Brashler, and Kathryn Parker, pp. 455–500. New Issues Press, Kalamazoo, MI.

Martin, Terrance *(cont.)*

2001   Animal Remains from the Windrose Site: 1994–1995 Investigations.
In *The Windrose Site: An Early Nineteenth Century Potawatomi Settlement in the Kankakee River Valley of Northeastern Illinois*, pp. 145–164. Reports of Investigations 56. Illinois State Museum, Springfield.

Martin, Terrance, and John C. Richmond

1990   Animal Remains from Feature 7 at Site 20GR187. Appendix 6 in Gratiot County Archaeology, Phase V, S89–273: Shin-gwah-koos-king/Bethany Mission (20–GR-186/187/199), by Scott Beld.

2002   Animal Remains from the Cater Site (20MD36), Midland County, Michigan. *Michigan Archaeologist* 48 (1–2): 87–116.

McCalla, Douglas

1985   The Internal Economy of Upper Canada: New Evidence on Agricultural Marketing before 1850. *Agricultural History* 59:397–416.

McCormick, William

1824   *A Sketch of the Western District of Upper Canada Being the Southerly Extremity of that Interesting Province.* Reprinted in 1980, edited by R. Alan Douglas. Occasional Papers No. 1, Essex County Historical Association. University of Windsor Press, Windsor.

McGeorge, W.

1924   Early Settlement and Surveys along the Thames River in Kent County. *Kent Historical Society Papers and Addresses* 6:5–31.

McInnis, Martin

1987   Marketable Surpluses in Ontario Farming, 1860. In *Perspectives on Canadian Economic History*, edited by Douglas McCalla, pp. 37–57. Copp Clark Pitman, Toronto.

1992   Perspectives on Ontario Agriculture, 1815–1830. In *Canadian Papers in Rural History*, edited by Donald Akenson, 8:17–127. Langdale Press, Gananoque, Ontario.

Merrell, James

1989a   *The Indians' New World Catawbas and Their Neighbours from European Contact through the Era of Removal.* University of North Carolina Press, Chapel Hill.

1989b   Some Thoughts on Colonial Historians and American Indians. *William And Mary Quarterly* 46 (1): 94–119.

Meyer, Melissa, and Kerwin Klein

1998   Native American Studies and the End of Ethnohistory. In *Studying Native America Problems and Prospects*, edited by Russell Thornton, pp. 182–216. University of Wisconsin Press, Madison.

Michigan Pioneer Historical Society Collections

1877–1920 40 vols. Lansing.

Miller, Charles, and George Hamell

1986   A New Perspective on Indian-White Contact: Cultural Symbols and Colonial Trade. *Journal of American History* 73:311–328.

Miller, George

1980   Classification and Economic Scaling of 19th Century Ceramics. *Historical Archaeology* 25 (1): 1–25.

1991   A Revised Set of CC Index Values for Classification and Economic Scaling of English Ceramics from 1787 to 1880. *Northeast Historical Archaeology* 29:1–22.

Monks, Gregory

1999   On Rejecting the Concept of Socio-Economic Status in Historical Archaeology. In *Historical Archaeology Back From the Edge*, edited by Pedro Paulo Funari, Martin Hall, and Siân Jones, pp. 204–216. Routledge, London.

Moore, Henrietta

1989   Problems in the Analysis of Social Change: An Example from the Marakwet. In *Archaeology as Long-Term History*, edited by Ian Hodder, pp. 85–104. Cambridge University Press, Cambridge.

Morantz, Toby

1992   Old Texts, Old Questions: Another Look at the Issue of Continuity and the Late Fur-Trade Period. *Canadian Historical Review* 73 (2): 166–220.

Moreland, John

2001   *Archaeology and Text*. Gerald Duckworth, London.

Morgan, Lewis Henry

1851   *League of the Ho-De'-No-Sau-Nee, Iroquois*. Sage and Brother, Rochester. Reprinted in 1962 as *League of the Iroquois*. Citadel Press, Secaucus, NJ.

Morrison, Beverly

1991   The Story Site: An Early Nineteenth Century Homestead in Brant County, Ontario. *KEWA* 91 (2): 2–26.

Morrison, Kathleen

2002   Historicizing Adaptation, Adapting to History: Forager-Traders in South and Southeast Asia. In *Forager-Traders in South and Southeast Asia Long Term Histories*, edited by Kathleen Morrison and Laura Junker, pp. 1–17. Cambridge University Press, Cambridge.

MPHSC. *See* Michigan Pioneer Historical Society Collections.

MSAR

1825–   *Missionary Society Annual Reports of the Canadian Conference Missionary Society, Auxiliary to the Missionary Society of the Methodist Episcopal Church.* United Church Archives, Toronto.

Murphy, Carl

1985   Charred Plant Remains from the Bellamy (AdHm-7) Site, 1984. Report in the Possession of the Author.

1991   A Western Basin Winter Cabin from Kent County, Ontario. *KEWA* 91 (1): 3–17.

Murphy, Carl, and Neal Ferris

1990   The Late Woodland Western Basin Tradition of Southwestern Ontario. In *The Archaeology of Southern Ontario to A.D. 1650*, edited by Christopher Ellis and Neal Ferris, pp. 189–278. Occasional

Murphy, Carl, and Neal Ferris *(cont.)*
    Publications of the London Chapter, Ontario Archaeological Society 5. London, Ontario.

Murray, Tim
2004   The Archaeology of Contact in Settler Societies. In *The Archaeology of Contact in Settler Societies*, edited by Tim Murray, pp. 1–16. Cambridge University Press, Cambridge.

Nassaney, Michael, and Eric Johnson
2000   The Contributions of Material Culture to Ethnohistory in Native America. In *Interpretations of Native North American Life: Material Contributions to Ethnohistory*, edited by Michael Nassaney and Eric Johnson, pp. 1–30. Society for Historical Archaeology/University Press of Florida, Gainesville.

Nassaney, Michael, and Ken Sassaman
1995   Introduction Understanding Native American Interactions. In *Native American Interactions: Multiscalar Analyses and Interpretations in the Eastern Woodlands*, edited by M. Nassaney and K. Sassaman, pp. xix-xxxviii. University of Tennessee Press, Knoxville.

Nelson, R.
1984   Midewin Medicine Bags of the Ojibwa. In *Papers of the Fifteenth Algonquian Conference*, edited by Wesley Cowan, pp. 397–408. Carleton University Press, Ottawa.

Neusius, Sarah
1996   Game Procurement among Temperate Horticulturalists: The Case for Garden Hunting by the Dolores Anasazi. In *Case Studies in Environmental Archaeology*, edited by Elizabeth Reitz, Lee Newsom, and Sylvia Scudder, pp. 273–288. Plenum Press, New York.

Nin.Da.Waab.Jig
1987   *Walpole Island: The Soul of Indian Territory*. Nin.Da.Waab.Jig. Walpole Island.

Oerichbauer, Edward
1982   Archaeological Investigations at the Site of a Northwest and XY Company Winter Post (47–Bt-26): A Progress Report. *Wisconsin Archeologist* 63 (3): 153–236.

Ohnuki-Tierney, Emiko
1990   Introduction: The Historicization of Anthropology. In *Culture through Time Anthropological Approaches*, edited by Emiko Ohnuki-Tierney, pp. 1–25. Stanford University Press, Stanford.

Olmstead, Earl
1991   *Blackcoats among the Delaware: David Zeisberger on the Ohio Frontier*. Kent State University Press, Cleveland, OH.

Orser, Charles
1996   *Historical Archaeology of the Modern World*. Plenum Press, New York.
2005   Network Theory and the Archaeology of Modern History. In *Global Archaeological Theory Contextual Voices and Contemporary Thoughts*, edited

by Pedro Paulo Funari, Andrés Zarankin, and Emily Stovel, pp. 77–96. Kluwer Academic/Plenum Publishers, New York.

Osborne, Brian, and Michael Ripmeester

1997   The Mississaugas between Two Worlds: Strategic Adjustments to Changing Landscapes of Power. *Canadian Journal of Native Studies* 17 (2): 259–291.

PAC.   *See* Public Archives of Canada Records Group.

PAO.   *See* Public Archives of Ontario Holdings.

Parker, Kathryn, and Lee Newsom

2001   Archaeobotanical Remains from the Windrose Site. In *The Windrose Site: An Early Nineteenth Century Potawatomi Settlement in the Kankakee River Valley of Northeastern Illinois*, pp. 133–143. Reports of Investigations 56. Illinois State Museum, Springfield.

Parmalee, Paul, and Walter Klippel

1983   The Role of Native Animals in the Food Economy of the Historic Kickapoo in Central Illinois. In *Lulu Linear Punctated: Essays in Honor of George Irving Quimby*, edited by Robert Dunnell and Donald Grayson, pp. 253–324. Museum of Anthropology Paper 72. University of Michigan, Ann Arbor.

Patterson, Thomas

2000   Archaeologists and Historians Confront Civilization, Relativism, and Poststructuralism in the Late Twentieth Century. In *History after Three Worlds: Post-Eurocentric Historiographies*, edited by Arif Dirlik, Vinay Bahl, and Peter Gran, pp. 49–64. Rowman & Littlefield, London.

Pauketat, Timothy

2001   Practice and History in Archaeology: An Emerging Paradigm. *Anthropological Theory* 1 (1): 73–98.

2003   Materiality and the Immaterial in Historical-Processual Archaeology. In *Essential Tensions in Archaeological Method and Theory*, edited by Todd Van Pool and Christine Van Pool, pp. 41–54. University of Utah Press, Salt Lake City.

Paynter, Robert

2000a   Historical and Anthropological Archaeology: Forging Alliances. *Journal of Archaeological Research* 9 (1): 1–37.

2000b   Historical Archaeology and the Post-Columbian World of North America. *Journal of Archaeological Research* 8 (3): 169–217.

Peers, Laura

1994   *The Ojibwa of Western Canada 1780 to 1870.* University of Manitoba Press, Winnipeg.

Phillips, Ruth

1984   Zigzag and Spiral: Geometric Motifs in Great Lakes Indian Costume. In *Papers of the Fifteenth Algonquian Conference*, edited by Wesley Cowan, pp. 409–424. Carleton University Press, Ottawa.

Pickering, Joseph

1831   *Inquiries of an Emigrant*. Effingham Wilson, London.

Plain, Aylmer

1973   A Study of the Family Connections to the Chippewa Indian Families
           who Moved to the Sarnia Indian Reserve from the Areas They Formerly
           Inhabited, Previous to the Time of Signing the Amherstburg Treaty,
           1827. Manuscript on file at the Walpole Island Research Centre, Walpole
           Island.

Prevec, Rosemary

1985   Bellamy Site AdHm-7 Faunal Report, Total Faunal Collection.

Priddis, Harriet (compiler)

1915   The Proudfoot Papers—Part II. *London and Middlesex Historical Society Part
           VIII* London, Ontario.

Prince, Paul

2002   Cultural Coherency and Resistance in Historic-Period Northwest-Coast
           Mortuary Practices at Kimsquit. *Historical Archaeology* 36 (4): 50–65.

Public Archives of Canada Records Group
           Ottawa.

Public Archives of Ontario Holdings
           Toronto.

Quaife, Milo (editor)

1928   *The John Askin Papers*. 2 vols. Burton Historical Collection, Detroit
           Library Commission, Detroit.

1958   *The Siege of Detroit in 1763*. Lakeside Press, Chicago.

Quimby, George

1966   *Indian Culture and European Trade Goods*. University of Wisconsin Press,
           Madison.

Quimby, George, and Alexander Spoehr

1951   Acculturation and Material Culture. *Fieldiana: Anthropology* 36 (6): 107–147.

Ramenofsky, Ann

1998   Evolutionary Theory and the Native American Record of Artifact
           Replacement. In *Studies in Culture Contact Interaction, Culture Change
           and Archaeology*, edited by James Cusick, pp. 77–101. Center for
           Archaeological Investigations Occasional Papers 25. Southern Illinois
           University Press, Carbondale.

Ray, Arthur

1988   Native Economic Dependency: Searching for the Evidence. In *Overcoming
           Economic Dependency*, D'Arcy McNickle Center for the History of the
           American Indian, Occasional Papers in Curriculum Series Number 9:95–
           100. Newberry Library, Chicago.

Redfield, Robert, Ralph Linton, and Melville Herskovits

1936   Memorandum for the Study of Acculturation. *American Anthropologist*
           38:149–152.

Reis, José Alberione dos

2005   What Conditions of Existence Sustain a Tension Found in the Use of
         Written and Material Documents in Archaeology? In *Global Archaeological
         Theory Contextual Voices and Contemporary Thoughts*, edited by Pedro
         Paulo Funari, Andrés Zarankin, and Emily Stovel, pp. 43–58. Kluwer
         Academic/Plenum Publishers, New York.

Rempel, John

1967   *Building with Wood and Other Aspects of Nineteenth-Century Building in
         Ontario*. University of Toronto Press, Toronto.

Resnick, Benjamin

1988   *The Williams Place: A Scotch-Irish Farmstead in the South Carolina Piedmont*.
         South Carolina Institute of Archaeology and Anthropology, Volumes in
         Historical Archaeology III. University of South Carolina, Columbia.

Richards, Patricia

1993   Winnebago Subsistence—Change and Continuity. *Wisconsin Archeologist*
         74 (1–4): 272–289.

Richardson, John

1848   *Tecumseh and Richardson: The Story of a Trip to Walpole Island and Port
         Sarnia*. Reprinted in 1924. Ontario Book Company, Toronto.

Richter, Daniel

1992   *The Ordeal of the Longhouse: The Peoples of the Iroquois League in the Era of
         European Colonization*. University of North Carolina Press, Chapel Hill.

1993   Whose Indian History? *William and Mary Quarterly* 50 (2): 379–393.

2001   *Facing East from Indian Country: A Native History of Early America*. Harvard
         University Press, Cambridge.

Ricoeur, Paul

1984   *The Reality of the Historical Past*. Marquette University Press, Milwaukee.

1989   *Time and Narrative*, vol. 3. Chicago University Press, Chicago.

Riddell, David

1984   Archaeological Investigations of the Thoren Site. Part of the Report on
         the 1982 Archaeological Activities of Archaeological Services Inc., edited
         by Ronald Williamson. Report on file with the Ontario Ministry of
         Culture, Toronto.

Rival, Laura

2002   *Trekking through History: The Huaorani of Amazonian Ecuador*. Columbia
         University Press, New York.

Rogers, Edward

1978   Southeastern Ojibwa. In *Handbook of North American Indians. Volume
         15: The Northeast*, edited by Bruce Trigger, pp. 760–771. Smithsonian
         Institution Press, Washington, DC.

1994   The Algonquian Farmers of Southern Ontario, 1830–1945. In *Aboriginal
         Ontario*, edited by Edward Rogers and Donald Smith, pp. 122–166.
         Dundurn Press, Toronto.

Rogers, J. Daniel

1990   *Objects of Change: The Archaeology and History of Arikara Contact with Europeans.* Smithsonian Institution Press, Washington, DC.

2005   Archaeology and the Interpretation of Colonial Encounters. In *The Archaeology of Colonial Encounters Comparative Perspectives*, edited by Gil Stein, pp. 331–354. School of American Research Press, Santa Fe, NM.

Ross, Brian

1998   Results of the 1995 & 1996 Survey of Camp Kitchikewana's Threatened Archaeological Assets, Beausoliel Island, Georgian Bay Islands National Park. Report on file, Parks Canada, Cornwall.

2004   Archaeological Mitigation of the Wanakita Site at Camp Kitchikewana, Georgian Bay Islands National Park. Report on file, Parks Canada, Cornwall.

Rotman, Deborah

2005   Newlyweds, Young Families, and Spinsters: A Consideration of Developmental Cycle in Historical Archaeologies of Gender. *International Journal of Historical Archaeology* 9 (1): 1–36.

Rubertone, Patricia

1996   Matters of Inclusion: Historical Archaeology and Native Americans. *World Archaeological Bulletin* 7:77–86.

2000   The Historical Archaeology of Native Americans. *Annual Review of Anthropology* 29:425–446.

2001   *Grave Undertakings: An Archaeology of Roger Williams and the Narragansett Indians.* Smithsonian Institution Press, Washington, DC.

Russell, Peter

1983   Forest into Farmland: Upper Canada Clearing Rates, 1822–1839. *Agricultural History* 57:326–339.

Sabathy-Judd, Linda

1999   *Moravians in Upper Canada: The Diary of the Indian Mission of Fairfield on the Thames 1792–1813.* Champlain Society, Toronto.

Sahlins, Marshall

1983   Distinguished Lecture: Other Times, Other Customs: The Anthropology of History. *American Anthropologist* 85 (3): 517–544.

1985   *Islands of History.* University of Chicago Press, Chicago.

Salisbury, Neal

1996   The Indians' Old World: Native Americans and the Coming of Europeans. *William and Mary Quarterly* 53:435–458.

Sassaman, Kenneth

2000   Agents of Change in Hunter-Gatherer Technology. In *Agency in Archaeology*, edited by Marcia-Anne Dobres and John Robb, pp. 148–168. Routledge, London.

2001   Hunter-Gatherers and Traditions of Resistance. In *The Archaeology of Traditions Agency and History Before and After Columbus*, edited by Timothy Pauketat, pp. 218–236. University Press of Florida, Gainesville.

Schmalz, Peter

1984   The Role of the Ojibwa in the Conquest of Southern Ontario, 1650–
        1751. *Ontario History* 76 (4): 326–352.

1991   *The Ojibwa of Southern Ontario.* University of Toronto Press, Toronto.

Scholliers, Peter

2001   Meals, Food Narratives, and Sentiments of Belonging in Past and Present.
        In *Food, Drink and Identity: Cooking, Eating and Drinking in Europe since the
        Middle Ages*, edited by Peter Scholliers, pp. 3–22. Berg, Oxford.

Schortman, Edward, and Patricia Urban

1998   Culture Contact Structure and Process. In *Studies in Culture Contact
        Interaction, Culture Change and Archaeology*, edited by James Cusick, pp.
        102–125. Center for Archaeological Investigations Occasional Papers 25.
        Southern Illinois University Press, Carbondale.

Schroeder, Sissel

2004   Current Research on Late Precontact Societies of the Midcontinental
        United States. *Journal of Archaeological Research* 12 (4): 311–372.

Schuyler, Robert

1978   Historical and Historic Sites Archaeology as Anthropology: Basic
        Definitions and Relationships. In *Historical Archaeology: A Guide to
        Substantive and Theoretical Contributions*, edited by R. Schyler, pp. 27–32.
        Baywood Press, Farmingdale.

Scott, James

1990   *Domination and the Arts of Resistance (Hidden Transcripts).* Yale University
        Press, New Haven, CT.

Shirreff, Patrick

1835   *A Tour through North America; Together with a Comprehensive View of the
        Canadas and United States.* Published by the author, Edinburgh. Reprinted
        in 1971, Benjamin Blom, New York.

Shoemaker, Nancy

1991   From Longhouse to Loghouse: Household Structure among the Seneca in
        1900. *American Indian Quarterly* 15 (3): 329–338.

2004   *A Strange Likeness: Becoming Red and White in Eighteenth-Century North
        America.* Oxford University Press, New York.

Silliman, Stephen

2005   Culture Contact or Colonialism? Challenges in the Archaeology of Native
        North America. *American Antiquity* 70 (1): 55–74.

Silverman, Marilyn, and P. H. Gulliver

1992   Historical Anthropology and the Ethnographic Tradition: A Personal,
        Historical, and Intellectual Account. In *Approaching the Past: Historical
        Anthropology through Irish Case Studies*, edited by Marilyn Silverman and
        P. H. Gulliver, pp. 3–72. Columbia University Press, New York.

Slight, Benjamin

1844   *Indian Researches; or, Facts Concerning the North American Indian.* J. E.
        Miller, Montreal.

Small, David
1999   The Tyranny of the Text: Lost Social Strategies in Current Historical
         Period Archaeology in the Classical Mediterranean. In *Historical
         Archaeology: Back from the Edge*, edited by Pedro Paulo Funari, Martin
         Hall, and Siân Jones, pp. 122–136. Routledge, New York.
Smith, Donald
1981   The Dispossession of the Mississauga Indians: A Missing Chapter in the
         Early History of Upper Canada. *Ontario History* 73 (2): 67–87.
Smith, G.
1914   Captain Joseph Brant's Status as Chief, and Some of His Descendants.
         Ontario Historical Society, Paper and Records 12:89–101.
Smith, Linda Tuhiwai
1999   *Decolonizing Methodologies Research and Indigenous Peoples*. University of
         Otago Press, Dunedin.
Smith, Michael
1992   Braudel's Temporal Rhythms and Chronology Theory in Archaeology.
         In *Archaeology, Annales, and Ethnohistory*, edited by Bernard Knapp, pp.
         23–34. Cambridge University Press, Cambridge.
Smith, William
1846   *Smith's Canadian Gazetteer*. H. & R. Rowsell, Toronto. Reprinted in 1970,
         Coles Canadiana Reprints, Toronto.
Snow, Dean
1994   *The Iroquois*. Blackwell Publishers, Cambridge.
1995   *Mohawk Valley Archaeology: The Sites*. Matson Museum of Anthropology,
         Occasional Papers in Anthropology 23. Pennsylvania State University,
         University Park.
Snow, Dean, Charles Gehring, and William Starna (editors)
1996   *In Mohawk Country: Early Narratives about a Native People*. Syracuse
         University Press, Syracuse, NY.
Sohrweide, Gregory
2001   Onondaga Longhouses in the Late Seventeenth Century on the Weston
         Site. *Bulletin Journal of the New York State Archaeological Association* 117:1–
         24.
South, Stanley
1977   *Method and Theory in Historical Archaeology*. Academic Press, New York.
Speck, Frank
1955   *The Iroquois: A Study in Cultural Evolution*. Cranbrook Institute of Science,
         Bulletin 23. Bloomfield Hills, MI.
Spector, Janet
1975   Crabapple Point (Je 93): An Historic Winnebago Indian Site in Jefferson
         County, Wisconsin. *Wisconsin Archeologist* 56 (4): 270–345.
1993   *What this Awl Means: Feminist Archaeology at a Wahpeton Dakota Village*.
         Minnesota Historical Society Press, St. Paul.

Spence, Michael

1994 Mortuary Programmes of the Early Ontario Iroquoians. *Ontario Archaeology* 58:6–20.

1996 A Comparative Analysis of Ethnic Enclaves. In *Arqueología Mesoamericana: Homenaje a William T. Saunders*, edited by A Mastache, J. Parsons, R. Santley, and M Puche, pp. 333–353. Universidad National Autónoma de México, Mexico City.

1999 Comments: The Social Foundations of Archaeological Taxonomy. In *Taming the Taxonomy: Toward a New Understanding of Great Lakes Archaeology*, edited by Ronald Williamson and Christopher Watts, pp. 275–281. eastendbooks, Toronto.

2005 A Zapotec Diaspora Network in Classic-Period Central Mexico. In *The Archaeology of Colonial Encounters Comparative Perspectives*, edited by Gil Stein, pp. 173–206. School of American Research Press, Santa Fe, NM.

Stahl, Ann

2000 What is the Use of Archaeology in Historical Anthropology? In *The Entangled Past: Integrating History and Archaeology*, edited by M. Boyd, J. Erwin, and M. Hendrickson, pp. 4–11. Archaeological Association of the University of Calgary, Calgary, AB.

Stein, Gil

2005 Introduction: The Comparative Archaeology of Colonial Encounters. In *The Archaeology of Colonial Encounters Comparative Perspectives*, edited by Gil Stein, pp. 3–32. School of American Research Press, Santa Fe, NM.

Stone, Lyle, and Donald Chaput

1978 History of the Upper Great Lakes Area. In *Handbook of North American Indians. Volume 15: The Northeast*, edited by Bruce Trigger, pp. 602–609. Smithsonian Institution Press, Washington, DC.

Stonefish, Darryl

1995a *Moraviantown Delaware History*. Moravian Research Office, Moraviantown Delaware First Nation.

1995b *Moraviantown Delaware Stories*. Moravian Research Office, Moraviantown Delaware First Nation.

Stothers, David, and Timothy Abel

1989 A Tabulation and Analysis of Stolen Antiquities from the Historic Ottawa Cabin at the Fry Site. *Ohio Archaeologist* 39 (1): 26–37.

Sturtevant, William

1978 Oklahoma Seneca-Cayuga. In *Handbook of North American Indians. Volume 15: The Northeast*, edited by Bruce Trigger, pp. 537–543. Smithsonian Institution Press, Washington, DC.

Surtees, Robert

1969 The Development of an Indian Reserve Policy in Canada. *Ontario History* 61 (2): 87–98.

Surtees, Robert *(cont.)*

1982   *Indian Land Cessions in Upper Canada, 1763–1862: The Evolution of a System*. PhD dissertation, Department of History, Carleton University, Ottawa.

1983   Indian Land Cessions in Upper Canada, 1815–1830. In *As Long as the Sun Shines and the Water Flows: A Reader in Canadian Native Studies*, edited by Ian Getty and Antoine Lussier, pp. 65–84. University of British Columbia Press, Vancouver.

1985   *A Cartographic Analysis of Indian Settlements and Reserves in Southern Ontario and Southern Quebec, 1763–1867*. Research Branch, Indian and Northern Affairs Canada, Ottawa.

1994   Land Cessions, 1763–1830. In *Aboriginal Ontario*, edited by Edward Rogers and Donald Smith, pp. 92–121. Dundurn Press, Toronto.

Sutton, David

2001   *Remembrance of Repasts: An Anthropology of Food and Memory*. Berg, Oxford.

Sutton, Richard

2003   Report on the 1991 Ministry of Transportation Stage 4 Excavation of the Dewar Site (AgHa-55), Highway 54, Seneca Township, Regional Municipality of Haldimand-Norfolk. Archaeological Assessments Report for and on file with the Ontario Ministry of Transportation, Toronto.

Tanner, Helen (editor)

1987   *Atlas of Great Lakes Indian History*. University of Oklahoma Press, Norman.

Taylor, Alan

2006   *The Divided Ground: Indians, Settlers, and the Northern Borderland of the American Revolution*. Knopf, New York.

Telford, Rhonda

1998   The Nefarious and Far-Ranging Interests of Indian Agent and Surveyor John William Keating, 1837 to 1869. In *Papers of the Twenty-Eighth Algonquian Conference*, edited by David Pentland, pp. 372–402. University of Manitoba, Winnipeg.

Thomas, Earle

1986   *Sir John Johnson, Loyalist Baronet*. Dundurn Press, Toronto.

Thomas, Julian

1996   *Time, Culture and Identity: An Interpretive Archaeology*. Routledge, New York.

Thornton, Russell

1998   Who Owns Our Past? The Repatriation of Native American Human Remains and Cultural Objects. In *Studying Native America Problems and Prospects*, edited by Russell Thornton, pp. 385–415. University of Wisconsin Press, Madison.

Thurston, Tina

1997   Historians, Prehistorians, and the Tyranny of the Historical Record:
        Danish State Formation through Documents and Archaeological Data.
        Journal of Archaeological Method and Theory 4 (3/4): 239–264.

Thwaites, Reuben (editor)

1896–   *The Jesuit Relations and Allied Documents: Travels and Explorations of the*
1901   *Jesuit Missionaries in New France, 1610–1791.* 73 vols. Burrows Brothers,
        Cleveland, OH.

Tilley, Christopher

1993   Introduction Interpretation and a Poetics of the Past. In *Interpretative
        Archaeology*, edited by Christopher Tilley, pp. 1–27. Berg, Providence.

Timmins, Peter

2003   Report of the 1999 Field School Excavations at the Thames Valley Trail
        Site (AfHh-288) London, Ontario. License report on file with the Ontario
        Ministry of Culture, Toronto.

Tobias, John

1983   Protection, Civilization, Assimilation: An Outline History of Canada's
        Indian Policy. In *As Long as the Sun Shines and the Water Flows: A Reader
        in Canadian Native Studies*, edited by Ian Getty and Antoine Lussier, pp.
        39–55. University of British Columbia Press, Vancouver.

Tooker, Elizabeth

1994   The Five (Later Six) Nations Confederacy, 1550–1784. In *Aboriginal
        Ontario*, edited by Edward Rogers and Donald Smith, pp. 79–91.
        Dundurn Press, Toronto.

Trigger, Bruce G.

1981   Archaeology and the Ethnographic Present. *Anthropologica* 23:3–17.

1985   *Natives and Newcomers: Canada's "Heroic Age" Reconsidered.* McGill-Queen's
        University Press, Montreal.

1986a   Ethnohistory: The Unfinished Edifice. *Ethnohistory* 33:253–267.

1986b   The Historian's Indian: Native Americans in Canadian Historical Writing
        from Charlevoix to the Present. *Canadian Historical Review* 67 (3): 315–342.

1989a   History and Contemporary American Archaeology: A Critical Analysis. In
        Archaeological Thought in America, edited by Carl C. Lamberg-Karlovsky,
        pp. 19–34. Cambridge University Press, Cambridge.

1989b   *A History of Archaeological Thought.* Cambridge University Press, Cambridge.

1991   Early Native North American Responses to European Contact: Romantic
        Versus Rationalistic Interpretations. *Journal of American History* 77 (4):
        1195–1215.

2003   *Archaeological Theory: The Big Picture.* Grace Elizabeth Shallit Memorial
        Lecture Series. Brigham Young University, Provo, Utah.

2006   *A History of Archaeological Thought.* Second Edition. Cambridge University
        Press, Cambridge.

Trigger, Bruce, and William Swagerty

1996   Entertaining Strangers: North America in the Sixteenth Century. In *The Cambridge History of the Native Peoples of the Americas: North America*, vol. 1(1), edited by Bruce Trigger and Wilcomb Washburn, pp. 325–398. Cambridge University Press, Cambridge.

Triggs, John

2004   The Mississauga at the Head-of-the-Lake: Examining Responses to Cultural Upheaval at the Close of the Fur Trade. *Northeast Historical Archaeology* 33:153–176.

Trouillot, Michel-Rolph

1995   *Silencing the Past: Power and the Production of History.* Beacon Press, Boston.

Trubowitz, Neal

1992   Thanks, but We Prefer to Smoke Our Own: Pipes in the Great Lakes-Riverine Region during the Eighteenth Century. In *Proceedings of the 1989 Smoking Pipe Conference: Selected Papers*, edited by Charles Hayes III, pp. 97–112. Research Records 22. Rochester Museum and Science Center, Rochester, NY.

Tuck, James

1971   *Onondaga Iroquois Prehistory: A Study in Settlement Archaeology.* Syracuse University Press, Syracuse, NY.

Turgeon, Laurier

2004   Beads, Bodies and Regimes of Value: From France to North America, c. 1500–c. 1650. In *The Archaeology of Contact in Settler Societies*, edited by Tim Murray, pp. 19–47. Cambridge University Press, Cambridge.

University of Western Ontario Regional Archives
        Wheldon Library, London, Ontario.

Upton, Del

1996   Ethnicity, Authenticity, and Invented Traditions. *Historical Archaeology* 30 (1): 1–7.

UWORA. *See* University of Western Ontario Regional Archives.

Van der Veen, Marijke

2003   When is Food a Luxury? *World Archaeology* 34 (3): 405–427.

Veenema, Michael

2002   *Challenge, Corruption, and Grace on the Road to Closure: The Moravian Mission of New Fairfield on the Thames, 1845–1903.* Master's thesis, Department of History, University of Western Ontario, London.

Vibert, Elizabeth

1997   *Trader's Tales: Narratives of Cultural Encounters in the Columbia Plateau, 1807–1846.* University of Oklahoma Press, Norman.

Wagner, Mark

1998   Some Think It Impossible to Civilize Them at All: Cultural Change and Continuity among the Early Nineteenth Century Potawatomi. In *Studies in Culture Contact Interaction, Culture Change and Archaeology*, edited by James Cusick, pp. 430–456. Center for Archaeological Investigations Occasional Papers 25. Southern Illinois University Press, Carbondale.

2001   *The Windrose Site An Early Nineteenth Century Potawatomi Settlement in the Kankakee River Valley of Northeastern Illinois.* Reports of Investigations 56. Illinois State Museum, Springfield.

2003   In All the Solemnity of Profound Smoking: Tobacco Smoking and Pipe Manufacture and Use among the Potawatomi of Illinois. In *Stone Tool Traditions in the Contact Era*, edited by Charles Cobb, pp. 109–126. The University of Alabama Press, Tuscaloosa.

Wall, Diana

1991   Sacred Dinners and Secular Teas: Constructing Domesticity in Mid-19th-Century New York. *Historical Archaeology* 25 (4): 69–81.

Wallace, Anthony

1969   *The Death and Rebirth of the Seneca.* Alfred A. Knopf, New York.

Walpole Island Heritage Centre

        Walpole Island First Nation.

Warrick, Gary

1998   The Archaeology of Early Nineteenth-Century Iroquoians on the Grand River, Ontario. Paper presented at the CAA Meetings, Victoria.

2000   The Precontact Iroquoian Occupation of Southern Ontario. *Journal of World Prehistory* 14 (4): 415–466.

2004   Archaeological Investigation of the Davisville Community, City of Brantford, Brant County: Results of the 2002 Test Pit Survey, Test Excavations of Davisville 7 site (AgHb-253) and Partial Excavation of Davisville 2 Site (AgHb-242). Report on file with the Ontario Ministry of Culture, Toronto.

Washburn, Wilcomb, and Bruce Trigger

1996   Native Peoples in Euro-American Historiography. In *The Cambridge History of the Native Peoples of the Americas: North America*, vol. 1(1), edited by Bruce Trigger and Wilcomb Washburn, pp. 61–124. Cambridge University Press, Cambridge.

Watts, Christopher

1997   *A Quantitative Analysis and Chronological Seriation of Riviere au Vase Ceramics From Southwestern Ontario.* Master's thesis, Department of Anthropology, University of Toronto, Toronto.

2006   *Pots as Agents: A Phenomenological Approach to Late Woodland Period (ca. AD 900–1300) Pottery Production in Southwestern Ontario, Canada.* PhD dissertation, Department of Anthropology, University of Toronto, Mississauga.

Weaver, Sally

1972   *Medicine and Politics among the Grand River Iroquois: A Study of the Non-Conservatives.* Publications in Ethnology 4, National Museum of Man, Ottawa.

Weaver, Sally *(cont.)*

1994a   The Iroquois: The Consolidation of the Grand River Reserve in the Mid-
          Nineteenth Century. In *Aboriginal Ontario*, edited by Edward Rogers and
          Donald Smith, pp. 182–212. Dundurn Press, Toronto.

1994b   The Iroquois: The Grand River Reserve in the Late Nineteenth and Early
          Twentieth Centuries. In *Aboriginal Ontario*, edited by Edward Rogers and
          Donald Smith, pp. 213–257. Dundurn Press, Toronto.

Weld, Sir Isaac

1799   *Travels through the States of North America and the Provinces of Upper and Low-
          er Canada during the Years 1795, 1796, and 1797.* 2 vols. John Stockdale.
          London. Reprinted in 1968 by Johnston Reprint Corporation, New York.

Weslager, Clinton

1972   *The Delaware Indians: A History.* Rutgers University Press, Piscataway, NJ.

1978   *The Delaware Indian: Westward Migration.* Middle Atlantic Press,
          Wallingford, PA.

White, Richard

1983   *The Roots of Dependency: Subsistence, Environment, and Social Change among the
          Choctaws, Pawnees, and Navajos.* University of Nebraska Press, Lincoln.

1991   *The Middle Ground: Indians, Empires and Republics in the Great Lakes Region,
          1650–1815.* Cambridge University Press, Cambridge.

1998   Using the Past: History and Native American Studies. In *Studying Native
          America Problems and Prospects*, edited by Russell Thornton, pp. 217–243.
          University of Wisconsin Press, Madison.

Whiteman, Darrell

1986   Using Missionary Records in Ethnohistorical Research. *Studies in Third
          World Societies* 35:25–60.

WIHC. *See* Walpole Island Heritage Centre.

Williamson, Christine

2004   Contact Archaeology and the Writing of Aboriginal History. In *The
          Archaeology of Contact in Settler Societies*, edited by Tim Murray, pp. 176–
          199. Cambridge University Press, Cambridge.

Williamson, Ronald, and David Robertson

1994   Peer Polities Beyond the Periphery: Early and Middle Iroquoian Regional
          Interaction. *Ontario Archaeology* 58:27–48.

Witthoft, John

1967   A History of Gunflints. *Pennsylvania Archaeologist* 36 (1–2): 12–49.

Wittry, Warren

1963   The Bell Site, Wn9, an Early Historic Fox Village. *Wisconsin Archeologist*
          44 (1): 1–57.

Wolf, Eric

1982   *Europe and the People Without History.* University of California Press,
          Berkeley.

Wood, David

2000   *Making Ontario Agricultural Colonization and Landscape Re-Creation before the Railway*. McGill-Queen's Press, Montreal.

Wray, Charles

1983   Seneca Glass Trade Beads c. A.D. 1550–1820. In *Proceedings of the 1982 Glass Bead Conference Selected Papers*, edited by C. Hayes III, pp. 41–49. Research Records 16. Rochester Museum and Science Center, Rochester, NY.

Wright, James

1966   *The Ontario Iroquois Tradition*. Bulletin 210. National Museum of Canada, Ottawa.

1967   The Pic River Site: A Stratified Late Woodland Site on the North Shore of Lake Superior. *Contributions to Anthropology V: Archaeology and Physical Anthropology*. Bulletin 224: 54–99. National Museum of Canada, Ottawa.

Wrong, George (editor)

1939   *Sagard: The Long Journey to the Country of the Hurons*. The Champlain Society, Toronto.

Wylie, Alison

1993   A Proliferation of New Archaeologies: "Beyond Objectivism and Relativism." In *Archaeological Theory: Who Sets the Agenda?*, edited by Norman Yoffee and Andrew Sherratt, pp. 20–26. Cambridge University Press, Cambridge.

1995   Alternative Histories: Epistemic Disunity and Political Integrity. In *Making Alternative Histories the Practice of Archaeology and History in Non-Western Settings*, edited by Peter Schmidt and Thomas Patterson, pp. 255–272. School of American Research Press, Santa Fe, NM.

1999   Why Should Historical Archaeologists Study Capitalists? In *Historical Archaeologies of Capitalism*, edited by Mark Leone and Parker Potter Jr., pp. 23–50. Kluwer Publishers, New York.

2002   *Thinking from Things: Essays in the Philosophy of Archaeology*. University of California Press, Berkeley.

Yerbury, John

1986   *The Subarctic Indians and the Fur Trade, 1680–1860*. University of British Columbia Press, Vancouver.

Index

acculturation, 25; as cultural subordination, 11–13; and master narratives, 10–12, 16, 22, 25; and normative view of cultures, 11
agency, 19–20; and material culture, 21, 24
Alexander, Rani, 26–27
Algonquians. *See* Delaware (nation); Ojibwa; Potawatomi
American Revolution. *See* Revolutionary War
Amherstburg, 53
Amikwa (territorial group), 34
Anishnabeg peoples (Algonquian speaking), 3, 5, 34; assumptions of historic social change, 54; precontact archaeology of, 32–33. *See also* Ojibwa
Annales school of history, 18–19
anthropological history. *See* ethnohistory
archaeological history: concept of, 1–2, 18–22; and continuum of contact histories, 26–28; and "Native-lived" colonialism, 22–25, 167–75; precontact and postcontact, 18, 21–22; reflexivity in, 9–10, 18; role of written records in, 30–31
Ausable River, 36, 37

Battle of Fallen Timbers, 82
Beaver Wars, 116
Bellamy site, 41, 178n9; faunal and floral assemblage, 43–45, 73; material culture, 52, 53, 55, 69, 150,

182n13; population estimates, 56–57; settlement pattern, 49–52
Binford, Lewis, 50–51
Bkejwanong. *See* Ojibwa: Walpole Island reserve
Bond Head, Francis, 178n13
Bourdieu, Pierre, 20, 169
Brant, John, 159
Brant, Joseph, 114, 122–31 passim, 135, 138, 143, 145, 151, 159, 163, 165, 181n10, 182n20
Brantford, 125–26, 149, 151, 182n14
Braudel, Fernand, 18–19
British Indian Department. *See* Indian Department
Burlington, 129, 131

Cadillac, Antoine Laumet de Lamothe, 35
Campbell, Patrick, 127, 129–30
Canajoharie, 124, 127
Canotung, Joseph, 32, 39
catastrophic bureaucracy, 59–62, 169–71; and the Delaware, 109; and the Iroquois, 125, 136, 150; and the Ojibwa, 65, 76
Cayuga (Iroquois nation), 3, 5, 114, 124, 126, 128, 147, 156, 181n9; settlements along Grand River, 126–27, 131, 133
change and continuity: relationship between in historical trajectory, 172–74
Chatham (Ontario), 84, 90

Oppelt, Gottfried, 94, 103
Outchibous, 34

Parke, Thomas, 133
Petun (Iroquoian nation), 3, 114, 116–17
Point Pelee, 36
Pontiac, Chief, 35, 81
Potawatomi, 3, 5, 44, 45, 66, 179n17, 180n10, and connection to the Western Basin Late Woodland Tradition, 33
Powless families, 143–46, 173, 182n19; archaeology of homes at Mohawk Village, 145–64, 182n20
practice theory, 20
Proctor, General, 85

Quimby, George, 23

Revolutionary War, 81, 83, 124–25, 170
Richelieu River, 181n5
Rogers, J. Daniel, 24; and processes of "maintenance," "replacement," and "adoption," 58
Rondeau Bay, 38, 102
Royal Proclamation of 1763, 81
Rubertone, Patricia, 23, 25

Sabathy-Judd, Linda, and "circles of grace," 89
Sandusky, 83, 98
Sandusky Bay, 39, 178n8
Sandwich (Township), 93
Sarnia, 65
Sauk, 5
Saulteaux (Ojibwa), 34–35
Schnall, John, 91, 93, 94, 95, 96, 101
Seckas (Sekahos), Chief, 35
Seneca (Iroquois nation), 3, 5, 114, 116–21, 123, 133, 181n9
Sensemann, Gottlieb, 79, 85, 95, 102
settlement-subsistence activities, importance of: in archaeological histories,

28–29; as social choices and dispositions, 29; in understanding written records, 29–30
Shawnee, 80, 83
Shirreff, Patrick, 132, 134
Silliman, Stephen, 27, 168
Six Nations. See Iroquois: Six Nations
southwestern Ontario: Ojibwa territorial communities in, 37; nineteenth century changes in cleared land, 64; population increases, 63. See also study area
Speck, Frank, 154, 202n13
Spector, Janet, 24
St. Anne's Island, 39
St. Anne's Odawa. See Odawa
St. Clair River, 36–37, 42, 73
study area, southwestern Ontario, 2–4
Susquehannock (Iroquois nation), 117
Sydenham River, 36–56 passim, 79, 84, 177n3, 178n8, 179n18

Talfourd, Froome, 66
Tecumseh, 85
terminology: issues in use of, 4–6
territory, problematic concept, 6
Thames River (Ontario), 36–52 passim, 79–110 passim, 170
Tinaouatoua, 118
Tiononderoge. See Fort Hunter
Treaty of Paris, 82, 124, 181n7
Treaty of Stanwix, 81–82
Tuscarora (Iroquois nation), 5, 133, 181n8
Tuscarora Township, 125–26, 136, 139–41
Tuscarora Village, 126–27, 133

Unami-Unalachtigo. See Delaware (nation)

Vogler, Jesse, 90, 108–10; commented on by Anna Jameson, 79, 90

About the Author

Neal Ferris holds the Lawson Chair of Canadian Archaeology at the University of Western Ontario in London, Ontario, where he is cross appointed with the Department of Anthropology and the Museum of Ontario Archaeology. His research focus has been on the Aboriginal and non-Aboriginal archaeology of Northeastern North America, in particular the Late and Terminal Woodland Traditions of the Great Lakes, and of the European colonizers, rural settlers and the Indigenous Aboriginal peoples of the Northeast, concentrating primarily on archaeology as the history of lived experience through patterns and processes of settlement-subsistence, social organization, interaction, agency and identity within and between communities. Prior to being appointed the Lawson Chair, Neal Ferris was employed for twenty years by the Ontario government as a provincial archaeologist, where he developed and conducted research on various contemporary issues facing the practice of archaeology today. He has coedited an award-winning synthesis of Ontario archaeology; contributed chapters to edited volumes published in Canada, the United States and Europe; and published articles in regional, national and international journals such as *Ontario Archaeology*, the *Canadian Journal of Archaeology*, and the *Revista de Arqueología Americana*.